FLORIDA STATE
UNIVERSITY LIBRARIES

JAN 15 2001

TALLAHASSEE, FLORIDA

SHEDDING LIGHT ON THE DARKNESS

MODERN GERMAN STUDIES
A Series of the German Studies Association

General Editor: Gerald R. Kleinfeld, Arizona State University

This series offers books on modern and contemporary Germany, concentrating on themes in history, political science, literature, and German culture.

Volume 1
> *Germany's New Politics: Parties and Issues in the 1990s*
> Edited by David P. Conradt, Gerald R. Kleinfeld, George K. Romoser, and Christian Søe

Volume 2
> *After Unity: Reconfiguring German Identities*
> Konrad H. Jarausch

Volume 3
> *Beyond 1989: Re-reading German Literature since 1945*
> Keith Bullivant

Volume 4
> *Gender and Germanness: Cultural Productions of Nation*
> Edited by Patricia Herminghouse and Magda Mueller

Volume 5
> *Power Shift in Germany: The 1998 Election and the End of the Kohl Era*
> Edited by David P. Conradt, Gerald R. Kleinfeld, and Christian Søe

Volume 6
> *Shedding Light on the Darkness: A Guide to Teaching the Holocaust*
> Edited by Nancy A. Lauckner and Miriam Jokiniemi

SHEDDING LIGHT ON THE DARKNESS

A Guide to Teaching the Holocaust

Edited by

Nancy A. Lauckner and
Miriam Jokiniemi

Berghahn Books
NEW YORK · OXFORD

D804.33
.S54
2000

Published in 2000 by
Berghahn Books

© 2000 Nancy A. Lauckner, Miriam Jokiniemi

All rights reserved.
No part of this publication may be reproduced in any form
or by any means without the written permission of Berghahn Books.

Library of Congress Cataloging-in-Publication Data

Shedding light on the darkness : a guide to teaching the Holocaust / edited by Nancy A. Lauckner, Miriam Jokiniemi.
   p. cm.
   Includes bibliographical references (p.) and index.
   ISBN 1-57181-208-3 (alk. paper)
   1. Holocaust, Jewish (1939-1945)--Study and teaching (Higher)--United States. 2. Holocaust, Jewish (1939-1945)--Study and teaching (Higher)--Canada. I. Lauckner, Nancy Ann, 1941- II. Jokiniemi, Miriam.

D804.33 .S54 2000
940.53'18'071173--dc21
                                            00-027751

British Library Cataloguing in Publication Data

A catalogue record for this book is available from the British Library.

Printed in the United States on acid-free paper.

Contents

Acknowledgments — vii

Introduction — ix
    Nancy A. Lauckner

Part I

1. The Holocaust through Literature and Film — 3
    David Scrase

2. The Well-Utilized Survivor — 17
    Susan E. Cernyak-Spatz

3. Victims and Perpetrators: The Many Voices of the Holocaust — 29
    Thomas Freeman

4. Designing within and around Limits: The Holocaust, Madonna, and Me — 42
    Linda Feldman

5. The Difficulty of Breaking the Silence: Teaching the Holocaust in a Program of German Literature and Culture — 59
    Dagmar C. G. Lorenz

6. Four Genres and One Question: Why? — 77
    Steven R. Cerf

7. The Holocaust and Resistance in German Literature — 92
    Gisela Brude-Firnau

8. Inserting a Short Course on the Holocaust into German Offerings at a Small Liberal Arts College — 107
    Nancy M. Decker

9. Teaching the Shoah in Context: A Course on Jewish German Relations — 124
    Karen Remmler

10. German Myths and Jewish Traumas: Teaching Postwar
 Cultural History 1945–1995   140
 Florentine Strzelczyk

11. Witness Grete Weil: An Intensive Summer Graduate
 Seminar   157
 Laureen Nussbaum

12. A Graduate Seminar on the Holocaust and the Third
 Reich as Reflected in Postwar German Literature   174
 Nancy A. Lauckner

Part II

13. The Nazi Period, the Holocaust, and German-Jewish
 Issues as Integral Subjects in a German Language Course   191
 Karin Doerr

14. The Holocaust in an Introductory German Literature
 Course: Problematic Responses as a Catalyst for
 Curricular Change   200
 Miriam Jokiniemi

15. Beyond Cultural Literacy:
 "Interactive Autobiography" as Holocaust Pedagogy   211
 William Collins Donahue

16. The Teaching (and Not Teaching) of "the Disaster"   225
 Leslie Morris

Important Historical Readings on the Holocaust and
the Nazi Era   237
    Compiled by *Ronald Webster*

List of Contributors   241

Index   243

Acknowledgments

In a cooperative project of this kind, there are always many people to thank for their help in making it possible. First of all, we extend our sincere gratitude to our contributors, whose work it is our pleasure to showcase in this volume and without whose essays the book would not exist. They all worked very hard to produce the essays, undertook the requested revisions cheerfully and in a spirit of cooperation, and willingly and promptly answered the multitude of detailed questions the editors asked in the process of completing the manuscript. The opportunity to develop good working relationships and even friendships with some of the most outstanding Germanists and German Studies specialists teaching the Holocaust in North American colleges and universities was a most rewarding "fringe benefit" of our work on this project, and it has been a great joy to see these essays on their ingenious courses blossom into a volume which exceeds our expectations and which, we believe, represents a significant contribution to Holocaust pedagogy in our profession.

Further, we thank Professors Irene Kacandes of Dartmouth College and Karin Doerr of Concordia University for their offer to help in various ways. We extend our sincere appreciation to James Hammons (formerly of the University of Tennessee Library, but now at Ball State University), Ulla Habekost of the Goethe Institute Toronto, and Irene Tencinger of the Faculty of Information Studies at the University of Toronto for their unstinting efforts in checking bibliographical details; and to William Ward of the University of Tennessee Library, Kathryn Elder of York University Libraries, Professor Gary Evans of the University of Ottawa, Andrés Abril and the Film and Video Department of the United States Holocaust Memorial Museum, and many others for their invaluable assistance in providing information on film and video desiderata.

We express our gratitude to Professors Scott Denham (Davidson College), Thomas Fox (University of Alabama), Sander Gilman (University of

Chicago), Patricia Herminghouse (University of Rochester), and Herbert Lindenberger (Stanford University), as well as to several of our contributors, for their advice and suggestions on publishers to contact. We also thank everyone who read all or part of our manuscript for their helpful comments. And, of course, we offer our sincere appreciation to Dr. Marion Berghahn for publishing this volume, to general editor Professor Gerald Kleinfeld for including it in the Modern German Studies series, to Shawn Kendrick and Christine Marciniak for their excellent copyediting and typesetting respectively, and to the staff members of Berghahn Books for their outstanding work in preparing the book to go to press.

We thank the colleagues at the University of Tennessee and York University who aided us with advice and support through the many stages of this project: Professors Carolyn R. Hodges, Peter Höyng, David Lee, Chauncey J. Mellor, Stefanie Ohnesorg, Gilya Schmidt, and Olga Welch of the University of Tennessee; Meredith Morris-Babb, previously, and Joyce Harrison, currently, of the University of Tennessee Press; Professors Ellen Anderson, David Johnson, Mark Webber, and Ronald Webster of York University; and Professor Michael Brown of the York University Centre for Jewish Studies. Further, we thank Saskia Zeegen and professional indexer Barbara Schon of Toronto for their invaluable work in preparing the Index, and Professor Margy Gerber of Bowling Green State University for her counsel at various stages. Finally, we express our deep appreciation to Charles Timothy Wiebe and Dr. Stephen W. Kercel for their helpful advice and support in their areas of specialization.

INTRODUCTION

This volume of essays on Holocaust teaching by North American Germanists marks the realization of an idea that we, its editors, began discussing in October 1994. As professors of German who had long been interested and involved in teaching and research about the Holocaust in our discipline, we knew that there were significant gaps in the scholarly resources on the Holocaust available to Germanists. Despite the outstanding and prolific Holocaust research that has been published over the years and continues to appear regularly, one area is markedly underrepresented: that of Holocaust pedagogy, especially as it relates to the fields of German and German Studies. Some scholars have presented conference papers and written journal articles on the topic, but generally these have been isolated studies. We recognized the need for a book that would collect essays by Germanists active in Holocaust teaching that would describe and discuss their Holocaust-related courses.

At the outset, two definitions are in order. The term "Holocaust," in its strictest sense, has long referred to the Nazi program of persecution, ghettoization, incarceration in concentration camps, and attempted annihilation of the Jewish population of Europe and the Soviet Union on the basis of "race." Contemporary historical research has now broadened our understanding of the term to include the genocide against the Roma and Sinti and the "euthanasia" of the physically and mentally impaired, the latter program of which ended officially in 1941 due to the bishops' protest and domestic outcry. Members of other population groups (Slavs, Communists, homosexuals, Jehovah's Witnesses, etc.) also suffered persecution, imprisonment, and murder or death at the hands of the Nazis, so their fate, too, figures in Holocaust research.

In their Holocaust-related German and German Studies courses, the contributors to this volume focus on the Jews as the primary victims of the Holocaust in terms of numbers and as the central targets of Nazi racial policy, although some contributors also treat other victims in class discussions as well as in readings or films. This focus reflects the practice in our discipline in such courses and the far greater availability of literary works and films on the Jews. Recognizing that the Nazi-originated and administered Holocaust affected all Jews under the Nazi sphere of influence, our contributors do not limit their attention to German Jews in these courses. While some of the courses study the perpetrators as well, many contributors do so only indirectly by discussing perpetrators who appear as characters in the literary works and films chosen. The proportion correctly represents the small percentage of Holocaust-related courses in German and German Studies that specifically treat the perpetrators.

The second definition needed is that of "German Studies." The paradigm shift from Germanistics to German Studies began in the mid-1980s and has become a strong trend in our discipline. The field expands the range of traditional German offerings and attracts more students by introducing courses with cultural and often historical content; thus courses related to the Holocaust are often found in a German Studies curriculum. At some institutions German Studies programs are truly interdisciplinary, involving the cooperation of faculty in German, history, cultural studies, film, and other areas of study, and providing a curriculum taught by faculty members from these areas. The field is also found in many colleges and universities, however, in which German departments and programs have changed their designation to "German Studies" and the German faculty, having broadened its area of expertise, teaches most or all of the German Studies courses itself. Both variants characterize the field of German Studies in the U.S. and Canada. In addition, many traditional German departments and programs that have not changed their name now teach many courses of the German Studies type. Recognizing the significance of the German Studies trend, the German government has established a number of North American centers to support teaching and research in the field: at Berkeley, Brandeis, Georgetown, Harvard, and the University of Wisconsin (Madison) and its teammate, the University of Minnesota, in the U.S.; and at York and its partner, the Université de Montréal, in Canada.

There are several important reasons why this long-needed book is especially valuable at this time. First, the strong current trend in our profession to replace traditional Germanistics programs in Canada and the U.S. with those in German Studies makes Holocaust courses an appropriate and essential component of these new curricula to complement and to enhance students' understanding of German literature, culture, and history. Therefore, the growing numbers of Germanists and German

Studies specialists who will both want and be expected to teach the Holocaust in the years ahead will need the resources and guidance that a book such as this can provide.

Second, disciplinary boundaries in the U.S. and Canada are more open than those in Europe, where historians teach the Holocaust and Germanists seldom have the opportunity. In North America, though, as explained above, Germanists do teach Holocaust-related courses in both German and German Studies. As we, a U.S. Germanist and a Canadian Germanist, formulated and discussed our plans for this volume, we quickly recognized that the North American environment in which we work represents an important element in our Holocaust teaching that both requires and deserves exploration which it has not thus far received. The circumstances we face, our students' preparation and expectations, our own educational backgrounds, the requirements of our institutions: all this creates radically different conditions for teaching the Holocaust than those confronting our colleagues in German-speaking countries. These advantages and disadvantages intrinsic to the North American context call for pedagogical approaches to Holocaust teaching that may differ considerably from those that such colleagues can use effectively. The contributors to this volume address both the benefits and problems inherent in teaching this subject as North American Germanists and demonstrate ways to meet the challenge based on their own classroom experience.

Third, because the time is inexorably approaching when all the Holocaust survivors still alive today will have died, it is important to look to that future and the particular circumstances in which it will place Holocaust teaching. When we lose the last people who personally experienced the Holocaust, we will no longer have in our classrooms their direct individual testimony that has brought the Holocaust home to our students with a vividness that nothing else can approach. It is very likely that revisionists will take advantage of this situation and that there will be a surge in Holocaust denial. Thus it is extremely important that there be ongoing, high-quality Holocaust teaching in the future, both to counter the deniers and to teach future generations about the Holocaust without the direct personal testimony of the survivors. We believe that Germanists and German Studies professors have a special obligation to be active in Holocaust teaching because of the historical responsibility for the Holocaust of the people whose language, literature, history, and culture they teach. This conviction, stated in the invitation to our contributors, has guided our project since its inception. We hope that this volume will serve our colleagues well by providing ideas, resources, and methods for their teaching in this challenging future.

Germanists, then, in traditional German programs and in German Studies departments, are the intended audience for which we have prepared this book that focuses on the teaching of the Holocaust within their discipline. It addresses neither Holocaust Studies nor Jewish Studies, yet we anticipate that readers from the various areas involved may find our contributors' essays and courses interesting and thought-provoking. Further, this volume is not meant for historians, who will find it quite different in focus, nature, structure, and documentation system from the practices that pertain in their own field. Our contributors have chosen readings, films, and assignments based on the approaches and methods of our discipline and their own goals for their particular students and classes, which differ from those that guide historians in creating their courses. We, of course, welcome historians who, cognizant of these differences, choose to read our book.

The essay contributors to this volume are Germanists in German and German Studies who have been teaching about the Holocaust for some time and have developed creative courses that provide Holocaust instruction to North American students. In selecting the people whom we wished to invite to participate in our project, we had several objectives. We wanted colleagues who would provide well-written scholarly essays containing valuable insights into Holocaust teaching on the basis of their own experience with a specific course or courses, but we were also looking for an interesting variety in the kinds of courses described and in the types of institutions where they are taught. Further, we sought both colleagues who teach in the U.S. and those who teach in Canada because of the North American concept of our volume. We developed a list of potential contributors by drawing on our own knowledge of Germanists teaching the Holocaust in our respective countries, on our awareness of their Holocaust-related scholarship in some cases and on bibliographies in others, and on colleagues who suggested other active Holocaust scholars whom we might wish to contact. In February 1996 we invited twenty-five people from this list to consider joining our project, and seventeen accepted promptly. We also extended an invitation to one colleague who had heard about the project and indicated great interest in participating, should we like another contributor. The volume now contains sixteen essays. Five of the authors are from Canada, and the remaining eleven from the U.S. The number of Canadian essay contributors is both adequate and representative, given the relatively small cohort of Canadian Germanists in comparison to the far larger one in the United States and given the correspondingly smaller proportions of Germanists in the two countries who engage in Holocaust teaching.

In addition to a focus on quality, our goal in selecting, editing, and organizing these essays has been to enhance the volume's representative nature and usefulness. The courses described run the gamut from intermediate language and literature offerings to advanced undergraduate and graduate courses. They are taught in institutions ranging from small private liberal arts colleges to large public universities in both countries, usually in a regular term, but in one case in a summer program and in another in a mini-term. With one exception, all the courses treated in detail here were taught under a German, foreign language, or German Studies rubric.

The abstracts that we received early in this project and the essays submitted later described a wide variety of Holocaust-related courses, as we had hoped, yet often both the courses and the manner in which the contributors discussed them were inventive beyond our anticipation. We reconsidered our intention to use essays only on courses in which the Holocaust was either the sole topic or a central aspect when the abstracts demonstrated that some of our contributors did not teach courses of this kind, yet they did teach about the Holocaust. The courses their abstracts described were of two types: (1) some were fairly standard undergraduate offerings (second-year German, third-year conversation and composition, and the like) to which the contributors had added a small but significant and often very creative, Holocaust component; (2) others were developed by colleagues who registered their philosophical opposition to teaching courses focusing solely or principally on the Holocaust, yet who had devised courses on other topics in which the Holocaust was an ongoing concern. Recognizing that the courses these contributors taught demonstrated important aspects of the Holocaust teaching being done by North American Germanists without which our book would be incomplete and unrepresentative, we expanded our volume to include two parts. The essays in Part I discuss courses in which the Holocaust is the sole or a central focus, while those in the smaller Part II, which are generally somewhat shorter, treat courses of the two different types outlined above.

Two of our contributors endured the Holocaust years in Europe, came to North America after the war, and became Germanists at U.S. institutions. Among their interests in teaching and scholarship has been the discussion of Holocaust-related matters, based both on scholarly sources and their personal experience. Susan E. Cernyak-Spatz of the University of North Carolina at Charlotte has contributed the essay "The Well-Utilized Survivor," in which she describes her course for undergraduates that treats Holocaust history, literature, and film. Spared the worst of the Holocaust, Laureen Nussbaum of Portland State University writes about a very different kind of course in "Witness Grete Weil: An Intensive Summer Graduate Seminar." This course on a single author whose oeuvre is marked by the Holocaust serves as an example of one means of providing students exacting and meaningful academic work on German literature of the Holocaust when little time is available. Although both Cernyak-Spatz and Nussbaum have ostensibly "retired," they continue to teach and write about the Holocaust or literature depicting it. Their contributions to this volume are valuable not only as descriptions of their own courses, but also as indications of what two individuals who survived the Holocaust era consider essential elements that Germanists must teach North American students about this dark chapter in human history.

In "The Holocaust through Literature and Film," David Scrase of the University of Vermont discusses his English-language course on Holocaust literature and film, which he developed as a needed complement to his university's history offerings on the Holocaust. This course serves a wide undergraduate audience both inside and outside his department. Although most of the contributors to this volume use films in their Holocaust courses, his course and that of Nancy M. Decker of Rollins College utilize this medium most extensively. Decker's essay, "Inserting a Short Course on the Holocaust into German Offerings at a Small Liberal Arts College," will be of interest to readers for several reasons: it describes a mini-term course on the Holocaust and thus, like Nussbaum's essay, presents a way of teaching a meaningful Holocaust course when limited time is available; it shows how one can begin teaching the Holocaust on a small scale initially outside the regular curriculum; and it draws heavily on World Wide Web resources that have begun to be essential for Holocaust teaching.

Besides Nussbaum, two other contributors in Part I offer essays on literature courses on the Holocaust taught in German and with all or virtually all readings in German. In his "Four Genres and One Question: Why?" Steven R. Cerf of Bowdoin College discusses his undergraduate seminar, which introduces advanced German majors and minors to Holocaust literature in German by systematically utilizing a genre-based approach as well as including art, music, and film. Nancy A. Lauckner of the University of Tennessee treats "A Graduate Seminar on the Holocaust and the Third Reich As Reflected in Postwar German Literature" and describes the challenges of teaching German Holocaust literature to students in a small German graduate program at a Southern university.

In addition to Scrase, three other contributors discuss undergraduate courses on Holocaust literature taught in English with readings in English. In her essay on "The Holocaust and Resistance in German Literature," Gisela Brude-Firnau of the University of Waterloo describes her course of the same title in which she uses German literature in English translation to explore the issue of resistance in the literary depiction of the Holocaust. Thomas Freeman of Beloit College writes in "Victims and Perpetrators: The Many Voices of the Holocaust" about his English-language course, which accommodates students with some knowledge of German and those with none, while providing a fourth hour of German instruction each week for those who do some readings in German. His essay also discusses the version of his course in which German is the language of instruction and of all the readings. From the University of Illinois at Chicago, Dagmar C. G. Lorenz contributes "The Difficulty of Breaking the Silence: Teaching the Holocaust in a Program of German Literature and Culture," in which she discusses frankly her difficulties in introducing and gaining acceptance for a Holocaust course in one of the largest German programs in the U.S. at Ohio State University. Lorenz offers an important historical perspective on Holocaust teaching in the North American context as differentiated from the situation that obtains in Germany and describes her quarter-length course which focused on the Holocaust in literature and film.

Three of the Part I essays present courses that treat the Holocaust from the standpoint of cultural studies. In "Teaching the Shoah in Context: A Course on Jewish German Relations," Karen Remmler provides insight into the rewards and challenges of teaching the Holocaust to diverse audiences by contrasting her experiences in teaching a similar course in English to a largely Jewish class of non-German majors at Amherst College and in German to a primarily non-Jewish group of German majors at Mount Holyoke College. In "German Myths and Jewish Traumas: Teaching Postwar Cultural History 1945–1995," Florentine Strzelczyk of the University of Calgary describes a course she taught at Queen's University. Strzelczyk's essay, which offers essential theoretical and pedagogical considerations for teaching the Holocaust within German cultural history as well as ideas for incorporating the Canadian context in doing so, will be of particular interest to colleagues just getting started in Holocaust teaching, because in it the author discusses a number of Holocaust-related units and subunits that are easily transposable into a variety of courses and that will spark the readers' own ingenuity. Similarly, "Designing within and around Limits: The Holocaust, Madonna, and Me," by Linda Feldman of the University of Windsor, will be very helpful to colleagues embarking on Holocaust teaching, because it offers practical advice on developing a course that meets students' needs and that deals effectively and creatively with the opportunities and limits of the local context. Feldman's use of cultural and literary "microtexts" and her four modules provide methods that readers can readily adapt to their own situations.

Although there are fewer essays in Part II, they demonstrate on a smaller scale as much variety as those in Part I. William Collins Donahue of Rutgers University complements Strzelczyk's pedagogical focus in his "Beyond Cultural Literacy: 'Interactive Autobiography' as Holocaust Pedagogy." Here he describes a Holocaust unit that he incorporated into his third-year Autobiography and Culture course and in which he effectively utilized a class visit by a Holocaust survivor to expose his students to essential information about the Holocaust in a way that caught their interest, while simultaneously developing their skills in listening to, speaking, reading, and writing German. Karin Doerr of Concordia University discusses in "The Nazi Period, the Holocaust, and German-Jewish Issues as Integral Subjects in a German Language Course" the methods by which she introduces information and supplementary materials on these topics into her intermediate-level, two-semester German Composition and Conversation course. Readers who teach such courses will find her methods useful in expanding the traditional subject matter, informing their students about Germany's past and present, and sensitizing students to threats to a civil society. In "The Holocaust in an Introductory German Literature Course: Problematic Responses as a Catalyst for Curricular Change," her compatriot Miriam Jokiniemi of York University explains how some disturbing student responses to the Holocaust in regard to both literature and current events served as the impetus for her reevaluation of her second-year literature course. By redesigning the course to treat diversity and universality, Jokiniemi developed a unit that has enabled her to teach German Holocaust literature successfully in a section on alterity and Otherness.

Finally, in "The Teaching (and Not Teaching) of 'the Disaster,'" Leslie Morris of the University of Minnesota describes two courses she taught at Bard College, one on postwar German literature in translation called History, Memory, Narrative, and the other a comparative literature course entitled Poetry of Place/Poetry of Exile. Though neither course focused on the Holocaust or offered a Holocaust unit as such, both emphasized considerations essential for students and teachers of the Holocaust: its basic unrepresentability and the concepts of displacement, exile, and borders. Readers of this provocative essay not only will think of new ideas for their own courses of this kind, but also will realize that all the contributors to this volume are succeeding in the vital task Morris articulates, that is, "teaching what cannot be taught."

We have chosen the method and structure of a three-part "package" for the essay contributions to this volume, because this approach is especially appropriate and useful for our target audience of Germanists in German and German Studies. Each contributor presents an essay, the first component of each package, describing a Holocaust-related course or courses that he or she has taught. In these essays each author explains his or her philosophy of Holocaust teaching; indicates what works were selected and why; discusses the kinds of assignments and class activities used, and student response to the various components of the course; describes what aspects of the course worked effectively and why, and which proved problematic and why; and comments on what changes he or she would make in the course in the future. The essay format thus offers the reader detailed and extensive information about the development and teaching of each course described, information that is of vital interest and importance to any Germanist who may wish to adapt one of these courses or some of the insights in the essays for his or her own classes. The essays are not intended to portray ideal or perfect courses, but rather to provide sixteen varied visions of effective German and German Studies courses that involve the Holocaust.

A second component of each package is the syllabus for the course discussed in the essay. Each contributor has provided the syllabus that he or she used, in accordance with our purpose of presenting actual courses and the syllabi that worked for the professors who taught these courses.[1] Most of the syllabi have been adapted for this volume by omitting nonessential matters of purely local concern (instructors' office hours, locations, etc.) and by making other adjustments to use the space most efficiently. We have also changed the arrangement by date (month and day), which many of the syllabi originally contained, to a week-by-week or day-by-day method. This method eliminates extraneous dates and shows clearly how much time is devoted to a particular discussion or work. Thus readers can see at a glance the duration and the order of each item used in the syllabus, both of which are essential considerations for colleagues seeking ideas for constructing courses of their own. The syllabi are intended as basic course overviews that complement the extensive discussions and explanations provided in the essays. Further, the syllabi enable readers of this volume to skim each course quickly in order to determine which essays may prove most pertinent to their needs, and readers interested in developing or revising their own Holocaust-related courses may choose to adapt one or more of the syllabi or parts of them.

The list of works cited after each syllabus, together with the parenthetical notes in the essay text and any explanatory notes needed, is the remaining component of each essay package. These lists are not to be construed as lists of recommended readings. Rather, each contributor's list contains all print, film, and electronic works mentioned, quoted, or paraphrased in his or her essay and used in his or her syllabus. We have used MLA documentation style for our volume because it is the standard for scholarship in language and literature and thus is both familiar to and well understood by our intended readers. The notes and each list of works cited provide the documentation and scholarly apparatus required by the MLA system. Further, each list serves the important additional function of giving the reader an alphabetized and easily accessible reference file of the works used by the individual contributor to prepare his or her course and essay.

While the procedure of presenting essay packages makes our volume both especially useful and easily usable for its intended readership in the ways just discussed, the method does have a disadvantage which readers should note. It can sometimes call attention to a literary, film, or cultural work not because of its quality, but rather because of its highly touted publication or release and its consequent ubiquity in scholarly or popular discourse on the Holocaust at the time the courses were being taught or the essays written. This is the case with the frequent references to Goldhagen's *Hitler's Willing Executioners* (1996), which came under severe attack in the scholarly debate unleashed by the book's publication. Students in courses at the time this book was published of course came to class talking about it. Our contributors and their students have followed the debate, and some colleagues will use the book as a means of teaching critical thinking when they next offer their course. In that context they will discuss the debate with their students. We would strongly recommend that anyone who takes this approach should expose students to Browning's *Ordinary Men* (1992; reissued 1998), an excellent and widely accepted treatment of the subject that both he and Goldhagen address. Robert R. Shandley's edited volume *Unwilling Germans? The Goldhagen Debate* (1998) provides useful material by compiling various opinions on this scholarly controversy.

To serve our primary audience, Germanists in German and German Studies, yet to make our volume accessible to others who may wish to read it, the editors have developed a translation policy. Thus, English translations of any long German quotations (of approximately sentence length or more) in these essays appear in the notes, but we translate neither most individual German words and phrases nor the syllabi of the courses offered in German with German readings. We reason that the vocabulary of these words and phrases, many of which are historical in nature, should be familiar to anyone who teaches or intends to teach a Holocaust course, and that any colleague who wishes to develop Holocaust courses taught in German with German readings must be sufficiently proficient in German to understand untranslated syllabi of such courses.[2]

For our volume, Ronald Webster, a German historian at York University, has graciously prepared a list of important historical readings on the Holocaust and the Nazi era. Located after the essay contributions, his list contains major works reflecting the latest and most widely accepted standard of historical scholarship, as well as works that are important for other reasons, such as their impact. He has provided this list for our readers to guide Germanists who wish to acquire historical background in preparation for teaching a Holocaust-related course as well as to help experienced teachers who want to expand the historical knowledge they already have on this period in order to revise an existing course or introduce a new one. The works he has listed will also be useful as sources of historical readings for students in German and German Studies courses related to the Holocaust.

When one undertakes to teach the Holocaust, there are certain basic guidelines to consider in order to achieve the most effective conditions for teaching the subject. Although careful preparation is important for every course, this element is especially crucial when one wishes to teach the Holocaust. It is essential that the instructor be well grounded in the historical facts and issues related to the Holocaust in order to be able to present it to his or her students in context. The most efficient way to gain the needed knowledge would be to enroll in a course or courses on the Holocaust and its era offered in History or Holocaust Studies departments, yet often professors find it difficult to engage in formal classroom studies once they are employed. However, they can educate themselves about the Holocaust through reading and research. In addition, there are numerous Holocaust centers and museums, summer programs offered by universities and other research institutions, many conferences and workshops on the Holocaust, and now much information available from electronic sources, so there is ample opportunity to gain the necessary historical background.

Further, if a German or German Studies professor teaches a Holocaust-related course and his or her institution offers a Holocaust or Third Reich course in history or Holocaust Studies, it would be wise to recommend that students take the latter course before enrolling in the German or German Studies course. This approach would give students the needed historical context for studying the Holocaust and might mitigate the problem that students sometimes react overly emotionally to literature and cultural documents related to the Holocaust. Many of our contributors decry their students' lack of historical knowledge; if students entered their classes well versed on Holocaust history, the professors could devote their class sessions to teaching the actual course content instead of having to allocate time to provide students with historical background information.

The above guidelines are offered as recommendations, not prescriptions. The conditions mentioned, particularly the availability of history and Holocaust Studies courses on the Holocaust and Third Reich, are not present at every institution. The Holocaust is far too important a subject—and the consequences of not teaching it potentially far too devastating—to deny German and German Studies professors the right and the opportunity to teach their Holocaust courses if their students cannot take or have not yet studied history courses on the Holocaust. The volume's editors view all Holocaust-related courses as "Holocaust courses," whether they focus on Holocaust literature, film, cultural history, art, music, or other aspects of the Holocaust. Further, we contend that because German and German Studies professors are well grounded in the language, literature, culture, and history of the country and people from which the Holocaust originated, they offer an essential context and perspective to students in their Holocaust courses. The essays in this volume present courses that provide an appropriate context and illustrate the outstanding contribution of North American Germanists and German Studies professors to Holocaust teaching.

We and our contributors share the sincere hope that this volume will support and promote the teaching of the Holocaust by North American scholars of German and German Studies in the challenging years ahead. The courses developed and described by our authors will, we believe, spark unique and creative variations by colleagues already experienced in Holocaust teaching who are seeking new ideas to enable them to modify and revise their existing courses or to design new ones, as well as provide support for those scholars who are venturing into Holocaust teaching for the first time, either because of their own convictions of its importance or because of a departmental assignment. We realize that some colleagues never treat the Holocaust in their courses because they feel insecure about approaching a daunting subject of such historical and human magnitude, especially if their own graduate education included no instruction on the Holocaust; we trust that their exposure to this volume and the assistance it offers will give them the confidence and courage they need to embark on Holocaust teaching. Thus, we see ourselves, our contributors, and our readers as partners in the challenging yet crucial undertaking of providing meaningful instruction on the Holocaust in German and German Studies programs of North American colleges and universities. It is our hope that by "shedding light on the darkness" we may contribute to fulfilling the moral obligation incumbent upon our discipline and that by teaching new generations about the Holocaust we will be honoring the memory of its victims.

Nancy A. Lauckner

Notes

1. In the case of essays in which a contributor discusses more than one course, we asked the author to provide a syllabus for only one of the courses treated. If readers would like to obtain a syllabus for one of the courses for which none is reproduced here, they should contact the professor who taught the course in question. The list of contributors includes authors' affiliations.
2. Readers should also note another convention established for this volume: contributors who provide parenthetical dates after titles of translated works refer to the date of first publication or release in the original language, usually German.

Works Cited

Browning, Christopher R. *Ordinary Men: Reserve Police Battalion 101 and the Final Solution in Poland*. 1992. Reissued [with a new afterword by the author]. New York: HarperPerennial, 1998.

Goldhagen, Daniel Jonah. *Hitler's Willing Executioners: Ordinary Germans and the Holocaust*. New York: Knopf, 1996.

Shandley, Robert R., ed. *Unwilling Germans? The Goldhagen Debate*. Minneapolis: University of Minnesota Press, 1998.

Part I

Chapter 1

THE HOLOCAUST THROUGH LITERATURE AND FILM

David Scrase

In view of the fact that Vermont is a predominantly rural state with a population less than one percent Jewish and that it lacks both noticeable ethnic divisions and any concomitant and significant history of racism or genocide, Vermont's state university began teaching the Holocaust rather early. It offered a course in the mid-1960s entitled Assimilation—Holocaust—Israel, and in the fall semester of 1978, a course devoted *entirely* to the Holocaust. The instructor for the former was Professor Raul Hilberg, who had come to Vermont in 1956 and wrote the bulk of his monumental work *The Destruction of the European Jews* while at the University of Vermont. Hilberg and Samuel Bogorad, a professor of English, taught the latter course.

For a number of years they continued to teach this Holocaust course as, essentially, a history and literature course located in the Department of Political Science. Hilberg dealt with the historical facts and data; Bogorad approached the subject through works of literature. They continued to offer this course, which was immensely popular, on a regular basis until Bogorad retired in 1985. At this point, Hilberg began to teach a course that spent the whole semester laying forth the facts of the Holocaust.

Aware that a gap needed to be filled, I then began to offer in the Department of German and Russian, on a more or less regular basis, a course in English called Hitler and After, which, we hoped, would raise our enrollments a little. Hitler and After treated works of German-language provenance in English translation. It was, therefore, limited to whatever was available. Books such as Brecht's *The Jewish Wife and Other Short Plays*, which contains three selections from *The Private Life of the Master Race* (Furcht und Elend des Dritten Reiches, 1938), and Günter Grass's *Cat and Mouse* remained readily available, as they still do. Jurek Becker's *Jacob the Liar* was quickly out of print for a while, however, soon to be followed by Rolf Hochhuth's *The Deputy* and Peter Weiss's *The Investigation*, and the course became steadily less viable.

Meanwhile, in 1991, Raul Hilberg retired. The university held a three-day symposium, with six papers given by some of the world's preeminent scholars of the Holocaust, to celebrate the retirement of a man many consider the doyen of Holocaust scholars. The Dean of the College of Arts and Sciences, Howard Ball, preferred to see the occasion less as the end of an era than as the beginning of a new one, an era in which a Holocaust course would not depend on the presence of someone who just happened to be qualified to teach it, but would be an integral part of a regular program of Holocaust Studies. This program has now been established. The Department of History has reserved a slot for a Holocaust historian, and this person teaches a survey course once a year, as well as smaller Holocaust-related seminars at the senior and graduate levels. Meanwhile I have developed a course on the literature and film of the Holocaust, which is directed at a general undergraduate audience and which incorporates works in English by European and American authors, not just works by German-language writers. Given the material, the course would be offered at many institutions under the rubric of German Studies or German. At the University of Vermont, however, all courses containing foreign literature read and discussed in English are designated "General Literature." This is the course I will describe in this essay.

One of the tenets of the earlier, all-German literature course had been *Vergangenheitsbewältigung* (coming to terms with the past)—inevitably so, in view of the amount of literature devoted to this theme in the postwar period, and the dominance of this tenet over the decades since 1945 to the present. With regard to the Holocaust, there is, of course, the general educational goal: to learn from history and the mistakes of the past. But the categorization of the participants into victims, perpetrators, bystanders, and both rescuers and resisters, is also pertinent. Since the students who take my course have not always taken the History of the Holocaust survey course, I find it necessary to provide some historical background.

Fortunately, I have at my disposal a textbook which the Center for Holocaust Studies at the University of Vermont compiled specifically as an introduction to the subject. *The Holocaust: Introductory Essays* contains three sections. The first, devoted to the facts, is entitled the "History of the Holocaust." Its five chapters deal with the "Emergence of Modern Antisemitism," "The Rise of the Nazis to Power," "Nazi Persecution in Germany and Austria," the "Final Solution," and "Rescue and Resistance." This section provides the essential background for the students as they read the literature and view the films. Although the literature and films duplicate much of the material in the textbook, this is good rather than bad, for the students more readily learn repeated facts. The movie *The Longest Hatred* (1991), for example, duplicates, reinforces, and underscores the material in the chapter on antisemitism.

The course begins with some introductory remarks and information and a showing of Alain Resnais's short film *Night and Fog* (1955). By showing this film in the first class, I expose the students to almost everything that is yet to come: the rise of the Nazis, the persecution of the Jews (although the word "Jew" itself does not appear in the film, which does not specifically show the victims of the Nazis to be Jews), the roundups and deportations, the camps and annihilations, and the question of guilt. The discussion of the film (which usually takes place at the following meeting, since the harrowing images at the end of the film leave most students speechless) centers on such questions as the historical progression of events and the deeper argument of functionalist versus intentionalist theories, on questions of cinematographic devices such as camera angle, on the uses and limitations of documentary material, and on Resnais and writer Jean Cayrol's left-wing political agenda. The meaning and history of the term "Nacht und Nebel" is essential in this regard.

Having used *Night and Fog* to outline the progression of the Holocaust and set the scene for the semester's viewing and reading, the course now examines the rise of the Nazis in Germany and uses three sources to do so. Robert Bernheim portrays the historical facts well in the textbook *The Holocaust: Introductory Essays* in his chapter entitled "The Rise of the Nazis to Power." (The textbook's Chronology and Glossary are a helpful resource now, as well as throughout the course.) Secondly, Leni Riefenstahl's *Triumph of the Will* (1935) provides a limited visual picture of the Nazi consolidation of power, and thirdly, Bertolt Brecht's three brief plays *The Jewish Wife*, *In Search of Justice*, and *The Informer* give a different view of Germany under the Nazis.

When we consider the blatant propaganda of *Triumph of the Will*, we discuss comparatively and in more detail the same questions of documentary and political agenda raised in preliminary fashion about *Night and Fog*. The euphoria of many Germans; their manipulation by Goebbels and other influential Nazi figures; the cult of the Führer and of Hitler as a god-like savior; as well as Riefenstahl's camera techniques are all the basis of what is generally a very stimulating discussion. It is left to me, with the help of the textbook, to point out that the picture of the Third Reich recorded by Riefenstahl is one-sided and limited.

At this point Brecht's short plays provide a welcome change of view. It is now that I vary my teaching method. Knowing that the rapid and cursory reading accorded *The Jewish Wife* by the average student leaves most of Brecht's subtlety unnoticed, I divide the class into groups of about five, with the assignment of writing out the unrecorded half of the four telephone conversations conducted by Judith Keith. I tell the students that two or three of these groups will have to read their telephone conversations to the class and explain or defend their interpretations. In addition to providing information about middle-class life in Germany in the 1930s, with all its blindness, paranoia, and mistrust, Brecht's *Private Life of the Master Race* enables us to begin distinguishing among the genres: fiction, drama, and poetry.

I then examine in its general historical context and in its specific twentieth-century manifestation the question of antisemitism, which appeared neither in *Night and Fog* nor *Triumph of the Will* and which formed only one aspect of the short Brecht plays. The TV movie *The Longest Hatred* evoked the general picture well, if somewhat tediously. This film explains the early Christian roots of antisemitism, its growth during the Middle Ages, its widespread presence throughout Europe, and its apparent waning through the Enlightenment and during nineteenth-century assimilation. It shows the modern outburst of antisemitism in the twentieth century, its extreme and vicious violence during the Third Reich, and its continued vehement existence even since the end of the Holocaust in the Middle East and elsewhere. Although the film provides useful information, Francis Nicosia covers this material comprehensively in his chapter of the course textbook.

But the film—almost universally criticized by the students as tedious, if informative—serves as a useful foil to the more evocative and artistic movies we view. The opposing aspects of documentary facts, "tedious" or not, on the one hand and of their artistic representation on the other provide for a continuation of the debate begun on the first day and destined to continue throughout the semester.

By week three of the fifteen-week course, it is time to deal with the war, the occupations, the concentration of Jews and others in camps and ghettos, and the deportations. Bernard Gotfryd's book *Anton the Dove Fancier* (1990) is the story of a Polish Jew who lived through the occupation, ghettoization, deportation, and labor in the work and death camps; who emigrated from Poland to the United States after liberation; and who, in the 1980s, finally recorded his experiences not as a linear account or memoir, but as a series of interconnected short stories devoted to specific people, events, and adventures. These stories cover a span of about fifty years from life in prewar Poland to survival in the aftermath of the Holocaust. Students have no difficulty relating the events in these stories to the historical developments outlined in the textbook. The way Gotfryd deals with these events, the *artistry* of his depiction, the striking turns in fortune, the surprise endings, all enable us to look at the subgenre of the short story and make distinctions among the novel, the memoir, and the short story.

Anton the Dove Fancier tells of life in Poland, of discrimination and antisemitism, and of deportation and death in a series of interdependent short stories told by a participant whose subjectivity and objectivity are never an issue, while Marcie Hershman's *Tales of the Master Race* (1991) provides a similar sequence of interdependent episodes of life in a provincial town in wartime Bavaria. The life of Germans rather than Jews, then, of perpetrators and bystanders rather than victims (with a few exceptions), is her subject matter, and everything is invented rather than remembered. In a sense Hershman's stories take up life in Germany where Brecht left off; wartime existence is portrayed rather than prewar life. Both Hershman and Gotfryd are gifted writers, and student response is enthusiastic; their stories repay careful analysis as well as providing gripping adventures. Hershman is additionally valuable inasmuch as she introduces the subject of euthanasia.

The first nondocumentary or nondocudrama that we view is Jan Kadar's *The Shop on Main Street* (1965). Life in Nazi-occupied territory is once again the topic, but in this case the emphasis is on "Aryanization" of Jewish businesses, and on the human weakness of someone faced with the moral imperative to help. The dreamlike sequences, the experimental slow-motion episodes, and other advanced camera techniques in this relatively early, still black-and-white film, together with its careful structuring, provoke interesting discussion of the cinema as an art form.

Having examined the treatment of the Holocaust in pre-Holocaust productions such as Brecht's short plays and *Triumph of the Will*, having discussed documentary as well as artistic treatment of the subject, and having looked at the literary genres and subgenres of drama and fiction, we now read poems touching on the Holocaust. Theodor Adorno's much quoted, and misunderstood, statement that poetry after Auschwitz is barbaric is a good place to begin. There is no paucity of high-quality poetry from which to choose, but I usually concentrate on Paul Celan and Nelly Sachs so that students can appreciate that Holocaust poetry exists *in German*, even though most of them must be content to read it in English.

Meanwhile the students watch Heinz Schirk's German TV docudrama *The Wannsee Conference* (1984). Here the emphasis is on the turn to total destruction, the legitimization and the full, deliberate implementation of the "Final Solution" after the onset of the extermination of the Jews by the mobile killing units from June 1941 on. The film brings the focus back to the perpetrators. It helps destroy the myth that it was the monster Hitler who alone willed the destruction of the Jews; it shows the "banality of evil" (Hannah Arendt's term to describe Adolf Eichmann) in the bureaucratic functionaries of the Third Reich; and it enables us to discuss the figures of Heydrich and Eichmann. The almost complete absence of moral thinking is again central. Camera craft and more complex use of various cinematic techniques are of less concern. Now, near the halfway point of the course, we examine the camps in more detail, especially the death camps.

But before coming to the literature of Auschwitz, as one might term the works by Elie Wiesel, Sara Nomberg-Przytyk, and Peter Weiss, we read the first story of survival by passing as a Gentile: namely Louis Begley's *Wartime Lies* (1991). Like so many other stories of survival by people who were children at the time, Begley's account was written and published decades after the events it describes. *Wartime Lies* very effectively sets forth the problems involved in passing as a Christian. Living the lie of pretending to be what one is not becomes an important topic in the course, one which is also central to Agnieszka Holland's film *Europa Europa* (1990), which students view at this time.

Gotfryd's *Anton the Dove Fancier* had dealt with life in the camps, including Maidanek and Mauthausen, from the perspective of one who had experienced them. The death camp known by name to most students before they take the course is Auschwitz. The one work we treat that many students have already read is Wiesel's *Night* (1958). This book enables us to examine, again, the survival of a child who is obliged to grow up quickly. We now explore in more detail the mutual support of parent and child, a topic which is central to Begley's *Wartime Lies* and, later in the course, to Nechama Tec's *Dry Tears*. But it is the pious Eliezer's religious crisis that is the main topic of discussion.

The next book we read, *Auschwitz: True Tales from a Grotesque Land* (1985) by Sara Nomberg-Przytyk, serves as a perfect foil to *Night*. Firstly, it describes the experiences of a woman in the women's camp, and, secondly, it presents the case of someone sustained and rescued through her continued faith in communism, as opposed to one who loses his formerly unquestioning faith in his God and in the innate goodness of humans. In terms of form, too, the two works present an interesting contrast. Unlike Gotfryd and more like Begley, Wiesel describes in linear fashion the course of events in his life during the last few years of the war. Nomberg-Przytyk, on the other hand, proceeds more along the lines of Gotfryd's *Anton the Dove Fancier* and Hershman's *Tales of the Master Race* by portraying events and people in self-contained episodes. Both Wiesel's novel and Nomberg-Przytyk's tales are seen by students as gripping and fascinating accounts of each author's camp experiences.

The next film, *The White Rose* (1982), takes us back to Germany but introduces the virtually new theme of resistance. Here, instead of the isolated incidents of resistance to German atrocities in the Holocaust often only hinted at in Gotfryd's *Anton the Dove Fancier*, we examine the attempt of a courageous group of Germans to educate others about what is happening, only to lose their lives as a result. We also discuss in detail the cinematographic accomplishment of director Michael Verhoeven. Perhaps because most students have to rely on subtitles, much of *The White Rose* is missed by the students—some even think that the group is a Jewish resistance group. They do, however, like the film, whereas they almost universally dislike the next work we read, namely Rolf Hochhuth's *The Deputy* (1963), which they find long, "boring," hard to read (possibly because of the blank verse), and confusing.

The Deputy focuses on courageous and futile resistance, as well as moral weakness. We discuss the actions of Gerstein, along with those of Riccardo and the historical resisters Provost Lichtenberg, Father Maximilian Kolbe, and Bishop Clemens von Galen. The portrayal of Pope Pius XII enables us to examine not only the role of the Vatican and the Roman Catholic Church but also of other religious groups, such as the Confessing Church on the one hand and the German Christians on the other. Although *The Deputy* as a "documentary drama" brings us back to a constant topic of the course—the use of factual documents in the preparation of creative art—I am now considering dropping the work because of student reaction to it.

The film *The Boat Is Full* (1981), directed by Markus Imhoof, raises the question of national as opposed to religious or moral stance, as well as the issue of personal intervention. At about this time I introduce in class the short film produced by B'nai B'rith entitled *The Courage to Care* (1986). This series of short interviews with survivors and rescuers explores the question of moral activism and the willingness to take a stand and help a human being in dire need. I encourage students to consider whether they would have acted, and how and when they might have demonstrated the "courage to care."

Nechama Tec, a survivor who came to this country after the war, did not write *Dry Tears* (1982) until nearly thirty years after the events she describes. Only a child when the Germans invaded and occupied Poland, Tec was obliged to grow up fast, and her account reveals her as a perceptive and intelligent observer of all that she experienced. Since she and her sister were blond-haired and blue-eyed, they both survived by living with Polish families and passing as Christians, a circumstance which enables the class to draw comparisons with the situation in Begley's *Wartime Lies*. In fact, the role of the lie in surviving is another constant topic throughout the course (see also the movie *Europa Europa*). Tec's parents looked more stereotypically Jewish and survived in hiding. *Dry Tears* accordingly illustrates the two aspects of surviving in wartime Poland: as a "Christian," and in hiding. Although *Dry Tears* has weaknesses as a literary narrative, the students respond much more to the gripping content and ignore the stylistic shortcomings. It is one of their favorite books.

The film *The Courage to Care* and Tec's *Dry Tears* together form the most uplifting part of the course inasmuch as they focus on survivors praising their rescuers. Peter Weiss's *The Investigation* (1965) plunges its readers to the very depths of depravity and suffering. After Wiesel's *Night* and Nomberg-Przytyk's *Auschwitz: True Tales from a Grotesque Land*, this play brings to a close the trio of works that stress life and death in Auschwitz. *The Investigation* as documentary drama directs our attention once more to the matter of factual documentation versus artistic creation. The play's debt to Dante's *Inferno* points to the need for a framework to facilitate understanding impossibly difficult and incredible material. Once again literary form and the questions it raises are of paramount importance.

The Holocaust contains a myriad of subthemes and tangential questions, many of which have surfaced, often more than once, by this point in the course. But *A Love in Germany* (1983), the movie based on the book by Rolf Hochhuth and directed by Andrzej Wajda with the collaboration of Agnieszka Holland, introduces new themes. The primary one concerns forced labor and the position of the slave workers deported from their homelands throughout Europe to factories and farms in the Reich. Another important question is fraternization and concomitant definitions of the "traitor." Not least interesting is the scene in which the German authorities attempt to make an Aryan out of the unfortunate and, at first, unsuspecting Pole. The framework of the film and the constant alternation between the present of the 1980s and the past events of the 1940s emphasize the postwar German need to come to terms with the past. Perhaps because of the subtitles, the back and forth between the present and remembered past, and a lack of appreciation for technical subtleties, the students dislike the film intensely.

The theme of coming to terms with the past lurks in the background of Claude Lanzmann's epic film *Shoah* (1985). Given the inordinate length of the film ($9\frac{1}{2}$ hours), the class is able to view only part of it. I usually choose the central part (tape three of the five videotapes), which shows the Chelmno survivor Simon Srebnik with the Christian Poles in front of the church after the service celebrating the birth of the Virgin. This section also contains surreptitiously filmed testimony given by Franz Suchomel, a guard at Treblinka. We accordingly hear from a victim, some bystanders, and a perpetrator, and we carefully examine Lanzmann's art with the camera, his seemingly naive but actually penetrating questions as an interviewer, and his careful structuring of the film sequences.

The course concludes with a short fictional piece, *The Shawl* (1989) by Cynthia Ozick, and the film version (1982) of a long fictional novel, *Sophie's Choice* (1979) by William Styron. Both works are genuine fiction, neither memoir nor autobiography, and neither author is a survivor or direct victim. These works deal with the "aftermath" of the Holocaust by examining the effects of the Holocaust on Rosa who, having survived Auschwitz after having seen her child die, finds other people oblivious to, and disinterested in, sufferings such as hers; and on Sophie, likewise a survivor who has lost her children, who finds her way back to life in the United States through the love of Nathan, whose schizophrenia, however, finally leads them both to their deaths. The Holocaust did not, of course, end in May 1945 with the defeat of Germany and the liberation of those camps still "functioning" up to the very end, but has continued for the survivors and victims, their families, the perpetrators and their families, as well as, above all, the conscience of the world through the decades following 1945.

Because my course carries the designation "writing intensive," I accordingly do not usually give exams but ask for a minimum of four and sometimes as many as six essays. The standard of writing of the students attracted to this course varies considerably. Many appreciate the emphasis I place on high-quality writing, some do not. The following examples will illustrate the kinds of essay topics I have used: (1) What picture of German society does Brecht present in his three short plays? Allude also to the film *The White Rose*, if you wish; (2) Rolf Hochhuth's play *The Deputy* contains a typology of evil. Assess some of the perpetrators as they appear in the play from this standpoint; (3) What are some elements in *Wartime Lies* that make Maciek's life as a survivor different from the lives of other survivors?; and (4) What are the main qualities of Cynthia Ozick's book that make it such a unique contribution to Holocaust literature?

As this essay has shown, my course covers more than the years of the camps, more than the war, more than the Third Reich. It goes back to the very beginnings of antisemitism and ends with the continuing effects of the Holocaust in the last years of the twentieth century. It does, to be sure, concentrate on the events of 1933 to 1945, and, through the material used, it covers most of the themes and subthemes, most of the categories and subcategories of the Holocaust: the victims, the perpetrators, the bystanders, the rescuers and resisters; the identification, expropriation, concentration, deportation, and extermination of the Jews of Europe; passing as a Gentile, hiding, euthanasia, Aryanization, the aftermath, and so on. In the fall semester of 1996, students were fortunate to be able to welcome two guest speakers to class. Professor Gerhard Weinberg delivered the University of Vermont's 1996 Raul Hilberg Lecture and then talked to the class about his memory of living as a small boy in Nazi Germany and experiencing antisemitism firsthand. And in our last class we welcomed Raul Hilberg himself, who spoke about "counterfactuality" in the portrayal of the Holocaust. We ended, therefore, more or less where we began: with the facts of documented history (Hilberg's love) and the art of created history (every literary scholar's love, including mine).

The University of Vermont **Prof. David Scrase**

GENERAL LITERATURE 161, THE HOLOCAUST IN LITERATURE AND FILM

Books: Bertolt Brecht *The Jewish Wife and Other Short Plays*
  Bernard Gotfryd *Anton the Dove Fancier*
  Marcie Hershman *Tales of the Master Race*
  Nechama Tec *Dry Tears*
  Elie Wiesel *Night*
  Sara Nomberg-Przytyk *Auschwitz: True Tales from a Grotesque Land*
  Louis Begley *Wartime Lies*
  Cynthia Ozick *The Shawl*
  Peter Weiss *The Investigation*
  Rolf Hochhuth *The Deputy*

Films: *Night and Fog*
  Triumph of the Will
  The Longest Hatred
  The Shop on Main Street
  The Wannsee Conference
  Europa Europa
  The White Rose
  The Boat Is Full
  A Love in Germany
  Shoah
  Sophie's Choice

Students will write four short (750 words) essays. Some films will be shown in full or in part in class, others at evening viewings.

Evening Viewing

Week 1
  Introduction: *Night and Fog* (film)

Week 2
  The 1930s: *Triumph of the Will* (film) *The Longest Hatred* (film)
  Brecht: *The Jewish Wife* *The Longest Hatred* (film)

Week 3
  Brecht: *The Informer, In Search of Justice*
  The Longest Hatred (film)

Week 4
    Gotfryd: *Anton the Dove Fancier*
    Discussion   *The Shop on Main Street* (film)

Week 5
    Hershman: *Tales of the Master Race*   *The Shop on Main Street* (film)
    The Shop on Main Street (film)

Week 6
    Poems   *The Wannsee Conference* (film)
    Discussion   *The Wannsee Conference* (film)

Week 7
    Begley: *Wartime Lies*   *Europa Europa* (film)
    The Wannsee Conference (film)   *Europa Europa* (film)

Week 8
    Wiesel: *Night*
    Europa Europa (film)

Week 9
    Nomberg-Przytyk: *Auschwitz*   *The White Rose* (film)
    Discussion   *The White Rose* (film)

Week 10
    Hochhuth: *The Deputy*   *The Boat Is Full* (film)
    The White Rose (film)   *The Boat Is Full* (film)

Week 11
    Tec: *Dry Tears*   *A Love in Germany* (film)
    The Boat Is Full (film)   *A Love in Germany* (film)

Week 12
    Weiss: *The Investigation*   *Shoah* (film)
    A Love in Germany (film)   *Shoah* (film)

Week 13

                                            Sophie's Choice (film)
    Shoah (film)   *Sophie's Choice* (film)

Week 14
    Ozick: *The Shawl*
    Sophie's Choice (film)

Week 15
    Conclusions

Works Cited

Print Sources

Becker, Jurek. *Jacob the Liar*. Trans. Leila Vennewitz. New York: Arcade, 1996.
Begley, Louis. *Wartime Lies*. New York: Ivy Books, 1991.
Bernheim, Robert. "The Rise of the Nazis to Power." Scrase and Mieder 35–50.
Brecht, Bertolt. *The Jewish Wife and Other Short Plays*. Trans. Eric Bentley. New York: Grove, 1965.
Gotfryd, Bernard. *Anton the Dove Fancier and Other Tales of the Holocaust*. New York: Washington Square Press, 1990.
Grass, Günter. *Cat and Mouse*. Trans. Ralph Manheim. New York: Harcourt, Brace & World, 1963.
Hershman, Marcie. *Tales of the Master Race*. New York: HarperCollins, 1991.
Hilberg, Raul. *The Destruction of the European Jews*. 1961. Definitive and revised ed. New York: Holmes & Meier, 1985.
Hochhuth, Rolf. *The Deputy*. Trans. Richard and Clara Winston. New York: Grove, 1964.
Nicosia, Francis R. "The Emergence of Modern Antisemitism in Germany and Europe." Scrase and Mieder 21–34.
Nomberg-Przytyk, Sara. *Auschwitz: True Tales from a Grotesque Land*. Trans. Roslyn Hirsch. Chapel Hill, NC: University of North Carolina Press, 1985.
Ozick, Cynthia. *The Shawl*. New York: Vintage, 1989.
Scrase, David, and Wolfgang Mieder, eds. *The Holocaust: Introductory Essays*. Burlington, VT: Center for Holocaust Studies at the University of Vermont, 1996.
Styron, William. *Sophie's Choice*. New York: Random House, 1979.
Tec, Nechama. *Dry Tears: The Story of a Lost Childhood*. 1982. With a new epilogue. New York: Oxford University Press, 1984.
Weiss, Peter. *The Investigation: A Play*. Trans. Jon Swan and Ulu Grosbard. New York: Atheneum, 1966.
Wiesel, Elie. *Night*. Trans. Stella Rodway. New York: Avon Books, 1960.

Films/Videotapes

The Boat Is Full. Dir. Marcus Imhoof. Video. Limbo Film, 1981.
The Courage to Care. Prod. Carol Rittner and Sondra Myers. Video. New York: Anti-Defamation League of B'nai B'rith, 1986.

Europa Europa. Dir. Agnieszka Holland. 1990. Video. Orion Home Video, 1992.

The Longest Hatred: The History of Anti-Semitism. Dir. Rex Bloomstein. Prod. Nucleus for Thames TV and WGBH. 1991. PBS. 21 April 1993. Video. WGBH-Boston Video, 1993.

A Love in Germany. Dir. Andrzej Wajda. 1983. Video. RCA Columbia Pictures Home Video, 1985.

Night and Fog. Dir. Alain Resnais. 1955. Video. Video Images, 1983.

Shoah. Dir. Claude Lanzmann. Video. Paramount Home Video, 1985.

The Shop on Main Street. Dir. Jan Kadar. 1965. Video. Ceskoslovensky Filmexport, distributed by Public Media [last known distributor, no date given].

Sophie's Choice. Dir. Alan J. Pakula. 1982. Video. CBS/FOX Video, 1984.

Triumph of the Will. Dir. Leni Riefenstahl. 1935. Video. Embassy Home Entertainment, 1986.

The Wannsee Conference. Dir. Heinz Schirk. 1984. Video. Prism Entertainment, 1988.

The White Rose. Dir. Michael Verhoeven. 1982. Video. MGM/UA Home Video, 1983.

Chapter 2

THE WELL-UTILIZED SURVIVOR

Susan E. Cernyak-Spatz

The March–April 1996 issue of *Martyrdom and Resistance* contains an article by Eric Epstein of Penn State University-Harrisburg. Entitled "Survivors Underutilized," it expresses Epstein's disappointment at the lack of participation by Holocaust survivors in U.S. classrooms (4). On this point I agree with Epstein, although I know from experience that not every survivor is capable of speaking to an audience or even of expressing himself or herself clearly. When Epstein, however, urges the teachers among his readers "not [to] squabble about imprecise details" (4), I must strongly disagree with him.

Precisely the need to clarify the details of the Holocaust as exactly as possible prompted me to develop a Holocaust literature course based on my dissertation and my personal experience. I wanted to see one positive result that I could wrest from my horrifying ordeal. I was determined to teach as many coming generations as I could about the Holocaust through literature as well as through my firsthand knowledge.

I had already attained a degree of prominence for being available for classroom lectures in the secondary schools and colleges in the Charlotte, North Carolina, area during the months preceding Yom Hashoah. I thereby increased the awareness of many secondary school teachers about the importance of delving into the history of the Holocaust within the framework of teaching World War II.

It became important to me to inform students not merely with books, but also with my personal knowledge, and for more than just one guest

---

Notes for this section can be found on page 24.

lecture in a history class, so I started teaching my course at the University of North Carolina at Charlotte in the late 1970s. The Department of Foreign Languages includes the course under the German 3050 rubric, which covers literature in translation for German majors. Not only does the course fulfill part of the requirement for the German major, but it can also be used to satisfy one of the humanities requirements. The course has increased steadily in enrollment, even after my retirement in 1992, so it cannot be said that the constituency consists of students from my language classes who take the course because they like my teaching. Most of the students are juniors and seniors. Probably one-third of a class might sign up to fulfill a humanities requirement and expect a do-nothing course—the students are quickly disabused of that notion. The rest come out of interest after they have seen the Yom Hashoah exhibit I mount every year in the university library or simply because they want to know more about a topic that is frequently discussed. That a real survivor is teaching the course provides an added incentive. I suspect that word-of-mouth reports of the impact the course has had on many previous students also play a part in boosting the enrollment.

My course has met with interest in other departments of the university. Thus I have lectured frequently in the Departments of Sociology, Religion, Geography, Engineering, and Women's Studies, and the course even led to my teaching and lecturing in Germany about the Holocaust. In 1992 the Dean of the Pädagogische Hochschule in Ludwigsburg, an exchange institution for my university, asked me to prepare a Holocaust seminar to be taught there in the fall of 1993. Since I would be retired by then, I wrote a proposal to the Fulbright Commission and received a one-semester grant. Professor Doerfel, the exchange coordinator at Ludwigsburg, prepared for my seminar by ordering fifteen copies of each book on the list I had sent to him, but sixty-seven students appeared for the first class meeting. Throughout the abbreviated semester (15 October to 21 December) there was no attrition in the number of participants.

In the fall of 1994 I undertook a tour of twenty-three lectures in sixteen German cities, beginning with Wuppertal and ending in Chemnitz in the new federal states. I spoke to the upper-level Gymnasium classes, i.e., to students approximately seventeen to eighteen years of age, and again the aforementioned impact of a speech by a survivor played a significant role. The German Gymnasium does teach the Holocaust in history, ethics, and religion courses, but every one of the professors in whose classes I spoke thanked me for the strong impression that my lecture had made on the students, none of whom had ever encountered an eyewitness who painted the reality of the "Final Solution" and of Auschwitz "in living color."

The survivor who is trained to put his or her personal experience into the historical and geographic context of the period is an invaluable tool in Holocaust teaching. Today's students, accustomed to technological perfection, must understand what the misuse of technical proficiency combined with the disregard for morality can produce, and one can only demonstrate this by establishing the historical background of the "Final Solution." In his introduction to Ebbo Demant's *Auschwitz—"Direkt von der Rampe weg ... ,"* Axel Eggebrecht quotes Henry Ormond, one of the attorneys for the plaintiffs at the Auschwitz trial at Frankfurt (20 December 1963 to 20 August 1965), as follows: "'Wenn die letzten Überlebenden der Hölle von Auschwitz nicht mehr Zeugnis ablegen könnten—und darauf wartet man in gewissen Kreisen—, dann wird Auschwitz in nicht zu ferner Zeit nur noch eine Legende sein'" (7).[1] Eggebrecht adds: "Seine Befürchtung traf nicht nur ein, sie wurde durch die Wirklichkeit weit überholt. ... Dann meldeten sich jene 'gewissen Kreise' unverfroren zu Wort. ... Und nun konnte man lesen, die Schrecken der Vernichtungslager habe es niemals gegeben, ... das alles seien Erfindungen böswilliger antideutscher Hetzer in West und Ost" (7).[2] This is the challenge that confronts us as survivors and educators: we cannot let Auschwitz become a legend.

Having lived in Berlin in 1933 and in Vienna in 1938, and having been interned at Theresienstadt and Auschwitz between 1942 and 1945 enables me to talk from my own experience about every phase of the Holocaust. My research activities have added to my ability to discuss virtually every aspect of the Third Reich. The only element absent from my "Third Reich education" is the Polish ghetto experience, a part that I consider myself incredibly fortunate to have missed. Thus, since my course is structured on the model of Dante's *Inferno*, in stages of descent into the hell of the ovens, I can contribute personal experience to treating every one of the stages.

When I introduced my course at UNCC, revisionists, the Ku Klux Klan, and neo-Nazis were rumored to be trying to infiltrate schools, and revisionists and deniers were sending their publications in hardback to university libraries at no cost. I had to do what I could to immunize as many students as I could reach against the poison of the deniers. Since the revisionists and deniers were thoroughly acquainted with the facts and data of Holocaust history, precision was important. Despite Epstein's claims, we cannot overlook "imprecise details" or selective memories.

I decided that a brief survey of the history of religious as well as racial antisemitism was an important precondition for the course. I prepared a condensation of George Mosse's *Toward the Final Solution*, which I have used for the introductory lectures ever since. It has proven invaluable as students then had and still have little knowledge about the origins of their own religion, much less those of religious or racial antisemitism.

My presentation of the development of racial antisemitism, which originated during the Enlightenment and increased during World War I and the Weimar Republic in Germany in particular, as well as in the rest of the Western world, helps students understand that some of their own prejudices derive from transmitted clichés and stereotypes. The discussion on stereotyping goes beyond stereotyping of Jews to include every kind of stereotyping with which our environment and background confront us.

My reading list for the course contains works chosen for the greatest verisimilitude. The Holocaust does not need fantasy. Unfortunately, many excellent books do not stay in print long enough because of low demand for them. Those dealing with pre-Holocaust and Holocaust periods in Germany and, especially, Berlin appear to have the lowest sales and therefore shortest shelf life. Inge Deutschkron's *Outcast*, Leonard Gross's *The Last Jews in Berlin*, and Ruth Andreas-Friedrich's *Berlin Underground 1938–1945* had very limited editions. Hans Peter Richter's *Friedrich* is eminently suitable, despite being considered a children's or young adults' book, because it describes perfectly the progression from normalcy to horror as it moves from 1925 to 1942, depicting the short and ever more reduced and deprived life of a child from age six to adolescence and death. This book has stayed in print, perhaps because high schools have used it.

There are not too many books on Theresienstadt in English that give an objective view of the False Front Ghetto. Arnost Lustig's *Night and Hope* is one of the few usable books. Unfortunately, it does not depict the conditions in the ghetto very fairly, since it fails to acknowledge the efforts of the Jewish administration of Theresienstadt to ameliorate the life of the inmates. Norbert Troller's *Theresienstadt: Hitler's Gift to the Jews* is probably the most detailed of the available books on the ghetto. I myself translated these handwritten diaries of an architect-artist who was in Theresienstadt from 1942 to 1944. Regrettably, the work is only obtainable in hardcover, and I prefer using paperbacks to make book buying cheaper for the students. With approximately eight books per course, that consideration is important.

Elie Wiesel's *Night*, Tadeusz Borowski's *This Way for the Gas, Ladies and Gentlemen*, and Primo Levi's *Survival in Auschwitz* are, in my view, the most important standard works for the Auschwitz camp, since they give three distinctly different views of it: one by a Jewish youngster, Wiesel, who is very self-absorbed and does not see much more than his immediate surroundings; another by an adult Christian, Borowski, who is a keen observer of the camp, including the women's camp, from his relatively secure position of being a Pole with good connections; and the third by Levi, whose compassionate and psychologically astute analysis of his fellow prisoners and his surroundings is probably the best that I have read. I hope all three works will remain in print. Ilona Karmel's *An Estate of Memory* is a very powerful, albeit harrowing, slightly fictionalized narrative of a women's labor camp with no extermination machinery, but with the chimneys of Auschwitz looming in the foreseeable future and becoming the women's ultimate destination. I sometimes use Nechama Tec's *Dry Tears* because it provides the feminine point of view as well as an example of Polish rescuers. *Dry Tears* is a well-written, unemotional illustration of the fact that, even in Poland, not everything was purely black or white.

Thomas Keneally's *Schindler's List* offers an excellent depiction of the Polish ghetto horrors. It is as graphic as students can stand, yet shows that the rescuer in German uniform did exist, albeit rarely. I especially stress the portion of the text that describes the turning point when Oskar Schindler changes from profiteering opportunist to compassionate rescuer. On the other hand, Reuven Dafni's *Final Letters* is such a wrenching portrayal of deportation, ghettos, and camps that the students understand that the rescuers were all the more daring in the face of the prevalent treatment of the Jews and the punishment that faced captured rescuers.

Peter Weiss's *The Investigation*, unfortunately also out of print, thematizes the trials of camp perpetrators in the postwar period. Each year, therefore, I copy excerpts illustrating the most distressing aspects of the work, such as "The Ramp," "The Swing," "The Bunker," and "The Fire Oven."

The reserve reading selections are primarily intended as resources for the research paper. The exception is Hans Askenasy's *Are We All Nazis?*, whose chapter on the Milgram experiment we discuss in detail. That class period always results in a lively debate on the question Askenasy raises. Otherwise I consider it unnecessary to use philosophical writers, such as Emil Fackenheim, Saul Friedländer, or Lawrence Langer, with students who need, first and foremost, to be informed about the facts, figures, and personalities of the Holocaust.

The course concludes with *The Wave*. This film narrates a series of events in a California high school that show how little it takes to turn normal young people of an impressionable age into elitist fanatics who disdain and persecute those who do not agree with them. The film as well as discussions of neo-Nazis, revisionism, and Bosnian "ethnic cleansing"—all of which show, in my view, the cataclysmic impact of the Holocaust on the second half of the century—bring us to the present and serve as a warning for all students of the time Ormond predicted: "'Wenn die letzten Überlebenden ... nicht mehr Zeugnis ablegen könnten ..., dann wird

Auschwitz ... nur noch eine Legende sein."'[3] As long as we are able, my fellow survivors and I will keep working to prevent that.

The films used in the course, including *The Wave*, are shown in chronological order, starting with the well-known allegory *The Hangman*. I follow this with *The Double Crossing*, a film on the ill-fated voyage of the SS *St. Louis*, which depicts an actual event in the pre-Holocaust period, and then with *Transport from Paradise*, the film made from a compilation of Arnost Lustig's short stories about Theresienstadt. *The Warsaw Ghetto*, a collection of SS-produced films made during the existence of the ghetto to document "the decline of a race," as the narrator of the film claims, probably has the strongest impact on nearly every class. The classic Auschwitz film, *Nuit et brouillard* (Night and Fog), is shown between the readings from Borowski and Levi. Screening *The Wave* on the last day of the course leaves the students with the disturbing reminder that the Holocaust is stretching its tentacles into the present. Most students indicate in their evaluations at the end of the semester that they regard the films as an invaluable addition to the course.

As the syllabus indicates, I do not give frequent tests, since I rely on the students to integrate the material instead of regurgitating memorized information on quizzes. The midterm examination, the first of two written submissions, includes a few essay questions on the material read up to that point and asks for character analysis, text analysis, and comparisons. It also requires a short opinion paper that elicits the students' reactions and reflections on the material presented thus far. One of the most interesting reactions came from a student who had been born in the city of Auschwitz. Her grandmother must have been a political prisoner in the camp there, since the young woman was not Jewish. She wrote:

> ... living 25 km away from the biggest death factory and having a grandmother who survived Auschwitz, but never talked about it [,] made me very curious about the real history of the Holocaust. This class has given me the opportunity to realize some important factors ... that modern society is willingly forgetting. I strongly believe that there should be more materials available to the public as a constant reminder of those who did not return. Better yet, students should be forced to take Holocaust history classes.

A German adult student in the spring 1995 UNCC Holocaust class had this reaction to the first half of the semester: "Of all the courses I have taken, the Holocaust class is by far the most impressive and moving experience for me. Already in early childhood I was made aware of the satanic deeds of the Nazis. I only now realize how superficial that information was. ..." A reentry student, an ex-soldier, had been to Dachau and wrote:

"I thought after [seeing] that exhibit I had a complete insight of the Holocaust. It sparked my curiosity that an actual survivor of the Holocaust taught a Holocaust class here at the university. How little I knew, I now realize." Several students wished that this were a two-semester class, as they felt that they did not get enough detailed information in one semester. Of course, the material has to be compressed so that both the literary material can be absorbed and the personal narratives included.

There is no final exam since the research paper takes its place. Each student gives me his or her topic during a personal interview. I have created a catalogue in which the entries are sorted by topics, such as Pre-Holocaust Germany, Nazi Law, Propaganda, Children in the Holocaust, False Front Theresienstadt, the Polish Ghettos, SS Mentality, Reactions (or rather inactions) of the Free World to the Holocaust, Rescuers in Germany As Well As in Occupied Countries, Women in Auschwitz-Birkenau, Women's Support Groups, the Economic Effects of the Holocaust, the Industrial Empire of Auschwitz-Birkenau, Medicine and Science, etc. Students receive from my catalogue three titles on their subject, and from those three books, all available in the library, they can find further material if they need it. The paper must be submitted in MLA form as much as possible and include footnotes and bibliography.

In a university whose student population is largely composed of commuters from the surrounding area in the middle of North Carolina, I have, at times, attracted the largest classes in the Department of Foreign Languages. This suggests that a Holocaust course that combines personal history, written history, and literature works for me and probably would work for other survivor-teachers in similar institutions. I am not sure if such a course would satisfy students in large cities where it might draw a greater number of Jewish students. The few Jewish students who have strayed into my classes in the last eighteen years, however, have known little more about the Holocaust than their classmates.

There is clearly an urgent need for instruction about the Holocaust, and the number of survivor-teachers is shrinking. Perhaps a speakers bureau should be established to make teachers like us available so that we might share our methods and our knowledge with those who will still teach the subject after we are gone and who might be able to use our methods and our experiences in the future. Unfortunately, much of the survivors' testimony of our contemporaries is tainted by selective memory, a phenomenon that increases with age if one does not keep up-to-date. Thus it is all the more important that those of us who are studying and keeping abreast of the literature of the Holocaust hand our knowledge on to the next generation so that the teaching may continue long after us.

Notes

1. "'When the last survivors of the Auschwitz hell cannot bear witness anymore—and certain groups are awaiting this moment—then Auschwitz will be merely a legend in the not too distant future'" [all translations in these notes by Susan E. Cernyak-Spatz].
2. "His fears did not only come true, they were far surpassed by reality. ... Then those 'certain groups' came forward brashly. ... And now we could read that the horrors of the extermination camps had never existed, ... all were merely an invention of evil anti-German rabble-rousers in the West and the East."
3. "'When the last survivors ... cannot bear witness anymore ..., then Auschwitz will only be a legend. ...'"

The University of North Carolina at Charlotte	Prof. Susan E. Cernyak-Spatz

GERMAN 3050-001, GERMAN LITERATURE OF THE HOLOCAUST

Week 1

Introductory Discussion
The Hangman (film), Intro. Notes

Week 2

Intro. Notes, start reading *Friedrich*
Continue *Friedrich*

Week 3

Continue *Friedrich*
The Double Crossing (film), read *Final Letters* as assigned

Week 4

Report and discussion of *Final Letters*, read *Night and Hope*
Night and Hope

Week 5

Night and Hope, read *Are We All Nazis?*
Are We All Nazis?

Week 6

Transport from Paradise (film)
Discussion of *Are We All Nazis?*, read *Schindler's List*

Week 7

Schindler's List
Schindler's List

Week 8

The Warsaw Ghetto (film), continue *Schindler's List*
Read *Dry Tears*; take-home exam (due next meeting)

Week 9

Continue *Dry Tears*
Dry Tears, read *This Way for the Gas, Ladies and Gentlemen*

Week 10

This Way for the Gas
This Way for the Gas

Week 11

This Way for the Gas, Night and Fog (film), read *Survival in Auschwitz*
Survival in Auschwitz

Week 12
Survival in Auschwitz
Survival in Auschwitz

Week 13
Select and discuss research topics, read *The Investigation*
The Investigation

Week 14
The Investigation
Research sources assigned

Week 15
The Wave (film), LAST Class Day
Final papers are due at my office in three days.

Reserve Reading List

Author	Title
Askenasy, Hans	*Are We All Nazis?*, 11–40, 101–9
Dafni, Reuven	*Final Letters*, 12–13, 14, 31–33, 44–59, 83–86, 102–4, 123–26
Dawidowicz, Lucy	*The War against the Jews*, 114–15, definition of "Einsatzgruppen"; 135, camp construction; 136, the Wannsee Conference; 137, Theresienstadt
Perl, William	*The Holocaust Conspiracy*, 11–35, 53–74. Illustrations: 119–45, 147–67
Rogasky, Barbara	*Smoke and Ashes*, 34–58, 73–96, 141–52
Wyman, David	*The Abandonment of the Jews*, 3–58

Required Texts

Borowski, Tadeusz	*This Way for the Gas, Ladies and Gentlemen*
Keneally, Thomas	*Schindler's List*
Levi, Primo	*Survival in Auschwitz*
Lustig, Arnost	*Night and Hope*
Richter, Hans Peter	*Friedrich*
Tec, Nechama	*Dry Tears*
Weiss, Peter	*The Investigation* (supplied by instructor)

Works Cited

Print Sources

Andreas-Friedrich, Ruth. *Berlin Underground 1938–1945*. Trans. Barrows Mussey. New York: Paragon House, 1989.
Askenasy, Hans. *Are We All Nazis?* Secaucus, NJ: L. Stuart, 1978.
Borowski, Tadeusz. *This Way for the Gas, Ladies and Gentlemen*. Trans. Barbara Vedder. 1967. Harmondsworth: Penguin, 1976.
Dafni, Reuven. *Final Letters*. New York: Paragon House, 1991.
Dawidowicz, Lucy. *The War against the Jews 1933–1945*. 1975. Ardmore, PA: Seth Press, 1986.
Deutschkron, Inge. *Outcast: A Jewish Girl in Wartime Berlin*. Trans. Jean Steinberg. New York: Fromm International Publishing Corp., 1989.
Eggebrecht, Axel. "Zur Einführung." *Auschwitz—"Direkt von der Rampe weg...." Kaduk, Erber, Klehr: Drei Täter geben zu Protokoll*. Ed. Ebbo Demant. Reinbek bei Hamburg: Rowohlt Taschenbuch Verlag, 1979. 7–12.
Epstein, Eric. "Survivors Underutilized." *Martyrdom and Resistance* (March–April 1996): 4, 14.
Gross, Leonard. *The Last Jews in Berlin*. New York: Simon & Schuster, 1982.
Karmel, Ilona. *An Estate of Memory*. New York: Feminist Press, 1986.
Keneally, Thomas. *Schindler's List*. New York: Simon & Schuster, 1982.
Levi, Primo. *Survival in Auschwitz: The Nazi Assault on Humanity*. Trans. Stuart Woolf. New York: Simon & Schuster, 1996.
Lustig, Arnost. *Night and Hope*. Trans. George Theiner. Evanston: Northwestern University Press, 1985.
Mosse, George. *Toward the Final Solution: A History of European Racism*. New York: Howard Fertig, 1978.
Perl, William. *The Holocaust Conspiracy: An International Policy of Genocide*. New York: Shapolsky Publishers, 1989.
Richter, Hans Peter. *Friedrich*. Trans. Edite Kroll. New York: Puffin Books, 1987.
Rogasky, Barbara. *Smoke and Ashes: The Story of the Holocaust*. New York: Holiday House, 1988.
Tec, Nechama. *Dry Tears*. Westport, CN: Wildcat Publishing Company, 1982.
Troller, Norbert. *Theresienstadt: Hitler's Gift to the Jews*. Trans. Susan E. Cernyak-Spatz. Ed. Joel Schatzky. Chapel Hill, NC: University of North Carolina Press, 1991.

Weiss, Peter. *The Investigation: A Play*. Trans. Jon Swan and Ulu Grosbard. New York: Atheneum, 1966.
Wiesel, Elie. *Night*. Trans. Stella Rodway. 1960. New York: Bantam Books, 1982.
Wyman, David. *The Abandonment of the Jews: America and the Holocaust, 1941–1945*. New York: Pantheon Books, 1984.

Films/Videotapes

The Double Crossing. Dir. Andy Marko and Nancy Partos. Prod. The Holocaust Memorial Foundation of Illinois and Loyola University of Chicago. Video. Ergo Media, 1992.
The Hangman. Dir. Paul Julian and Les Goldman. 1963. Video. CRM Films, 1965.
Nuit et brouillard (Night and Fog). Dir. Alain Resnais. 1955. Video. Classics Releasing, 1993.
Transport from Paradise. Dir. Zbynik Brynych. 1963. Video. Facets Video, 1987.
The Warsaw Ghetto. Prod. BBC Television. 1967. Video. Distrib. Social Studies School Service, Culver City, CA, [n.d.].
The Wave. Dir. Alex Grasshoff. Video. Films, Inc., 1981.

Chapter 3

VICTIMS AND PERPETRATORS
The Many Voices of the Holocaust

Thomas Freeman

On a recent trip to Washington, I visited the United States Holocaust Memorial Museum for the first time. I found that I knew the documents, photos, and relics on display so well from my teaching that it was hardly necessary to look at the captions and written explanations. The progression of the exhibits closely parallels the structure of my Holocaust literature course at Beloit College. Like my course, the museum exhibit starts with an overview of Jewish life in Eastern and Western Europe, using slides and films. The museum has an enormous collection of photo portraits of the population of an Eastern European *stetl*, arranged so that they seem to reach to the sky. The purpose of my overview of Jewish life before the Holocaust is to remind students that the genocide destroyed both people and an entire culture. My approach in this segment of the course is interdisciplinary. I give a brief introduction to Yiddish culture, language, literature, and music.

As I do, the Holocaust museum offers an introductory historical survey. I include a documentary slide presentation like that shown in the museum on Jewish life in Europe before the Holocaust; a discussion of traditional religious antisemitism and of ideological, racial antisemitism; and an overview of Hitler's rise to power and of the historical events of the Holocaust. Both the curators of the museum exhibit and I consider the persecution not only of the Jews but of other groups as well: Communists, Sinti and Roma, homosexuals, Freemasons, and Jehovah's Witnesses. Like the museum exhibit, I treat the inadequate American Jewish response and the role of the United States and other countries in refusing to take large numbers of Jewish refugees, as the plight of the refugee ship SS *St. Louis*, turned away off the shores of Cuba, illustrates. Other topics in my course that the museum displays also cover are the role of the resistance, the rescue of the Danish Jews, the Warsaw Ghetto uprising, the intervention of Wallenberg, the fate of Jews in various European countries, the liberation, and the war trials. The museum commemorates by country the names of non-Jews who helped Jews, and the varying sizes of the lists reveal at a glance the differing attitudes towards Jews among the nations where the Holocaust took place. Both the museum exhibit and my course portray the various stages of the Holocaust: the restrictive measures against Jews, deportation, the creation of ghettos, the murder of Jews in the concentration and the annihilation camps. I give more emphasis than the museum exhibit does to the forced collaboration of some Jews in the genocide: the Jewish councils, the Jewish police, and the Jewish Kapos. This is a central theme of Sobol's "concentration camp" musical *Ghetto* (1984), which I have discussed in detail elsewhere ("Die Kontroverse") and which I regularly read with my students.

The "heavy" architecture of the museum echoes in every detail the characteristic architecture of the camps and transforms the world into a kind of sacred "Holocaust space" in an enormous tomb-like memorial hall, somewhat similar to Yad Vashem in Jerusalem, with the names of the camps hewn onto the walls, illuminated by an eternal flame and the light of thousands of candles, which are lit by the visitors to the museum as they pass through. That is to say, visitors are invited to engage in a ritual act to give expression to their emotional response to the museum.

I have on occasion been able to provide students with an opportunity to participate in this sort of commemorative, ritual activity. For instance, on national Holocaust day, one class put together an all-campus event held in the College theater. It included singing Yiddish songs of the Holocaust, a talk by a survivor, and a candlelight vigil.

A basic problem in teaching the Holocaust is conveying past events as present, "living" reality. To each new generation of students, the Holocaust seems to recede further in time, becoming more remote historically. It moves into the realm of cowboys and Indians, which was a world of genocide that we have transformed into a mythic national adventure. One effective classroom exercise that addresses this problem requires small groups of students to pretend a Holocaust is threatening them in the U.S. and to discuss plans of action. After this, the entire class reconvenes to continue arguing the issues. One can do this exercise both at the beginning and the end of the course so that the students can compare how their plans of action have been modified by more detailed knowledge of the Holocaust.

I find the most effective way of conveying the Holocaust as a living reality is to have Jewish survivors and non-Jewish German eyewitnesses speak to my students. This moves the events out of the history books into the classroom. As time passes, these speakers will be people who experienced the Holocaust as children. When there are no more survivors, we will have to rely on the archives of recorded interviews, such as locally accessible ones made with Holocaust survivors living in Wisconsin or Steven Spielberg's Survivors of the Shoah Visual History Foundation. I sometimes play audio- and videotapes of survivors who visited my classes and have since died. However, I have found that a statement made by a person who is physically present has more impact than anything on a screen, probably because we associate film and TV screens so strongly with fantasy and fiction.

Thus, in my teaching, my comments about my own family's experiences in the Holocaust and even my secondhand account of stories survivors have told me, have a strong impact, enabling my listeners to see the Holocaust not from the outside, on a screen or the page of a document, but rather from the inside, through the eyes of the victims. This sort of live testimonial brings the Holocaust directly to my students, as do some of the memorabilia I pass around in class, ranging from a part of the electrified wire from one of the camp fences, to an ashtray labeled "International Military Tribunal Nürnberg 1945," to original Nazi propaganda materials—such as antisemitic books and magazines or SS "poetry" and instruction manuals.

Another way of literally bringing students into the world of the Holocaust is to take them to sites in Germany related to the Holocaust or Third Reich. When Beloit College students participate in our overseas seminar in Hamburg every two or three years, I take some students who have studied the Holocaust in my course to historical sites in Hamburg and around Germany. These have included Dachau, Sachsenhausen, Bergen-Belsen, and Neuengamme, Hitler's party rally parade grounds at Nuremberg, and, in Berlin, the execution cells at the Plötzensee Prison, the "archaeological" excavations of the Gestapo torture chambers, and the Wannsee Villa, where the Nazi elite made plans for the "Final Solution." Even at these sites, one can enhance the impact by having a former inmate guide the students. These guides not only show the camps, but also sites where deportations took place, or where Jews were confined before being deported. Thus, seminar students experience the Holocaust and the Third Reich in terms of places and spaces that have a powerful emotional effect. Since my students visit Berlin together with a group of German adult education students, they discuss the Holocaust with these Germans during our orientation meeting at the Wannsee Villa.

If we seek to understand why the Holocaust occurred, we must look into the minds of the perpetrators, and one might interpret this as representing their point of view. The degree of student interest in the motives of the perpetrators depends on the makeup of particular classes. When I first started teaching Holocaust literature in the mid-1970s at SUNY-Brockport, which at the time had several thousand Jewish students, the majority of the students in the course was Jewish, and my focus was primarily on the suffering of the victims and on the moral and theological issues raised by the Holocaust. I included guest lectures by the local rabbi on Jewish views of evil and suffering in response to the Holocaust. At Beloit College, a small liberal arts college in Wisconsin, most of the students in my Holocaust course are not Jewish. Because the course is part of the German program and counts toward the German major, many of the students come from a German-American background, reflecting the large German-American population in Wisconsin.

In the last few years, I have encountered a kind of resistance or backlash among these students, which expresses itself in resentment that such a course makes the Germans look bad and guilty and also reflects on their own identity as German Americans. This appears to be a broad phenomenon taking place at other schools as well. Some students want to avoid courses on the Holocaust, preferring those on contemporary German culture (*Völkerkunde*) that focus on quaint folk customs and regional variations in different parts of Germany in speech, character, and dress. They want courses that present positive views of Germany that make them feel good about themselves and their origins. Recently, students in our German Club who were taking a course on fascism in the History Department told me when I was planning the German literature offerings for the next semester: "We don't want to hear anything more about Hitler!"

Yet it is perhaps their identification with Germany that leads some of these students to be curious about the perspective of the perpetrators when they are confronted with the Holocaust. I have therefore accommodated their interest in the ever-evolving syllabus for my course. This interest in the perpetrators is understandably even more pronounced in Germany. As a Humboldt and Fulbright guest professor at the University of Hamburg, I had the opportunity both to attend courses on the Holocaust and to team teach one with a German colleague. My students there were, for the most part, members of the third generation since the Holocaust. There was clearly identification with the perpetrators, and in the discussions the students did draw upon their own family histories.

Initially, when I was just teaching Holocaust literature as the history of Jewish suffering from a Jewish perspective, I stressed such "classic" authors as Wiesel, Frankl, and Schwarz-Bart. My experiences with German university students and my use of texts that reflected their interests led me to incorporate more texts dealing with the minds of the perpetrators into my course in the U.S. I first introduced texts by major German authors who were Nazi sympathizers, such as Benn and Jünger, as well as the psychohistorical analysis of Nazi literature by Theweleit. This material was not always on the formal list of assigned reading, as I covered some of it in lectures or in handouts with excerpts. In addition, I have used documentary texts such as the memoirs of the commandant of Auschwitz with an article that gives a psychoanalytic reading of his autobiographical account (Zeilen), General Jürgen Stroop's report on his liquidation of the Warsaw Ghetto, and Peter Weiss's docudrama *The Investigation*, which contains the trial testimony of concentration camp guards. The analysis of the perpetrators in Hannah Arendt's study of Eichmann and in Adorno's study of the authoritarian personality provides another perspective. I also discuss the Milgram experiments and the Stanford study of the behavior of prisoners and guards (Haney, Banks, and Zimbardo). These works move into the realm of psychology and political and social philosophy and provide part of the interdisciplinary dimension of my course.

The fundamental question I wish to pose in this essay is what should be our goals in teaching the Holocaust? What is the proper balance between detached analysis with its implicit goal of rational "understanding" and responding to the genocide on an emotional level of sheer horror? When I first began teaching Holocaust courses, my students spent considerable time simply experiencing and discussing the emotions of horror evoked by the texts. In my course, I examine Holocaust literature as I do other literatures, raising questions about structure, perspective, style, imagery and symbolism, with the goal of better understanding both the content of the texts and the writing strategies of the authors. Perhaps one can find the proper balance by interspersing segments of objective analysis into a very emotional course as a means of breaking the tension. Here I find Lawrence Langer's book *The Holocaust and the Literary Imagination* a useful guide for my students despite its convoluted language.

Since my course is part of a German literature major, its function is not just to inform students about the Holocaust, but also to teach them to read and write and to discuss issues in German, as well as to learn techniques of literary criticism. It is part of a general college curriculum intended to teach critical thinking, methods of scholarly research, and argumentation. Thus, when we examine different historical accounts, such as those of Hilberg, Bauer, or Diner, we seek to uncover and criticize their underlying presuppositions. When we read Celan's "Todesfuge," students must write about the poem in the light of Adorno's assertion that there can be no aesthetically adequate literature portraying the Holocaust and that after Auschwitz only silence is appropriate.

Thus, on one level, my course must function as a vehicle for studying literature in German. But beyond this, a number of assumptions that underlie my philosophy of Holocaust teaching inform the course goals. Assuming that the Holocaust can be "explained," that it was not a random, purely irrational event that one can dismiss as an unfathomable twist of fate, I ask historical questions aimed at determining why the Holocaust occurred. This inquiry includes examining whether the Holocaust was unique in history or the repetition and continuation of earlier events. Was it an aberration or typical human behavior? I also consider the question of German "guilt" as raised by Hilberg, Arendt, and, most recently, Goldhagen, who indicts much of German society as enthusiastically involved. In addition, I discuss German repression and denial of guilt, Germany's so-called *Vergangenheitsbewältigung*, and the problem of survivor guilt among Holocaust victims and their children.

My students receive study questions on the readings to answer in short papers or prepare for discussion, and they also fill out vocabulary sheets that list technical terms and concepts covered in lectures. Other assignments include taking lecture notes to hand in, giving reports in class, and writing term papers based on library research or, where appropriate, on interviews with relatives who were survivors or witnesses. The witnesses may include relatives who were members of the Allied forces, or German or Jewish relatives who moved to the United States after World War II. In addition, students keep journals of responses to readings and films, class discussions, and visits by survivors.

It would be unthinkable for me not to treat the Holocaust in my courses since I am Jewish and most family members of my parents' generation were murdered in the Holocaust, and since I have studied and taught Yiddish and Jewish Studies and have published on Yiddish and Holocaust literature. However, because I am the only German language and literature professor at Beloit College, I generally cannot offer a Holocaust course in English outside of the German program. In order to reach more students, I did experiment with this one semester, offering the course in English, requiring students who wanted German credit to do the readings, exams, and papers in German, and giving them an extra session each week in German. This meant using texts available in both English and German. Although this arrangement doubled my usual enrollment, the German students felt shortchanged, so I did not repeat this attempt.

Students respond to the course in written evaluations that include comments and suggestions, papers and course diaries, as well as observations during discussions. Their reactions vary according to their academic competence and differing backgrounds, e.g., adult education students versus younger undergraduates, Jewish students versus non-Jewish students, students from German versus non-German family backgrounds, African-American, gay and lesbian, Latino, Asian-American, Native American, German exchange students, and exchange students from other countries more or less affected by the Holocaust.

Because of the limited number of literature courses I can offer, I present literature of the Holocaust as part of the wider context of German and European literature since 1933. My course includes fascist literature, German exile literature about Nazi Germany and the persecution of the Jews, and Holocaust literature. Thus, I must usually condense into one syllabus material that could benefit from several semesters of study. Understandably, students are overwhelmed by the material.

I try to alleviate the pressure imposed by the expectation that they read the material in German by having the same texts available on reserve in English. My students tend to write the translations of the words and phrases they have looked up onto the German text, so I can often tell how they have prepared for class. Even if I do not make these texts available in English, resourceful students can obtain them. Because we usually do some translation practice, it becomes readily apparent if students have not looked up words either in the dictionary or using the translation. The classes are small, consisting of five to ten students whom I know well. I try to treat them as responsible adults interested in mastering the language and learning about the subject matter. Most of my advanced students participate in our overseas program and are genuinely concerned about being prepared.

As we work with a generation of students nurtured on television who cannot even cope with reading a lengthy text in English, there are ways we can adjust our courses. Some of the works I consider important are long novels. If students become engaged with a lengthy text so that extended discussions seem productive, I spend more time on the work and omit something else. This elicits both praise for my "flexibility" and reproach for not adhering strictly to the syllabus.

To deal with the problem of too much material, I have tried using anthologies of Holocaust literature, but I find that the excerpts are too short to convey the impact of the full works. I consider Schwarz-Bart's *The Last of the Just* one of the most moving portrayals of Jewish life in Germany and France before and during the Holocaust, but it is a long novel that students find difficult to "get into." The excerpts provided in anthologies are not necessarily the passages I want to discuss, and the larger context is missing. Creating my own handouts cuts students' book expenses but raises problems with copyright laws, and students feel overwhelmed with piles of materials that are easy to lose. Charlotte Delbo's *Trilogie*—like Schwarz-Bart's novel, available in a German translation from the French—presents a similar problem. Well written, with a complexity that lends itself to literary analysis, it is a fragmented text of self-contained episodes, so one can successfully read individual segments without reference to the rest of the novel. I intend to use it again because it provides the perspective of a non-Jewish woman in the camps who describes the fate of Jews and other groups of prisoners.

My goal in the course is to lead students to the material, provide a forum for discussion, and invite them to think for themselves, to do their own learning, that is, to teach themselves. By virtue of its material, my course engages students on an emotional level. In their confidential course evaluations students comment favorably on this. They also express approval for the incorporation of language instruction, including conversation, reading, and vocabulary practice, and for my use of a combination of discussions, lectures, videotapes, and readings. Students generally react favorably to my use of a broad range of perspectives, including that of the perpetrators, although one Jewish student regretted that we had not read more "Jewish literature." They recognize that in order to withstand the voice of evil one must confront it directly. This is necessary so that we can better understand the Holocaust and ensure that it does not happen again.

Beloit College   **Prof. Thomas Freeman**

GERMAN 250, LITERATURE AND THE THIRD REICH

1. Course Goals: This course is designed both for students with knowledge of German who wish to do some of the readings in German and for students with no knowledge of German who wish to do the readings in English. The classes will be conducted in English, except for the fourth hour which will be held in German and will provide German students with thirteen hours of lectures and discussions in German in the course of the semester. The goal of the course is to acquaint students with the position of authors considered acceptable in Hitler's Germany, the plight of authors in exile, and the fate of those caught up in the Holocaust.

2. Grading and Attendance: You are expected to attend all classes since your participation in discussions will determine part of your grade.

3. Exams, Reports, Paper: There will be two tests and a final exam. In addition, students will present in class a brief (fifteen-minute) report on a topic of their choosing related to the subject matter of the course. There will also be a short (a few pages) final paper. This paper may be on the same topic as your report, so that, in effect, the report can serve as a way for you to test out your ideas for your paper before you turn it in.

4. Texts: We will read only parts of some books.
  1. Ernst Jünger, *The Storm of Steel*
  2. Gottfried Benn, *Primal Vision*
  3. Stefan Zweig, *The World of Yesterday*
  4. Bertolt Brecht, *The Jewish Wife and Other Short Plays*
  5. Bertolt Brecht, *Fear and Misery in the Third Reich*
  6. Bertolt Brecht, *The Resistible Rise of Arturo Ui*
  7. Nelly Sachs, Poetry
  8. André Schwarz-Bart, *The Last of the Just*
  9. Victor Frankl, *Man's Search for Meaning*
  10. Peter Weiss, *The Investigation*
  11. Hannah Arendt, *Eichmann in Jerusalem*
  12. Rolf Hochhuth, *The Deputy*

5. Films: *Die Blechtrommel* (The Tin Drum) and perhaps other feature films in German related to our topic will be shown outside of class.

Reading Assignments
Section I—Literature in the Third Reich

Week 1
Introduction to the course.

Week 2
Jünger, 1–91.
Jünger, 92–160. Fourth hour, German session.

Week 3
Jünger, 161–243.
Jünger, 244–319. Fourth hour, German session.

Week 4
Benn, vii-xxvi, 29–38, 46–53.
Benn, 54–62, 63–83, 83–101, 135–46. Fourth hour, German session.

Week 5
Benn, Poetry, 213–93.

Section II—Literature of Exile

Week 5
Quiz, first hour. Zweig, 304–57. Fourth hour, German session.

Week 6
Zweig, 358–440.
Brecht, *Fear and Misery in the Third Reich* (Brecht's *The Jewish Wife and Other Short Plays* includes *The Jewish Wife* and, among other short plays, *The Informer* and *In Search of Justice*, which you may want to use as well). Fourth hour, German session.

Week 7
Brecht, *Arturo Ui* (first half).
Arturo Ui (second half). Fourth hour, German session.

Section III—Literature of the Holocaust

Week 8
Quiz. Schwarz-Bart (I recommend the whole book, but we will concentrate on part III to the end). Parts III and IV, 91–225.
Schwarz-Bart, parts V and VI, 229–340. Fourth hour, German session.

Week 9
   Schwarz–Bart, parts VII and VIII, 341–422. Sachs, Poetry.
   Frankl, 1–148. Fourth hour, German session.

Week 10
   Frankl, 151–213. Weiss, *The Investigation*, 1–131.
   Weiss, 132–270. Fourth hour, German session.

Week 11
   Hochhuth, *The Deputy*, 7–165.
   Hochhuth, 165–352. Fourth hour, German session.

Week 12
   Arendt, *Eichmann*, 1–82.
   Arendt, 82–150. Fourth hour, German session.

Week 13
   Arendt, 151–205.

Week 14
   Arendt, 206–98.
   Reports. Fourth hour, German session.

Week 15
   Reports.
   Review. Fourth hour, German session.

Week 16
   Final exams and deadline for papers.

Works Cited

Print Sources

Adorno, T. W., et al. *The Authoritarian Personality*. New York: Harper, 1950.
Arendt, Hannah. *Eichmann in Jerusalem: A Report on the Banality of Evil*. New York: Viking, 1964.
Bauer, Yehuda. *A History of the Holocaust*. New York: F. Watts; Little, Brown; 1982.
Benn, Gottfried. *Primal Vision: Selected Writings*. New York: New Directions, 1960.
Brecht, Bert[olt]. *Fear and Misery in the Third Reich*. Ed. N. Ostrovskaya. Moscow: Mezhdunarodnaya Kniga, 1942.
_____. *The Jewish Wife and Other Short Plays*. Trans. Eric Bentley. New York: Grove, 1965.
_____. *The Resistible Rise of Arturo Ui*. Trans. Ralph Manheim. London: Methuen, 1976.
Celan, Paul. "Fugue of Death." Trans. Christopher Middleton. *Modern German Poetry, 1910–1960*. Ed. Michael Hamburger and Christopher Middleton. New York: Grove, 1962. 318–21.
_____. "Todesfuge." 1952. *A Reader in German Literature*. Ed. Robert Spaethling and Eugene Weber. New York: Oxford University Press, 1969. 215–16.
Delbo, Charlotte. *Trilogie*. Trans. Eva Groepler and Elisabeth Thielicke. Frankfurt am Main: Stroemfeld/Roter Stern, 1990.
Diner, Dan. "Negative Symbiose. Deutsche Juden nach Auschwitz." *Babylon* 1.1 (1986): 9–20.
Frankl, Victor E. *Man's Search for Meaning: An Introduction to Logotherapy*. Part one trans. Ilse Lasch. New York: Pocket Books, 1963.
Freeman, Thomas. "Die Kontroverse um Sobols Musical *Ghetto*." *Auseinandersetzungen um jiddische Sprache und Literatur. Jüdische Komponenten in der deutschen Literatur—die Assimilationskontroverse*. Ed. Walter Röll and Hans-Peter Bayerdörfer. Akten des VII. Internationalen Germanisten-Kongresses Göttingen 1985. Tübingen: Max Niemeyer Verlag, 1986. Vol. 5 of *Kontroversen, alte und neue*. Ed. Albrecht Schöne. 81–83.
Goldhagen, Daniel Jonah. *Hitler's Willing Executioners*. 1996. New York: Vintage, 1997.
Haney, Craig, Curtis Banks, and Philip Zimbardo. "Interpersonal Dynamics in a Simulated Prison." *International Journal of Criminology and Penology* 1 (1973): 69–97.

Hilberg, Raul. *Die Vernichtung der europäischen Juden. Die Gesamtgeschichte des Holocaust.* Ed. Ulf Wolter. Trans. Christian Seeger et al. Berlin: Olle & Wolter, 1982.

Hochhuth, Rolf. *The Deputy.* Trans. Richard and Clara Winston. New York: Grove, 1964.

Hoess, Rudolf. *Commandant of Auschwitz: The Autobiography of Rudolf Hoess.* Trans. Constantine FitzGibbon. London: Weidenfeld and Nicolson, 1959.

Jünger, Ernst. *The Storm of Steel.* Trans. Basil Creighton. 1929. New York: Howard Fertig, 1975.

Langer, Lawrence. *The Holocaust and the Literary Imagination.* New Haven: Yale University Press, 1975.

Milgram, Stanley. *Obedience to Authority.* New York: Harper and Row, 1974.

Sachs, Nelly. *In the Habitations of Death.* Trans. Michael Hamburger et al. New York: Farrar, Straus and Giroux, 1967.

Schwarz-Bart, André. *The Last of the Just.* Trans. Stephen Becker. New York: Atheneum, 1960.

Sobol, Joshua. *Ghetto.* Berlin: Quadriga Verlag, 1984.

Stroop, Jürgen. *The Report of Jürgen Stroop.* Trans. D. Dabrowska. Warsaw: Jewish Historical Institute, 1958.

Theweleit, Klaus. *Männerphantasien.* 2 vols. Munich: dtv, 1995.

Weiss, Peter. *The Investigation: A Play.* Trans. Jon Swan and Ulu Grosbard. 1966. New York: Atheneum, 1981.

Zeilen, Joachim. "Psychogramm des Kommandanten von Auschwitz." *Psyche* 4 (1991): 335–62.

Zweig, Stefan. *The World of Yesterday.* 1943. Lincoln: University of Nebraska Press, 1964.

Films/Videotapes

Die Blechtrommel (The Tin Drum). Dir. Volker Schlöndorff. 1979. Video. Kino International Corp., 1996.

Chapter 4

DESIGNING WITHIN AND AROUND LIMITS
The Holocaust, Madonna, and Me

Linda Feldman

My connection with Holocaust teaching began precipitously, and quite against my better judgment, in November 1987, when I casually picked up the student newspaper at a leading Ontario university and read an account of a talk given by a survivor of the Shoah. The reporter noted with apparent wide-eyed innocence that the speaker had been incarcerated at the Madonna [Majdanek] concentration camp. Madonna?! At this juncture, the reader was wide-eyed, too. The startling coupling of chastity and pop-star eroticism in place of historical dehumanization and degradation sounded a particularly imperious note given the recent memory wars, then exemplified by the *Historikerstreit*, the Bitburg incident, and German Chancellor Helmut Kohl's fateful remark in Israel about being the beneficiary of the "Gnade der späten Geburt" (see Bark and Gress 423–25).

The reporter's error brought home to this reader, as nothing else had, the difference that ten years could make in one's relationship to history. If for me the Holocaust, which had resulted in the deaths of well over one hundred relatives, was increasingly present, especially in the silence engulfing my family, it was clearly absent from the consciousness of a reporter barely half a generation younger than I. The mistake was all the more significant as it represented a gap of knowledge not just of the campus journalist, but of the editorial staff as well. Faced with what was in all

---

Notes for this section can be found on page 54.

likelihood a representative rather than an idiosyncratic slip, I was forced to examine my ethical and pedagogical responsibilities toward myself, my discipline, and my students. In the end, despite misgivings that my family background might convert my course into an exercise in narcissistic necrophilia, I submitted a proposal for what I hoped would be a less perilous special topics offering—The Holocaust and Aesthetic Theory. Offered in the spring of 1989 under the aegis of the Western Literature and Civilization program of the department with which I was then affiliated, the course, which attracted over seventy students, enjoyed a modest success. Thanks to the popularity of Madonna, my teaching career had taken on a new direction.

The Second Time Around

Fast forward to the present: The Holocaust and Aesthetic Theory is *not* the course that will be discussed in this article. Indeed, given the economically, educationally, and culturally privileged status of the University of Western Ontario's student clientele, it is safe to assume that, once transplanted to a much less favored institutional setting, this course would not have flourished. The second time around would thus necessarily be another first time around. I was willing, but was I able? The pathway to offering an alternate course on the Holocaust in my new institution was obstructed by a potentially lethal combination of impediments. As exemplified by the Madonna reference, one major problem was going to be the students' unfamiliarity with history, but this factor was predictable. Other difficulties, many of them all too familiar to colleagues affiliated with smaller, fiscally beleaguered schools and universities, included:

- a personnel situation so strapped that the mounting of a new departmental course would stretch individual workload norms and program obligations beyond the tolerable and permissible level;
- a lack of discretionary decanal funding to subsidize any additional teaching stipends that might become necessary as a result of the implementation of the course;
- a complex range of pedagogical issues and problems related to the aims, content, and intended clientele of the course; and, finally,
- political considerations at the disciplinary and institutional levels.

Taken together, these limitations seemed to suggest that the likelihood of mounting a course on Holocaust Studies was going to be slim at best.

That a new course was in fact offered in 1996 and 1998 demonstrates that success is an achievable goal, even when "everything is wrong and nothing is right." In this instance, the ability to design within and around limits, a process that will be outlined in the following sections, proved critical to success. While the particular combination of barriers at my institution means my account can have no general prescriptive value, I hope that the coping strategies developed to deal with individual problems will be helpful to those facing similar challenges.

A Self-Financing Scenario

The institutional context in which the new course was created is typical of many urban campuses. Located in Windsor, Ontario, a city dominated by the automobile industry, the university has in the past decade increasingly favored academic sectors catering to high technology and manufacturing. Within the relatively disadvantaged arts faculty, the foreign languages have long since been amalgamated, with each of the sections reduced to skeletal staffing. For German, this means a teaching complement of $2\frac{1}{2}$ people, one of them the head of the department. Given the necessity of offering a fixed number of language, civilization, and senior literature courses for program students (majors, minors, honors students) each term, there is no room for add-on innovations and sharply curtailed curricular maneuverability. Introducing a lower-level English-language service course on the Holocaust would thus entail generating extra funds so that the course instructor could be freed from some other mandatory teaching responsibility that term. But where in the midst of a financial crisis particularly hurtful to the arts faculty could $3,500 be found? The solution ultimately lay in the ad hoc development of an "Adopt-a-Course" financing strategy.

Fund raising for a course was, and still is, unique on our campus. As a creative solution to our needs, it was purely the child of chance. However, the chain of events leading up to the Adopt-a-Course principle, is, in its very typicality, worth considering for its potential applicability elsewhere. It all began when a Holocaust survivor, recently retired from the Economics Department, approached the German section in need of a translator. He explained that the courageous Austrian woman who had saved his life during the war was going to be the recipient of an award at the annual fund raiser of the Detroit Holocaust Center. One translating commitment grew into four more public engagements, as various community groups invited the rescuer to address them. The productive collaboration between the retiree, who was the woman's host, the department head, and the German section resulted in several discussions on possible ways to commemorate her valor; the retired colleague was willing to provide seed money for that purpose. One suggestion was to set up an essay contest in the rescuer's name; the other, to introduce a course on Holocaust Studies. In short order, two university accounts, to which charitable donations could be made, were set up. Thanks to the benefactor, financing of the course for a first round was assured.

If fund raising for the course was to succeed in the long term, however, it was clear that other sources of revenue would have to be identified. Two other fortuitous circumstances suggested possible avenues for exploration. First, the donor was currently cochairing the city-wide Yom Hashoah committee, which draws from a broad range of community organizations, including the district labor council, Christian and Jewish denominations, the local Jewish Community Center, the separate (Catholic) and public school boards, the municipal multiculturalism committee, the municipal race relations board, etc. Since I was slated to teach the course, the donor invited me to join the committee, thus providing me with access to rich resources in people, ideas, and, through them, possible sources of funding.

In addition, and quite coincidentally, I was serving as the local interviewer for the Visual History Foundation's Survivors of the Shoah Oral History Project, an undertaking that in the course of two years brought me into the homes and lives of almost one-half of the approximately fifty Shoah survivors in my community. Often I came to know their children as well. Both parents and children frequently expressed a deep interest in the course and its future, and although it has not yet been necessary to approach them for financial support, they would likely be responsive.

A check from a student following the trial run of the course made me aware of a third group of possible benefactors: former class participants. Since the Holocaust course was given in the late afternoon so that the broader community could participate, a significant number of registrants were in fact working people or modestly comfortable retirees, for whom tuition was free. Their enthusiastic response to the course would seem to indicate that should broader fund-raising efforts be necessary, they, too, would form an identifiable group for targeting. Since the course will be given on a two- to three-year rotation, there is a comfortable lead-up time in which to raise the necessary funds.

When one reviews the evolution of the Adopt-A-Course principle, certain key points emerge: the ability to remain open to a chance opportunity, the necessity of considering unconventional approaches to problem solving, the usefulness of developing and identifying potentially supportive contacts among community groups and individuals sympathetic to a course of this nature, and the support and good will of administrative structures at the home institution. Though in our experience much happened by chance, this need not be the case.

Lest this description of Adopt-A-Course be interpreted as a wholesale endorsement of the principle: it is not. The curricular "mallification" of the university, with its emphasis on satisfied customers, scarcely needs the reinforcement provided by the Adopt-A-Course approach. In addition, there is the question as to whether such a precedent may provide a justification for further erosion of baseline budgets in the particularly hard-pressed humanities. In fiscally precarious times, anything is possible. Moreover, that a course on the Holocaust housed in our department could not get guaranteed financing was also very disturbing. However, faced with the choice of writing memos for several years with no assurance of success, or seizing the unexpected opportunity to launch the course immediately, we regarded decisive action as the better alternative. Indeed, the past success of the course can only add to the department's bargaining hand in future negotiations to regularize its financing.

Student-Centered Design

Published syllabi in Holocaust Studies give testimony to the imagination, intellectual rigor, and individualistic approaches of course creators.[1] A survey of these course offerings, many of which exhibit an admirable depth as well as breadth, leads to the inescapable conclusion that the *what* is being stressed over the *how* or *for whom*, especially at the upper level. The absence of the students from these descriptions bespeaks a clientele whose assumed reading and writing skills mark them as firmly entrenched in middle-class Euro-Canadian and Euro-American cultural traditions. For the teachers of such students, the *what* may, in fact, achieve pedagogical primacy. With greater accessibility to university education, however, increasing numbers of students do not conform to this conventional norm. What planning strategy is the instructor to follow in such cases?

My response was the development of the student-centered, rather than curriculum-centered, course, To Auschwitz and Beyond: Reflections on the Meaning of the Holocaust, a new subtitle I generated for German 15-234, which was the only second-year, English-language service course available for adaptation. The unconventional shifting of emphasis away from the *what* to the *for whom* becomes more comprehensible when we examine the specificities of the intended clientele. The chief challenges that I have to take into account when giving this course include:

- the neo-Canadian background of the majority of students, many of whom do not have English as their first language;
- the lack of educational depth in the students' family backgrounds. Many are the first in their families to attend a university; often, working-class families are not particularly supportive of postsecondary education, which drains the family budget either overtly or covertly;
- the entrenched passivity fostered by authoritarian family structures and the school system. Students are unwilling to talk or voice an opinion, and their body language signals the desire to be overlooked;
- a low level of traditional cultural literacy. Many of these students do not read at all outside of school; preferred recreational reading is mostly Michael Crichton, Danielle Steele, and Stephen King; and for the most part, their extracurricular cultural experiences are exclusively with the products of mass culture;
- ignorance of history, a state encouraged by a provincial high school curriculum that allows students to obtain a high school diploma with only two courses in Canadian history;
- high prioritization of outside jobs, which are necessary to secure an education in a period of spiraling costs;
- low intellectual horizons. Most students see university study as a pathway to a job and are interested in securing the highest return for the least effort;
- poorly developed reading skills and, as a consequence, virtually absent critical skills.

Adjunct complications to be taken into account for planning purposes are the lack of any formal prerequisites for this course, and, in the case of program students, the de facto abolition of the formerly obligatory introductory-level German literature course due to recent administrative enforcement of class size minima at the 200-level. Given these limitations, it became apparent that the course would have to be multipurpose, teaching a multiplicity of skills as well as conveying selected discrete knowledge. In other words, defining the *for whom* would set further parameters for the *how* and the *what*. The course would have to foster reading, critical, and participatory skills; increase sensitivity to the use and function of language; promote literary awareness; and provide a chronological sequence of texts largely drawn from the German-language cultural sphere. As a backdoor into further literary and cultural studies, it would have to prove its relevance to the lives of the participants.

Teaching the *What*

The trial run of this one-semester course of fourteen weeks had thirty-nine contact hours, somewhat more than usual, thanks to a Tuesday/Thursday cycle that avoided time lost by Canadian Thanksgiving. The first week consisted of one session on "Why Give a Course on the Holocaust?" I tried, by tracing my involvement with the Holocaust on both a personal and professional basis, to convey to the students a sense of my own evolution and, with it, the changing corpus of information that I apprehend and transmit. By inserting my subjectivity so strongly, I tried to deconstruct their concept of knowledge as being monolithically authoritarian and, hence, unchallengeable. Then I posed the corollary question "Why Take a Course on the Holocaust?" and had them fill out a short questionnaire to give me a first demographic snapshot of the class. In addition to the usual information about their age, year of study, languages spoken or read, and area of concentration, I asked them why they were interested in taking this course and what it was they hoped to learn. I also asked them to list any materials they might have read on the Shoah. Their answers were a way of quickly checking whether our mutual expectations were well matched, or whether it would be necessary to refine course content and student expectations in order to avoid frustration or disappointment.

Following the introductory session came four equally long modules, the contents of which can be easily varied as the need arises. The first module, "The Discursive Framework Leading up to the Holocaust," dealt with the origins and evolution of stereotypes of the Jew in German culture. We began with an examination and discussion of pictorial representations of Jews in the Middle Ages and early modern period because most junior (lower-division) students feel more comfortable with images and are more likely to contribute to a class discussion at this early stage; a dynamic is thus established that will likely carry through the rest of the course. The second week was devoted to the theme of "Constructing the 'Master Race.'" New pictorial material from the eighteenth to twentieth centuries was introduced and rounded out by texts drawn from philosophy (Mendelssohn, Kant, Herder, Hegel on Jews) and racial science. Students were encouraged to analyze and, if possible, explain the shifts they perceived in the discourse on Jews. For most, the vicissitudes of anti-Jewish attitudes were a complete revelation and a conscious collision with a historical process extending beyond their own lifetimes. The first module closes with a discussion of the mechanics of the Holocaust, "The 'Final Solution' to the 'Jewish Question.'" The students work largely with historical documents: the minutes of the Wannsee Conference, Kogon's account of concentration camp routine, a chronology of the Holocaust, flow charts of administrative organization both in Germany and the Generalgouvernement, excerpts from the Warsaw diary of Adam Czerniakow. From experience, I have learned that this segment of the course cannot be glossed over: it is the presentation of details that first makes the concept of systematic mass extermination comprehensible. Unlike me, my students never saw on television the liberation of Bergen-Belsen by Canadian troops: they have no resources of familiar images to fall back on.

The second module, "Holocaust Narrative in Its Ethical Dimensions," invites the students to think through the implications of the Holocaust on contemporary life. I discuss the challenge to humanism and the arts presented in the Celan-Adorno exchange and reinforce it by contrastive samples of writing—and behavior—by Melita Maschmann and Hannah Senesh, Elie Wiesel and Rudolf Höss. The very different language used by these writers is probed in detail, with students elaborating on the differences and seeking to explain what these differences say about the values and priorities of each writer. We also discuss excerpts from the writings of Anne Frank and Jona Oberski, with an eye to understanding why one has become a part of the school curricular canon while the other has not. Finally, we look at the impact the Shoah has had on notions of legal accountability (Nuremberg, Vietnam, the Russell war tribunal, the World Court indictment of perpetrators of mass murder in Bosnia); science (the question of duress in scientific experimentation); religion (liberation theology, the revaluation of Simone Weil and the exculpation of the Jews); politics (the creation of the state of Israel, policies on refugee claimants); etc. Newspaper clippings related directly or indirectly to the Holocaust are brought in. The students learn that the Holocaust is not something that happened "back then," but something whose ramifications reach into central parts of our lives. At this point, I tie the section into the essay contest named after the rescuer previously mentioned in this chapter. In this way, students have six weeks in which to generate ideas for an essay entry on moral courage.

The third module, "Inventing Meaning: Making Sense of the Holocaust in Fiction," traces individual responses to the extermination of the Jews and initiates the shift from documentary to creative material. I begin by stressing the particularity of the response, even in a process engulfing millions, by pointing to Jean Améry and Primo Levi's contrasting assessments of the value of intellectualism as a means of survival. Highly contrastive fictional text samples heighten the sensitivity of students, who must play off Tadeusz Borowski's cynicism in his short story "The People Who Walked On" versus Hasidic retention of faith in three legends recorded by Yaffa Eliach, or Peter Weiss's underplayed and moving portrayal of Lili Tofler in *The Investigation* against the erased Jewishness of the Christocentric portrayals of the toyshop owner in Günter Grass's *The Tin Drum* or Jan Lobel in Luise Rinser's novella *Jan Lobel from Warsaw*. I call the predicament of the children of survivors to student attention with excerpts from Maxim Biller's "Die Nachmann-Juden" and the sample chapter "Auschwitz (Time Flies)" from Art Spiegelman's *Maus II*. The excerpts represent a broad range of text types, styles, and genres; with the appropriate lead-on questions, the students develop a greater sensitivity to how language and genre choice shapes what is or is not being said. With practice, they become less passive in their reading behavior as they finally accept the deliberative nature of creative writing and seek to unravel both its intentionality and its effects upon them.

"Memory Shifts," the final module, deals with the inevitability of reassessments and reevaluations of the past. We examine the process of revisioning from several quarters: political (the Bitburg incident, the fight over the Carmelite convent at Auschwitz); historical (the historians' controversy, the reception of Daniel Goldhagen's *Hitler's Willing Executioners* by the popular versus the academic readership); and literary (excerpts from Fassbinder's "Garbage, the City and Death," Saul Friedländer's juxtaposition of the Intifadeh and the Holocaust in *When Memory Comes*). The revisionism of neo-Nazi groups is also discussed, with a visit to the Web site of one of Canada's most notorious Holocaust deniers.[2]

Finally, we look at the broadened use of the term "Holocaust" to describe other mass exterminations, e.g., those of the Armenians in Turkey, the First Nations in Canada, the Hutus in Rwanda, the Muslims in Bosnia, the Cambodians under Pol Pot. To what extent is the use of the term justified in these cases? The module aims at trying to foster an appreciation of the concept of the Holocaust both in its particularity for Jewish history and self-understanding, and in terms of the technological paradigm for mass murder that it establishes.

The final session of the course, "Conclusion: Reghettoizing the Holocaust," raises the question of how and where teaching about the Holocaust occurs. I look at resistance to teaching the Holocaust or to listening to stories about the Holocaust, a resistance already present in the immediate postwar period. Though it is the central event of the twentieth century, I point out that the Holocaust is in danger of becoming invisible rapidly, particularly with the passing of the generation directly involved in it. The high school history curriculum mentions it en passant. I then elaborate on why it is important that the Holocaust be remembered and point to how it has become symptomatically invisible on our local campus. The plea for the centrality of the Holocaust to an understanding of twentieth-century German cultural studies forms the final thesis of the course.

Teaching the *How*

If, by positioning myself publicly to my discipline and my teaching area, I tried to illustrate the subjective interaction we have with the material that we teach, it was of highest priority to have students position themselves to what they were supposed to be learning. For about a third of the class of twenty, this was no problem: four were survivors and the other two retirees. Their life experience and the change of pace that a university course provided made them willing to take positions on almost anything said in class. However, their very keenness to participate risked intimidating the primary target audience of the course, namely the younger undergraduates.

To deal with the heterogeneity of the class, I relied heavily on discussion groups of five. The mature students were distributed among the five groups so that they could not form a distinctive bloc. The barriers between them and the younger students eroded quickly, as they got acquainted in group discussions. Each group appointed a spokesperson for each session; the spokesperson could not serve in that capacity again until everyone else in his or her group had carried out that responsibility once. In that way, even the most reticent students had to organize, coordinate, and articulate the ideas presented in their group discussion, and then elaborate on or defend them in any subsequent general class discussion.

I worked with short texts, usually two to five pages in length, which I term "micro-texts."[3] When necessary, I generated the translations, a task that could be irritatingly time-consuming. Micro-texts had the advantage that the groups could discuss them thoroughly in class. Depending on how complex my teaching goals were for the hour, the groups could either work independently on the same task, or a class task could be divided into component parts that were then assigned individually to the various groups.

To monitor the students' progress, I sporadically asked them at the end of the hour to hand in a sheet listing three new things they had learned. Alternately, I gave some statement and asked them to comment on it based on the discussion held that day. These exercises not only served to ensure maximal attentiveness, but also gave me the opportunity to see if the students were following the new material well. In addition, students practiced comprehension and critical skills by completing two short reading assignments. The first and easier entailed summarizing an essay, while the second required students both to summarize and to critique an argumentation.

The heterogeneity of the class composition posed a challenge. There were two Polish students whose sensitivities to some of the materials became increasingly apparent; a Tunisian student unhappy with the evolution of Middle Eastern politics; and intellectually, a wide spread between the extremely naive ("But wasn't it illegal to kill Jews?") and the extremely sophisticated. Among the younger students, only one, to my knowledge, had a Jewish background.

I tried to take their positionality into account by giving them as much latitude as possible in terms of their major assignment. They could either write a comparative essay on two Holocaust memoirs—an assignment I phrased as drearily as possible in the hope of dissuading them from choosing it—or generate their own project, be it an interview or independent research. Students could work in pairs, provided the input of each was clearly identifiable. The results of the assignment were extremely interesting. One student did a study of revisionist Web sites and handed in a binder containing a wide spectrum of useful printouts she had made in the course of her Web surfing. The Tunisian student wrote on the implications of the Holocaust for the Arab world. The two Polish students, particularly upset with *Maus*, did an interview with a local Polish priest who had been interned in Auschwitz during the war because of his resistance activities. Another student's grandmother, who had kept her Jewish roots a secret until she found out he was taking this course, allowed him to interview her about her experiences in the war.

Other students conducted interviews with survivors whom I had earlier contacted in order to solicit their participation. The parameters for the interview were simple: the students had to focus on areas in which they felt their knowledge was deficient. Their first task was to prepare a list of questions that they then presented to me and that they had to justify. The interview itself was to be forty-five minutes long, but tended to last an hour. Students also prepared a protocol in which they evaluated what had gone well, what had gone poorly, and what they had learned from their experience. The interviews differed markedly, depending on the sophistication of the students involved, but feedback indicated how important the experience of talking to a survivor had been to many of them, personally as well as intellectually. I realized that the authenticity of their experience would allow them to testify to the reality of the Shoah long after the survivors themselves were no more. For the future, I kept copies of their taped interviews.

In Retrospect

In many respects, the course functioned miraculously well, especially considering how much improvisation was necessary to adapt to a new clientele. Particularly, the choice of micro-texts, which allow a line-by-line, word-by-word dissection, proved to be of great pedagogical value, as students tackled the task of reading actively and attentively. The juxtaposition of highly contrastive texts was also useful and provocative; on more than one occasion I entered the class to find students already embroiled in arguments about that day's scheduled readings. Class discussions were spirited and lively and often gratifyingly well argued.

The broad parameters of the major assignment will be retained, since they seem to have achieved their goal of allowing the students to pursue their interests in ways that made the course more relevant to them. However, every trial run reveals areas in need of adjustments. Some changes I plan to implement are: an obligatory sourcebook on the history of the Holocaust and an anthology of Holocaust literature. The former is especially necessary since there is currently no history course to which I can direct students and since most have little or no background in European history. I will add the latter for assignment purposes, since an anticipated increase in class size will result in the need for an increased number of personalized reading assignments.

The discomfort of the Polish students also raises the question of how to cope more effectively in class with questions of resistance and collaboration in Eastern Europe. A revised teaching strategy is particularly urgent since Eastern European immigration to Canada is on the rise and already manifest in German enrollments at our university. In future, the questions and sensitivities of these students will be addressed in the second module on "Holocaust Narrative in Its Ethical Dimensions," where we can examine comparative victimhood and initiate a discussion on the psychology of the rescuer versus that of the collaborator.

Notes

1. See, e.g., Gideon Shimoni, ed., *The Holocaust in University Teaching*.
2. I recommend that readers who want information about Holocaust revisionism and denial for themselves or their students consult *The Nizkor Project*. This very reputable Canadian project maintains an excellent listing of antiracist materials and other useful sources for Holocaust educators.
3. Since readers who wish to adapt this technique will want to make their own selections, my syllabus and list of works cited identify the works from which I excerpted the micro-texts, but not the inclusive page numbers.

The University of Windsor **Prof. Linda Feldman**

GERMAN 15-234, MASTERPIECES OF GERMAN LITERATURE
TO AUSCHWITZ AND BEYOND:
REFLECTIONS ON THE MEANING OF THE HOLOCAUST

Week 1
Why Give a Course on the Holocaust?

Module 1: **The Discursive Framework Leading up to the Holocaust**

Week 2
Constructing the Jew as an Alien "Other"

Week 3
Constructing the "Master Race"

Week 4
The "Final Solution" to the "Jewish Question"

Module 2: **Holocaust Narrative in Its Ethical Dimensions**

Week 5
The Challenge of the Holocaust to Western Civilization and Culture

Week 6
Anne Frank, Jona Oberski. Rudolf Höss, Elie Wiesel

Week 7
Melita Maschmann, Hannah Senesh. Moral Imperatives, Moral Dilemmas

Module 3: **Inventing Meaning: Making Sense of the Holocaust in Fiction**

Week 8
Jean Améry, Primo Levi

Week 9
Tadeusz Borowski, Yaffa Eliach. Luise Rinser, Günter Grass, Peter Weiss

Week 10
Art Spiegelman, Maxim Biller

Module 4: **Memory Shifts**

Week 11
Historians' Controversies

Week 12
   Literary Revising and Revisionism

Week 13
   Other Holocausts? (Armenians, Cambodians, First Nations, Bosnians)

Week 14
   Conclusion: Reghettoizing the Holocaust

Works Cited

Print Sources

Adam, Peter. *The Arts of the Third Reich*. London: Thames and Hudson, 1992.

Améry, Jean. "At the Mind's Limits." *At the Mind's Limits: Contemplations by a Survivor on Auschwitz and Its Realities*. Trans. Sidney Rosenfeld and Stella P. Rosenfeld. 1980. New York: Schocken, 1986. 1–20.

Bark, Dennis L., and David R. Gress. *Democracy and [I]ts Discontents*. 1989. 2nd ed. Oxford: Blackwell, 1993. Vol. 2 of *A History of West Germany*. 2 vols. 1989. 423–25.

Biller, Maxim. "Die Nachmann-Juden." *Die Tempojahre*. Munich: dtv, 1991. 171–74.

Borowski, Tadeusz. "The People Who Walked On." *This Way for the Gas, Ladies and Gentlemen*. Selected and translated by Barbara Vedder. 1967. Introduction by Jan Kott translated by Michael Kaendel. Harmondsworth: Penguin, 1988. 82–97.

Czerniakow, Adam. *The Warsaw Diary of Adam Czerniakow: Prelude to Doom*. Ed. Raul Hilberg, Stanislaw Staron, and Josef Kermisz. Trans. Stanislaw Staron and the staff of Yad Vashem. New York: Stein and Day, 1979.

Eliach, Yaffa, ed. *Hasidic Tales of the Holocaust*. New York: Oxford University Press, 1982.

Fassbinder, Rainer Werner. "Garbage, the City and Death." *Plays*. Edited, translated, and with an introduction by Denis Calandra. New York: PAJ Publications, 1985. 161–89.

Frank, Anne. *The Diary of a Young Girl*. Trans. B. M. Mooyaart-Doubleday. Garden City, NY: Doubleday, 1952.

Friedländer, Saul. *When Memory Comes*. New York: Farrar, Straus and Giroux, 1979.

Goldhagen, Daniel Jonah. *Hitler's Willing Executioners: Ordinary Germans and the Holocaust*. New York: Alfred A. Knopf, 1996.

Grass, Günter. *The Tin Drum*. Trans. Ralph Manheim. 1962. New York: Vintage, 1990.

Grunberger, Richard. *The Twelve-Year Reich: A Social History of Nazi Germany 1933–1945*. New York: Holt, Rinehart and Winston, 1971.

Hitler, Adolf. *Mein Kampf*. Trans. Ralph Manheim. 1943. Boston: Houghton Mifflin, 1971.

Höss, Rudolf. *Death Dealer: The Memoirs of the SS Kommandant at Auschwitz*. Ed. Steven Paskuly. Trans. Andrew Pollinger. 1992. Foreword (1985) by Primo Levi. New York: Da Capo, 1996.

Holliday, Laurel, ed. and compiler. "Hannah Senesh." *Children in the Holocaust and World War II: Their Secret Diaries.* New York: Pocket Books, 1995. 311–33.

Kogon, Eugen. *The Theory and Practice of Hell: The German Concentration Camps and the System behind Them.* Trans. Heinz Norden. 1966. New York: Octagon, 1976.

Levi, Primo. "The Intellectual in Auschwitz." *The Drowned and the Saved.* Trans. Raymond Rosenthal. New York: Summit, 1988. 127–48.

Maschmann, Melita. *Account Rendered: A Dossier on My Former Self.* London: Abelard-Schuman, 1965.

Mosse, George. *Nazi Culture: Intellectual, Cultural and Social Life in the Third Reich.* New York: Grosset and Dunlap, 1966.

Oberski, Jona. *Childhood.* Trans. Ralph Manheim. 1983. N.p.: Coronet; Hodder and Stoughton, 1984.

Rinser, Luise. *Jan Lobel from Warsaw.* Trans. Michael Hulse and Luise Rinser. Edinburgh: Polygon, 1991.

Rose, Paul Lawrence. "The German Moralists and the Jewish Question: Kant, Herder, and Hegel." *Revolutionary Anti-Semitism in Germany from Kant to Wagner.* Princeton: Princeton University Press, 1990. 91–116.

Shimoni, Gideon, ed. *The Holocaust in University Teaching.* Holocaust Series. Prepared in association with the International Center for University Teaching of Jewish Civilization, Jerusalem. Oxford: Pergamon, 1991.

Spiegelman, Art. "Auschwitz (Time Flies)." *Maus II: A Survivor's Tale: And Here My Troubles Began.* New York: Pantheon, 1991. 39–74.

Weiss, Peter. *The Investigation: A Play.* Trans. Jon Swan and Ulu Grosbard. New York: Atheneum, 1966.

Wiesel, Elie. *Night.* Trans. Stella Rodway. 1960. Foreword by François Mauriac. New York: Bantam, 1982.

Electronic Source

The Nizkor Project. Dir. Kenneth McVay. November 1998 <http://www.nizkor.org/>.

Chapter 5

THE DIFFICULTY OF BREAKING THE SILENCE

Teaching the Holocaust in a
Program of German Literature and Culture

Dagmar C. G. Lorenz

Following the much publicized broadcast of the Hollywood TV series *Holocaust* (1978), Alfred Hoelzel published a pioneering article on teaching the Holocaust and Holocaust literature as an integral part of German curricula in the United States. He suggested that such courses be taught in English so as to reach students campus-wide. I was immediately persuaded by Hoelzel's concept. German as the language of instruction does limit the audience of any given course to German majors, German exchange students, and occasional participants from departments other than German who have sufficient language proficiency. Because the Holocaust and its prehistory and aftermath are of utmost significance to Central European culture, history, and identity—both Gentile and Jewish—I designed a course on Germanophone Holocaust literature and film, to be taught in English. In 1985 the Department of German at Ohio State offered this course for the first time on a trial basis. Designated a free elective, it neither fulfilled a requirement nor was an integral part of the program.

Under the circumstances enrollment was low, but not too low. There were eleven participants from vastly different areas of study who had signed up for a variety of reasons: some needed extra credit hours and the class fit into their schedule; others were motivated by personal or academic reasons. Several participants were nontraditional students, among them a

---

The note for this section can be found on page 71.

Columbus businessman, a recent convert to Judaism, and a senior citizen enrolled in a special study program. Despite, or perhaps precisely because of, some of the students' unconventional background and motivation, the course turned out to be a success. Intrigued both by the texts and the films, the students were usually well prepared for the individual class sessions and performed well on the exams. This encouraged me to fine-tune the syllabus further and submit the course to the departmental Undergraduate Studies Committee for consideration for permanent status. I felt that once integrated into the departmental curriculum and designated to fulfill humanities and general education requirements, the course would attract a larger clientele. In the following years, attendance in German 399 has fluctuated between twenty and forty-five students, the more typical figures being twenty-three to twenty-five. This mid-size format lends itself to my preferred teaching format, a combination of lectures, discussions, student presentations, guest speakers, and film screenings.

Establishing a course on the Holocaust in my department required a long-term commitment to teach the class. The department had to endorse the course and provide funding for advertisement and materials, among them films, slides, and library books. Because of the interdisciplinary aspects involved in the course, I had to consult with other academic units and instructors. Some of my departmental colleagues rejected the very notion of integrating a course on the Holocaust into the German curriculum. My mandate from the department was weak when I began to contact other departments and individuals who might have a vested interest in the subject matter. Luckily I encountered no objections to the course outside the Department of German. The respective colleagues in History, Yiddish, and Jewish Studies were supportive, and some of them supplied me with suggestions and materials for the final version of my course proposal. Yet on the departmental level I was asked to provide rewrite after rewrite before German 399 was finally approved. There were no further delays on the college and university level.

When I designed German 399, the ambiance at OSU and, more generally, in the state of Ohio was different from today's. Although some parts of academe were seriously discussing ethnicity and multiculturalism, these issues did not play the same role in language and literature departments that they do today. It was a fortunate coincidence that my project got underway parallel to an initiative undertaken by Dagmar Celeste, the wife of the then governor of Ohio, Richard Celeste, to enhance Holocaust awareness. Statewide programs on the Holocaust were gaining momentum. Previously, Ohio State had offered only a few isolated courses on the Holocaust. They included an infrequently taught lecture course in the

Department of History and scattered courses on the Weimar Republic and the Nazi era, one of them in the Department of German. Nonetheless, while it is proper to speak of additions to the Holocaust curricula and programming, there was no proliferation of courses about the Holocaust. There were at best a new interest and openness sparked by a growing awareness of cultural diversity and an increasing body of Holocaust literature, both scholarly and popular.

In the early 1980s I had offered a proseminar for undergraduates and graduates about Holocaust literature and film, and, soon thereafter, a seminar on antisemitism in German literature. The enrollment in both courses was slightly above average. Several of the course participants went on to explore individual authors of the Holocaust era and aspects of the Holocaust experience. Some wrote about related topics in their theses, dissertations, and research projects. Most of the students in these courses approached Holocaust literature with the same attitude as they do any topic of German cultural and literary studies: with some curiosity, but basically detached. A few students, however, expressed misgivings about the reading material. Some of them maintained that the aesthetic quality of Holocaust texts did not warrant extensive study. Others wondered if the authors studied in class were relevant to their future careers as German teachers; the works on the syllabus were not on the Master's reading list. The majority, however, welcomed the exposure to nonliterary media and the texts themselves. By and large, students who reacted negatively to the readings also objected to the nonliterary methodologies and perspectives involved in the analysis of Holocaust literature and films.

The negative student attitudes corresponded to similar ones among colleagues. This led me to believe that it had been wise on my part not to engage in Holocaust research, scholarship, and teaching before being awarded tenure. Several senior colleagues characterized my work on Holocaust authors as trendy; some considered the study of German Judaica in general peripheral to the discipline; others felt this way about Holocaust and exile literature in particular. Aside from their professional position, some colleagues cautioned me that, as a native speaker of German and a Germanist who proposed to teach a course on the Holocaust, I would provoke negative responses from the Jewish community and OSU's Melton Center for Jewish Studies. Many colleagues inquired whether the Department of History minded our department's invading its territory, and they recalled instances when historians had protested the Department of German's teaching German civilization. Some even foresaw problems if my planned course should succeed: if German 399 were to become popular among students, I might be obligated to teach it, even if I no longer wanted to do so. I would be condemned, so to speak, to teach a course on the Holocaust in perpetuity. No one suggested that other faculty members might want to teach the course from time to time. Some people predicted that the depressing subject matter of the Holocaust would have a negative effect on my health and emotional well-being. Yet, if we should have to discontinue German 399, they warned me, this would jeopardize the reputation of the department as a whole: the failure of a Holocaust course in the Department of German would be an indictment not only of the instructor but of the entire department.

A significant faculty group in the department was skeptical as to whether a Holocaust course was in the best interest of the German program. These colleagues argued that positive aspects of German culture attract German students. Building a successful program required highlighting those facets of German life that appeal to Midwestern students, many of whom define themselves as ethnic Germans. To avoid alienating these students, the Holocaust would best be left to historians and scholars of Jewish Studies. Moreover, a few of my colleagues suggested that teaching such a potentially controversial course might make me the target of hostility. These apprehensions were, indeed, realized in a small way. When I started teaching and lecturing about the Holocaust, I began to receive letters of protest from revisionist scholars. One weekend in 1987 a large bulletin board in the hallway next to my office was burned. The board had contained information about my course and other Holocaust programs. The OSU campus police tried but failed to produce a suspect.

The concepts that underlie German 399 reflect in part the insights I gained as a graduate student at the University of Cincinnati (1970-74). Scholars of German and Austrian Jewish literature and exile literature commanded a strong presence in the Department of Germanic Language and Literature and taught these subjects in their historical context. In addition, the department's interaction with the nearby Hebrew Union College fostered interest in the Holocaust on the part of faculty and students. The publications by scholars at the University of Cincinnati contributed to establishing the foundation for Holocaust studies in *Germanistik*. The work of some of my former professors, in some cases motivated by personal experiences, stimulated my interest in the Nazi era, which in the Federal Republic continues to be euphemized as "the most recent past." Ruth Klüger, a prominent German scholar and a survivor of Auschwitz, writes in her autobiography *weiter leben*:

> Über die Geschichte der sogenannten "jüngsten Vergangenheit," (die mit den Jahren nicht älter zu werden scheint und daher irgendwie so zeitlos ist wie das Jüngste Gericht) ist so viel geforscht und geschrieben worden, daß wir sie

langsam zu kennen meinen, während die Geschichte der Vergangenheitsbewältigung noch aussteht. (198)[1]

Presentations by exile authors and Shoah survivors—Frank Zwillinger, Hilde Domin, and Jakov Lind among others—in Guy Stern's course on exile literature, in-depth study of Paul Celan's poetry in Jerry Glenn's seminars, and discussions with Ruth Klüger, who taught at UC in the early 1970s, changed my previous outlook on *Germanistik,* which I had formed as a student at the University of Göttingen during the 1968 student riots. Although the New Left debates of the late 1960s heightened the understanding of fascism, they did not consider the effects of National Socialism on its intended victims and thus failed to provide access to the special challenges of Shoah literature.

Positions taken by exchange students in my classes show that this kind of approach to the Holocaust experience is still common in Europe. Their contributions to the discussion often reveal impressive background knowledge about National Socialism, but they lack information about the victims. Often this results in intriguing exchanges of ideas between international and American students. So do their disagreements about literary and aesthetic conventions. The films in German 399 invite comparisons between Hollywood and European filmmaking. These discussions are especially productive in the case of films from different eras indicative of different cultural awareness, for example, Agnieszka Holland's *Europa Europa* and Peter Lilienthal's *David,* produced with the collaboration of Jurek Becker. The latter film is informed by the conflicting agendas of a traditional and a more progressive Marxist author and filmmaker, and it differs in pace and plot from films made in the United States. Since copies of both works are in the departmental film library, they are very accessible for students.

In German 399 the fact that most students have little or no proficiency in German, and that the required texts are translations from German into English, limits debates on aesthetic issues. Having to rely on translations is a problem indeed. Many texts have not been and are not likely ever to be translated. Those that have been, are, for the most part, overpriced. Only the most popular works stay on the market. Until recently, it was possible to use supplementary duplicated materials. With rising copyright fees, the library reserve shelves will, once again, be the most realistic, albeit not the most efficient, solution. The required readings for German 399, some of them excerpts, as well as the films require contextualization in terms of language, culture, and aesthetics. Literature majors are eager to engage in debates on literary matters. Informed by the critical discourse of their discipline, they can be expected to address the genre, language, or the form of given works.

Particularly in the case of poetry, translation is a problem. To illustrate the difficulties faced by translators, we read Paul Celan's poem "Todesfuge" in several translations, notably Michael Hamburger's and John Felstiner's. In addition, students capable of dealing with the German original provide alternative versions. Here and in other cases, culture-specific literary conventions call for a discussion, for example, of postwar existentialism or the literature of the absurd in the case of Ilse Aichinger; GDR history and thought in that of Becker; and the antifascist resistance, the Frankfurt Auschwitz Trials, and documentary drama in that of Weiss. These discussions offer students the opportunity to examine aesthetic and genre categories in their historical context.

I point out that the text-oriented approaches favored by postwar Germanists—New Criticism and the *werkimmanente Interpretation*—could be and were used to marginalize Holocaust literature. These approaches excluded ideologically uncomfortable texts from the canon on the grounds that they did not satisfy aesthetic norms. Measured by the critical tools provided by Wolfgang Kayser and Emil Staiger, prominent scholars of the *werkimmanent* school, Shoah literature, excluding all but the most elusive poetry, would have to be dismissed as unpoetic.

Marxist theory places Shoah literature into a peripheral position for different reasons. Most Marxists make no distinction between National Socialism and other forms of fascism and consider antisemitism a secondary issue. Occasionally—increasingly less frequently in recent years—students challenge from a Marxist perspective the material presented in German 399. I encourage anyone desiring to do so to explore the differences between National Socialism and Italian or Spanish fascism in their research projects. Several works read in class can serve as a point of departure for such studies, notably Peter Weiss's *Investigation* and Anna Seghers's "The Excursion of the Dead Girls." Many students struggle with these texts because they resist the notion that the alliance between the lower middle class and industry, pitted against the working class, resulted in the Holocaust and World War II. Jewish students in particular object to the representation of Jews as victims of circumstance.

Jurek Becker's *Bronstein's Children*, as well as his earlier novel *Jacob the Liar*, elicit positive responses. Written from the point of view of narrators living in former East Germany, these works reveal the repression of Jewish life and identity in a socialist state, Becker's own experience. A former GDR citizen, Becker was aware of the discrepancy between Marxist theory and socialist reality and challenged the practices and beliefs that forced him and other Holocaust survivors into silence and self-denial. Many students identify with Becker's college-age protagonist in *Bronstein's Children*, and they enjoy the combination of mystery, love, and the generational conflict brought on by the unresolved past.

Some of the factual information in German 399 takes the student by surprise. Unaccustomed to thinking in historical terms and conditioned to view the Holocaust as an isolated event, students are not necessarily aware of the history of anti-Judaism and antisemitism. German majors know little about Ashkenazic history, embedded in, but distinct from that of the surrounding Christian nations until the Age of Enlightenment and the Haskalah. Both German and Jewish Studies students are shocked by the Judeophobia and xenophobia in Martin Luther's treatise *The Jews and Their Lies,* to which leading Nazi figures attributed model character. Students who know Luther as the translator of the Bible and view him as a progressive religious reformer have difficulty reconciling these roles with his attitude toward the Jews. Luther's pamphlet clearly needs to be contextualized within the Christian discourse on the Jews and the reformer's own time. References to or student reports on Sander L. Gilman's book *Jewish Self-Hatred* or his article "Chicken Soup," about the gentrification of Christ and the disenfranchisement of Jews from the Christian discourse, are useful to achieve this goal.

To explain why National Socialism was favorably received by so many different constituencies, it is not enough to refer to social and economic factors. A larger context involving language, intellectual and religious history, and habits of thought needs to be established. Even then some students refuse to believe that prominent persons such as Luther or Richard Wagner wrote virulent anti-Jewish diatribes. The antisemitic literature written between 1850 and 1900 takes students aback. When I lecture on the rise of racist antisemitism to demonstrate the global scope and the pseudoreligious dimensions, students frequently seek further information from me on the topics included.

The class also reads historical texts revealing Jewish views on German-Jewish history. Heinrich Heine's novel fragment "The Rabbi of Bacharach" offers an assessment of European Jewish history since Roman times by one of the most prominent nineteenth-century German-Jewish authors. For an impression of a Jewish woman's experience, I mention the *Education of Fanny Lewald,* the autobiography of a nineteenth-century, Jewish-born best-seller author. Today's students find it hard to relate to the conflicting emotions of hope, frustration, and despair in the works of Heine, Lewald, and Jakob Wassermann (*My Life as German and Jew*), particularly the recurrent lament over the Jewish history of persecution, coupled with an affirmation of German-Jewish coexistence. Sensitized by the historic overview presented in the first session in conjunction with Erich Fried's parable *Arden Must Die* (1967), the libretto of Alexander Goehr's opera, students are aware that German-Jewish identity is a complex issue. They realize that after the Shoah the problems have deepened. Nadja Seelich's film *Kieselsteine* (Pebbles), Jurek Becker's novel *Bronstein's Children*, and the autobiographies to which I refer interested students highlight the different internal reference points of Jews and Gentiles raised after the Shoah and illustrate that the relations between German-speaking Jews and non-Jews are not "normal."

Time and funding permitting, I invite an American-born advanced graduate student or junior faculty member as a guest speaker to discuss their experience of Jewish life in contemporary Germany and Austria. Otherwise I suggest reading selected texts in Sander L. Gilman and Karen Remmler's anthology *Reemerging Jewish Culture in Germany: Life and Literature since 1989* or from Dagmar C. G. Lorenz and Gabriele Weinberger's *Insiders and Outsiders: Jewish and Gentile Culture in Germany and Austria*. Sometimes I schedule visits by resource persons after showing films such as *Kitty: Return to Auschwitz*, a British documentary featuring the death camp survivor Kitty Hart, filmed on location in Auschwitz; Leni Riefenstahl's Nazi propaganda film *Triumph des Willens* (Triumph of the Will); and Alain Resnais's *Night and Fog*, a documentary of the camps, told by a former prisoner and replete with original footage. Thus prepared, the students possess basic information and concepts to examine the tenuous relationship between Jews and non-Jews in German-speaking countries. Throughout the course, we revisit these issues from a variety of perspectives and in the context of different paradigms: emancipation and assimilation, nationalism, and revolutionary movements. Simultaneously arising Jewish patterns or Jewish responses to European developments are explored as well, namely, the construction of the "German citizen of Mosaic Faith," cosmopolitanism, Zionism, Marxism, Jewish-German nationalism, and religious conservatism.

In conjunction with Heine, the seemingly reprehensible behavior of the protagonist Rabbi Abraham sparks questions concerning the Jewish experience in Germany: the rabbi saves himself and his wife by secretly abandoning his community, knowing that those left behind will perish in an imminent pogrom. The story meets with spontaneous disapproval, thereby initiating the discussion of certain views that recur in the works of Holocaust survivors, who place surviving and the duty to bear witness above any heroic impulses. In this context I also refer to *The Diary of Anne Frank* and Bruno Bettelheim's criticism of Jewish responses to the Nazi terror, and recommend to German-speaking students an admittedly problematic text, Brigitte Schwaiger and Eva Deutsch's *Die Galizianerin*. All of these works call for a reexamination of the potentially suicidal and destructive heroic ethos, so closely associated with notions of Germanness and inspired in part by nineteenth-century readings of medieval epics such as the *Nibelungenlied*. In contrast, Heine's work suggests that self-preservation is of greater value than self-destructive, albeit noble, gestures. This attitude foreshadows that of many Shoah memoirs. In addition, the unfinished condition of "The Rabbi of Bacharach" calls for a discussion of the situation of German-Jewish authors. While some students hold, as do many critics, that Heine lost interest in his subject matter, others follow my argumentation that the language and narrative patterns capable of portraying the experience of a Jewish protagonist had not been developed when Heine made one of the first attempts at writing a German-Jewish novel. In that context we also talk about the Nazis' attempt to eradicate this tradition by repressing, outlawing, and destroying it.

The lack of the appropriate means of communication remains a topic throughout the course. The inability of Holocaust survivors to articulate their experiences, the difficulty of venturing into uncharted linguistic and conceptual territory, and the unwillingness of most German speakers to deal with texts contradicting their expectations as readers are addressed in conjunction with the opaque texts of Aichinger, Celan, and Nelly Sachs, as well as Edgar Hilsenrath's provocative novel *Story of the Last Thought*. The former authors' silence as well as the latter's depiction of brutality and use of obscenity constitute an attack on the widespread refusal to deal with mass murder and genocide. The highly symbolic literature of many first-generation Shoah survivors—no less so than the shocking revelations in Weiss's *Investigation*, Jakov Lind's *Soul of Wood*, and Hilsenrath's *Story of the Last Thought*—requires careful preparation. Most students are not equipped to interpret dense lyrical texts or to deal with profanity and sacrilege literature in an academic setting.

I schedule Riefenstahl's *Triumph of the Will* and Resnais's *Night and Fog* one immediately following the other in order to show the inextricably entwined extremes of National Socialism. Many students have seen one or both films, hence the emotional impact of these works on them is less intense; a critical discussion immediately after the screening is possible. Nonetheless, Resnais's images affect some students to the point of tears. Conversely, others are drawn into the pageantry and the vibrant atmosphere artfully created in *Triumph of the Will*, even in the abbreviated fifty-minute version shown in German 399. Yet, on most students *Night and Fog* has a sobering effect. The discussion ranges from content-related questions and ethical issues regarding the acceptance of Nazi leaders by the German population and the extent to which the persecutions and the genocide could be foreseen, to issues of representation and authenticity. The fact that Resnais's film never mentions the terms "Jew" and "Jewish" leads to the matter of reception: how did Germans react to Holocaust films, how did they deal with their history? The discussion invariably turns to the practice of casting victims and perpetrators as opposites, as living in different worlds. The material presented subsequently in class causes students to reexamine and question their initial assumptions. They recognize increasingly more problems and formulate more sophisticated questions.

Perhaps because of the reputation of German as a demanding field of study, German 399 draws many intellectually adventurous students, prepared to challenge, debate, discuss, and refute. As a result, the overall quality of students' presentations and papers is excellent, the pace of instruction fast, and the grades are, relatively speaking, high. Besides students from German and Jewish Studies, with which German 399 has been cross-listed for several years, the course attracts majors from different fields in the humanities and the arts and sciences, from business, psychology, premed, prelaw, criminology, and education. Some students bring specific expectations to German 399. Depending on their expectations, my German accent and at times unidiomatic use of English may at first inspire confidence or apprehension. In addition to students who take German 399 because it fulfills a requirement and those who enroll by default, the course attracts participants with specific agendas. Since German 299, a humanities course on Weimar and Nazi Germany, precedes it, at least in theory, and Holocaust courses in other academic units complement it, some students already have a significant amount of information about the Shoah and Nazi Germany.

I have heard from colleagues who teach Holocaust courses in Hebrew and history that some students' preoccupation with Holocaust literature because of their family history or religion interferes with the objectives of a university course: students emotionally engaged in Holocaust topics may be dissatisfied with an academic discussion of the Shoah. They may resent the course requirements, examinations, presentations, and term papers, or the analytic approach and methodology. Their disappointment may translate into below-average course and teaching evaluations and high drop-out rates. Except for occasional off-scale ratings, German 399 has received consistently positive evaluations, and retention has been good. Perhaps as a result of my detailed introduction, consisting of a survey of the syllabus and a preview of the topics and the general approach, students who sense that the class does not meet their needs tend to leave during or after the first session.

I warn students that some of the texts, images, and films in the course are explicit, displaying violence, racism, and sexual material because these materials are essential to treating the Shoah and its representation by writers and artists, but I emphasize that there will be no gratuitous display and lengthy descriptive discussions of blood and gore. Instead, German 399 focuses on ways in which words and images process the experience and threat of genocide, and on the difficulty of conveying these events in the language of the perpetrators. Finally, when defining the course parameters, I establish that for ideological and historical reasons the prime targets of Nazi racism and genocide were the Jews of Germany, Europe, and, ultimately, the world. For that reason, I begin with a review of anti-Judaism and antisemitism, and the Jewish history in German-speaking countries, including emancipation, secularization, and assimilation; I then present an overview of the ascent of German nationalism, racism, and Nazism.

Aside from scheduling problems, the amount of reading material and course assignments, aversion to the instructor, or disinterest in the course material, a small minority of students have stated over the years more troublesome reasons for leaving the course, including the failure to highlight Nazi figures and Nazi history or military history; the application of the term "Holocaust" exclusively to the genocide perpetrated against Jews, Sinti, and Roma (rather than to all of the disasters of World War II, including the bombing of Dresden); and the fact that Jewish Holocaust survivors, exile authors, and children of survivors and exiles created most of the texts and films used in German 399. There were occasional requests for giving "equal time" to the Nazi standpoint, and criticism that the course neither sets "the record straight" nor reflects "a German point of view." In some cases these reactions resulted from a lack of awareness, in others, from ethnocentric, militaristic, and antisemitic attitudes. Occasionally, students attracted to Germany and things German by their fascination with National Socialism and white supremacism chose German 399 because they were looking for a forum for their ideological position.

I am undecided whether it is preferable for right-wing extremist students to stay in the course. If they do not, they may avoid confronting materials that challenge and could potentially modify their point of view altogether. However, they may also sit through the course, as some did, passive-aggressive and resentful, spending most of their intellectual energy on resisting the course content. The more assertive ones may resort to bullying and manipulation, making every attempt to subvert the class.

By incessantly arguing with the instructor, asking irrelevant or loaded questions, assuming threatening postures or making subtle threats, some hostile students have attempted to undermine the course agenda, to disrupt the program outlined in the syllabus, to discredit the stated educational goals, and even to cause the instructor to abandon her position.

Clearly, the absence of dissent would deprive the course of much needed intellectual stimulation. Yet in a class whose subject matter affects some students on a deep emotional level, there is always the risk that debates fueled by prejudice and resentment might exceed the limits of acceptable discourse. In my twelve years of teaching German 399 I have experienced volatile group dynamics. A firm believer in the right of individuals to express themselves (as long as no one else's rights are infringed upon), I refrained from overmanaging the classroom. Perhaps because I did not censor student presentations and discussions, the class as a whole eventually struck a balance and ensured a productive give and take. By questioning extreme views, eliciting alternative opinions from less forthcoming participants, and communicating in a collegial and responsible manner, the students established a constructive learning atmosphere every time I taught the course.

When designing German 399, I was concerned that, even though I was born after 1945, problems might arise from my German background. Instead I have found that my point of view generated great interest precisely because it derives from my experience of growing up in a culture where Jewish history and the Shoah were rarely discussed. Students with prior interest in the Holocaust also appreciate the opportunity of studying literary and cultural documents by German-speaking authors who are on the periphery of contemporary Jewish Studies in the United States. For the most part, the students in German 399 have had little exposure to the history of German Jewry, the extensive cultural ties between German Jews and Gentiles, and the continued Jewish presence in German-speaking countries today. The problems involved in constructing and preserving Jewish identity in a culture that engineered the Holocaust fascinate many Jewish students. They are eager to explore the ways in which Shoah survivors and the following generations come to terms with the dilemma of living, returning, or relocating to the country where Jews were persecuted and killed a few generations earlier.

Over the years, the Department of Germanic Languages and Literatures at OSU has undergone a transformation from a single-focus program to one concerned with multicultural perspectives and minority discourses. In the academic year 1995/96 the department merged with Yiddish and Ashkenazic Studies, formerly housed in the Department of

Judaic and Near Eastern Languages. Years of informal collaboration with the Yiddish faculty preceded this move, which allows Germanic Languages and Literatures to offer undergraduate and graduate programs, including the Ph.D., in German and Yiddish. In this cooperation, German 399 was an important factor—Yiddish students have traditionally attended the course. As a result of the departmental merger, German 399 has moved into a more central position in its home unit, which now accommodates in an unprecedented fashion the academic interests of students of German and Yiddish languages, literatures, and cultures.

Note

1. "So much has been researched and written about the history of the so-called 'most recent past' (which over the years does not seem to age and for that reason somehow seems as timeless as Judgment Day) that we gradually assume we know all about it, while the history of the process of coming to terms with the past has not yet begun" [translation by Dagmar C. G. Lorenz].

Ohio State University **Prof. Dagmar C. G. Lorenz**

GERMAN 399, THE HOLOCAUST IN GERMAN LITERATURE AND FILM

Week 1
Introduction: Historical Perspectives
Erich Fried, *Arden Must Die*
film: Kitty Hart, *Kitty: Return to Auschwitz*

Week 2
from: Martin Luther, *The Jews and Their Lies*
from: Heinrich Heine, "The Rabbi of Bacharach" (Der Rabbi von Bacharach)
films: Leni Riefenstahl, *Triumph of the Will*; Alain Resnais, *Night and Fog*

Week 3
from: Otto Weininger, *Sex and Character*
from: Jakob Wassermann, *German and Jew*; Hugo Bettauer, *City without Jews*
TV series: *The Oppermanns*

Week 4
The Oppermanns continued
Discussion of the film *The Oppermanns*; the representation of pre-Shoah German-Jewish society in a post-Shoah TV film

Week 5
Lion Feuchtwanger, *The Oppermanns* (novel)
Theodor Herzl, *The Jewish State*
Frau Anna Fest, "A Job in Its Own Category" (from: Alison Owings, *Frauen*)
Rudolf Hoess, *Commandant of Auschwitz*

Week 6
film: *David* (Peter Lilienthal, Jurek Becker)
Peter Weiss, *The Investigation*
Distribution of take-home midterm

Week 7
Take-home midterm due
Jakov Lind, *Soul of Wood*
film: *Trial at Nuremberg*
Anna Seghers, "The Excursion of the Dead Girls"

Week 8
    Ilse Aichinger, "Rahel's Clothes"
    Paul Celan, "Death Fugue"
    Jurek Becker, *Bronstein's Children*

Week 9
    Bronstein's Children
    film: Nadja Seelich, *Kieselsteine* (Pebbles)

Week 10
    Edgar Hilsenrath, *The Story of the Last Thought*

Course Requirements:

One oral report to be held in class. This report will be revised and submitted as a brief research paper (ca. four to six pages). At least three secondary sources (critical studies, books, newspaper articles, journal articles) are to be cited according to MLA style. One take-home midterm, one final exam in class. Grading: **Final** 30%, **Midterm** 25%, **Oral Report** 15%, **Paper** (Revised Report) 20%, **Class Participation** 10%.

Required Texts:

Becker, Jurek	*Bronstein's Children* Harcourt Brace (U.S.)
Botwinick, Rita Steinhardt	*A History of the Holocaust* Prentice-Hall (U.S.)
Feuchtwanger, Lion	*The Oppermanns* Carroll & Graf (U.S.)
Hilsenrath, Edgar	*The Story of the Last Thought* Sphere Books (England)
Lind, Jakov	*Soul of Wood* Methuen (England)
Weiss, Peter	*The Investigation* M. Boyars (England)

and a course packet of supplemental duplicated materials

Works Cited

Print Sources

Aichinger, Ilse. "Rahel's Clothes." Unpublished trans. by Dagmar Lorenz. [German: "Rahels Kleider." *Schlechte Wörter.* Frankfurt am Main: Fischer, 1976. 52–58.]

Becker, Jurek. *Bronstein's Children.* Trans. Leila Vennewitz. New York: Harcourt, Brace, Jovanovich, 1988.

―――. *Jacob the Liar.* Trans. Melvin Kornfeld. New York: Harcourt, Brace, Jovanovich, 1976.

Bettauer, Hugo. *City without Jews.* Trans. Salomea Neumark Brainin. New York: Bloch Publishers, 1991.

Bettelheim, Bruno. "The Ignored Lesson of Anne Frank." *Surviving.* New York: Knopf, 1979. 246–57.

―――. *The Informed Heart: Autonomy in a Mass Age.* New York: Avon; Glencoe; Free Press, 1960.

Botwinick, Rita Steinhardt. *A History of the Holocaust: From Ideology to Annihilation.* Upper Saddle River: Prentice-Hall, 1996.

Felstiner, John. *Mother Tongue, Holy Tongue: On Translating and Not Translating Paul Celan.* Eugene, OR: University of Oregon Press, 1986.

Feuchtwanger, Lion. *The Oppermanns.* Trans. Lion Feuchtwanger. New York: Carroll & Graf, 1962.

Frank, Anne. *Anne Frank: The Diary of a Young Girl.* Trans. B. M. Mooyaart-Doubleday. 1952. New York: Bantam Books, 1993.

Gilman, Sander L. "Chicken Soup, or the Penalties of Sounding Too Jewish." Lorenz and Weinberger 15–29.

―――. *Jewish Self-Hatred: Anti-Semitism and the Hidden Language of the Jews.* Baltimore: The Johns Hopkins Press, 1986.

Gilman, Sander L., and Karen Remmler, eds. *Reemerging Jewish Culture in Germany: Life and Literature since 1989.* New York: New York University Press, 1994.

Goehr, Alexander. *Arden Must Die: An Opera on the Death of the Wealthy Arden of Faversham in 2 Acts.* Libretto by Erich Fried. Trans. Geoffrey Skelton. London: Schott, 1967.

Hamburger, Michael, trans. *Poems of Paul Celan.* New York: Persea Books, 1995.

Heine, Heinrich. "The Rabbi of Bacharach: A Fragment." *Jewish Stories and Hebrew Melodies.* Trans. Charles Godfrey Leland. Updated by Elizabeth Petuchowski. New York: Markus Wiener Publishing, 1987. 19–80.

Herzl, Theodor. *The Jewish State.* Trans. Harry Zohn. New York: Herzl Press, 1970.

Hilsenrath, Edgar. *The Story of the Last Thought*. Trans. Hugh Young. London: Sphere Books, 1991.
Hoelzel, Alfred. "The Germanist and the Holocaust." *Die Unterrichtspraxis* 11 (1978): 54–58.
Hoess, Rudolf. *Commandant of Auschwitz*. Trans. Constantine FitzGibbon. London: Pan Books, 1961.
Klüger, Ruth. *weiter leben. Eine Jugend*. Göttingen: Wallstein, 1992.
Lewald, Fanny. *The Education of Fanny Lewald: An Autobiography*. Trans. Hanna B. Lewis. Albany: State University of New York Press, 1992.
Lind, Jakov. *Soul of Wood*. Trans. Ralph Manheim. London: Methuen, 1985.
Lorenz, Dagmar C. G., and Gabriele Weinberger, eds. *Insiders and Outsiders: Jewish and Gentile Culture in Germany and Austria*. Detroit: Wayne State University Press, 1994. 15–29.
Luther, Martin. *The Jews and Their Lies*. Los Angeles: Christian Nationalist Crusade, 1948.
Owings, Alison. "Frau Anna Fest: A Job in Its Own Category." *Frauen: German Women Recall the Third Reich*. New Brunswick, NJ: Rutgers University Press, 1993. 315–41.
Sachs, Nelly. *O the Chimneys: Selected Poems*. Trans. Wolfgang Hildesheimer. New York: Farrar, Straus, and Giroux, 1969.
Schwaiger, Brigitte, and Eva Deutsch. *Die Galizianerin*. Vienna: Zsolnay, 1982.
Seghers, Anna. "The Excursion of the Dead Girls." Trans. Elisabeth Rütschi Herrmann and Edna Huttenmaier Spitz. *German Women Writers of the Twentieth Century*. Ed. Elisabeth Rütschi Herrmann and Edna Huttenmaier Spitz. Oxford: Pergamon Press, 1978. 39–52.
Wassermann, Jakob. *My Life as German and Jew*. Trans. Salomea Neumark Brainin. New York: Coward McCann, 1933.
Weininger, Otto. Chapter XIII, "Judaism." *Sex and Character*. Authorized trans. from the 6th German ed. New York: AMS Press, 1975. 301–30.
Weiss, Peter. *The Investigation: Oratorio in 11 Cantos*. 1966. Trans. Alexander Gross. London: M. Boyars, 1996.

Films/Videotapes

David. Dir. Peter Lilienthal. 1979. Video. Kino International Corp., 1982.
Europa Europa. Dir. Agnieszka Holland. 1991. Video. Alliance, 1992.
Holocaust. Dir. Marvin Chomsky, Herbert Brodkin, and Robert Berger. Four-part television series. NBC. 16–19 April 1978. Video. Republic Entertainment, Inc., 1994.

Kieselsteine (Pebbles). Dir. Lukas Stepanik. Screenplay, Nadja Seelich. Video. Cinéart. Filmverleih Hans Peter Hofmann, 1982. [For help in locating this, try the Austrian Institute in New York.]

Kitty: Return to Auschwitz. Dir. Peter Morley. Video. Films Incorporated, 1979.

Night and Fog. Dir. Alain Resnais. 1955. Video. Hollywood Attic, 1996.

The Nuremberg Trial. Documentary. 1996. Video. WinStar Home Entertainment, Fox Lorber Associates, Inc., 1997.

The Oppermanns. Dir. Horst Meyer. Video. Pantoffelkino, 1986.

Trial at Nuremberg: A Documentary. Jewish Heritage Collection. CBS. 1958; Wolper Productions. Films, Inc., 1964. Video. WTL Productions, 1992.

Triumph des Willens (Triumph of the Will). Dir. Leni Riefenstahl. 1935. Video. Connoisseur Video Collection, 1992.

Chapter 6

FOUR GENRES AND ONE QUESTION: WHY?

Steven R. Cerf

I first offered my course "Der Holocaust und die Literatur" in German in 1988 as German 398, the German Department's capstone "problems seminar" for advanced majors and minors at Bowdoin College; I gave it again in 1993 and am planning to offer it again soon. I have also offered German 51, an English-language course on Literature and the Holocaust as a comparative literature class six times over the last twelve years. Enrollment in the German class averages approximately twenty students per course, and each time the department has closed the English-language class at fifty. Although the larger class in English, because of its very nature, allows students to cover far more reading material, the German-language class has a specificity and concentration all its own.

Introduction: Why Teach the Holocaust through Literature?

Bowdoin College in Brunswick, Maine, has an enrollment of approximately 1,500 students and a faculty numbering 130 full-time professors; I am the only faculty member teaching courses on the Holocaust and the literary imagination. Why? As a survivor's child (my father survived Sachsenburg in Chemnitz, and my maternal grandparents and numerous other relatives were deported to their deaths in Eastern Europe), I knew that a frighteningly astounding paradox drew me to pursue studies in Germanistics: never before in Western civilization had a nation with such a history of cultural and civilizing forces acted, on so large and calculated a scale, in such barbarously genocidal fashion. It is the "Why?" behind this paradox that continues to preoccupy me as teacher and scholar. Although I repeatedly taught *Furcht und Elend des Dritten Reiches*, *Andorra*, and the poetry of Paul Celan and Nelly Sachs in my introductory German literature courses in the 1970s, it was not until I joined a year-long self-help group for children of survivors (1978–79) that I had the courage to offer entire courses exclusively on the Holocaust. Clearly, with such high-affect material with which I was personally so involved, it was necessary for me to work through my emotional connection to this period in order to present my courses with the equanimity and balance essential to the liberal arts.

Why use literature to examine the Holocaust? For the simple reason that because the Nazis employed so many lies to tarnish the truth about humanity and humanistic concerns, it has been the task of post-World War II imaginative writers to render the truth as fiction. On the first day, I tell students about that nameless famous statesman who, after reading a new biography about himself, was delighted that his secret, which had forever shaped his life and all of his activities, had not been detected. In imaginative writing there are no such gaps—a true literary work has a totality and a structural integrity that is both whole and unique. Finally, I remind the students that as the Nazi propaganda ministry was notorious for corrupting the language in its dissemination of lies, it was obligatory for post-World War II German-language imaginative writers, regardless of where they resided, to use language with consummate precision. My primary source of information on the Nazi abuse of language is the canonical *LTI* by Viktor Klemperer.

I have structured the German-language course I teach according to genres: the memoir, the drama, the poem, and the novel. By beginning with the memoir, I immediately ask the student to personalize, to cathect with the victims' lives. The drama follows as the most socialized and socializing of literary genres; it is the genre that depicts the societal roles that the Holocaust created: victimizer, victim, and bystander. The examination of poetry in the course focuses on those images that artists evoke to connote the horrors of the Holocaust. The final portion of the semester deals with the role of prose fiction, particularly the novel. This unit serves as a review and as a means to fill in details of the events. Clearly the most difficult and tortuous of the literary genres dealing with the Holocaust, the novel can be studied only after an examination of the basic facts of this period.

In their evaluations, the students refer to the course as an "eye opener"; many had previously had no idea about the vast continent-wide and systematic organization that had been set up in the Third Reich to do away with "undesirables." And several students found many of the human rights issues raised in the course still relevant to their own concerns as citizens of a culturally diverse nation.

The Memoir

By choosing both Anne Frank's *Tagebuch* and Elie Wiesel's *Night* (the only English-language full-length text read in the course), I begin the semester by letting students hear the voices of the victims themselves. In much the same way as the United States Holocaust Memorial Museum in Washington, DC, gives each visitor a photograph of a victim, I present the students in German 398 with the individualized human dimensions of the suffering that went on in the lives of the innocent victims. After years of searching, my mother and I found a photograph of her mother—my grandmother—in front of her deportation car in Nuremberg; as part of the introductory lecture to the course each student receives a copy of my grandmother's picture.

The choice of these two memoirs is crucial for both their similarities and their differences. The similarities concern the youth of both victims and their having been thrust into almost instant adulthood. Both are brilliant writers able to capture the day-to-day hardship they endure with immediacy and lyricism. A further similarity is their connection with a caring family, which allows them to grow and provides, at least temporarily, some form of security.

The differences are just as remarkable: the Franks' secular humanistic household stands in sharp contradistinction to the Orthodox Jewish home of the Wiesels; Anne narrates her diary in the present tense, while Wiesel writes his chronicle in the past; Anne does not survive, whereas Wiesel does; and each author includes gender-specific concerns. In class discussions, the students immediately cathect with both writers because of their proximity to them in age and because of their own material dependence on their parents. Furthermore, the ability of both writers to mature so dramatically captures the interest of undergraduates, themselves inhabiting a world between youth and adulthood.

Very often discussions of these works deal with formalistic considerations: the dramatic immediacy of a diary versus the highly selective choice of events in a personal chronicle told in the preterite. Other formalistic concerns about the *Tagebuch* relate to Anne's choice of images and the descriptive detail she is able to muster. In Wiesel's case, effective discussions have ensued detailing what he had to omit in order to make his work so hauntingly pithy. I also present and discuss as important background material the historical implications of the occupation of the Netherlands and of the delayed deportation of the Jews from Hungary, using information culled from Lucy S. Dawidowicz's *The War Against the Jews: 1933–1945*.

We read the S. Fischer German-language paperback translation of Anne Frank's diary because it contains some fiction she was writing as well as helpful photographs, writing samples, and room plans, and because the German is closer to the original Dutch than is the English. Two reasons govern my choice of the English-language translation of the Wiesel text from the original French: (1) it is essential to present the immediacy of the description of Auschwitz early in the course, and (2) Wiesel is both a Holocaust survivor and one of the foremost champions of human rights living in North America today.

Teaching materials that have proven particularly helpful for this first unit have included Alain Resnais's documentary *Night and Fog*, Miep Gies's book on Anne, and Elie Wiesel's videotaped interview with Bill Moyers entitled *Facing Hate*. In the course of teaching German 51 in fall 1996, I screened Jon Blair's tape of the 1996 Academy Award-winning documentary *Anne Frank Remembered* and compared Elie Wiesel's recent more discursive and comprehensively informative *All Rivers Run to the Sea: Memoirs* with his lyric *Night*. The glossary of Yiddish and Hebrew terms at the back of Yaffa Eliach's *Hasidic Tales of the Holocaust* is particularly helpful for non-Jewish readers when encountering Wiesel for the first time.

Many of the students reading Anne Frank's *Tagebuch* for a second time—several had first encountered it in junior high school or in high school—comment that they are *now* able to comprehend the responsible and balanced world vision that she evokes in the second half of the work in contrast to the Nazis' triumphalist hysteria. That these students are now older, coupled with the amount of background information they can synthesize as a result of their increased maturity, allows them to understand the different levels on which to read Anne's piercingly truthful work.

The Drama

The entire class reads four dramas: Bertolt Brecht's *Furcht und Elend des Dritten Reiches*, Max Frisch's *Andorra*, Carl Zuckmayer's *Des Teufels General*, and, toward the very end of the semester, Frisch's *Biedermann und die Brandstifter*. We study the first three plays immediately following the first unit devoted to the memoir. They constitute the first actual German-language imaginative writing dealing with the Holocaust assigned in the course.

The Brecht drama, with its short scenes focusing on the all-encompassing Nazi totalitarianism and racism that permeated daily life in Germany, depicts the early domestic Nazi "experiments" over the six-year period before the actual outbreak of World War II. Further, the contemporaneous nature of Brecht's play, many of the scenes of which had their source in newspaper accounts, helps to focus student attention on the role of German exile literature. With the prescience of a great artist, Brecht, through each catastrophe presented, uncannily anticipates the continent-wide genocide that the Nazis were to carry out after the invasion of Poland.

The discussions surrounding *Andorra* have often been the most animated: Frisch as a literary heir to Brecht's Epic Theater, with the Swiss playwright's pointed, often discrete and didactic, shorter scenes and sociopolitical background, creates intellectual interest. Also, an entire society's role in racial persecution is a theme that cries out for examination. Students find it astounding that all of society's institutions collapse in the wake of totalitarianism: education, the law, business, medicine, religion, etc. In many ways, this play is one of the finest examples of *Problemdichtung* in the course as it generates so many more questions than answers. We discuss both the positive and negative roles of Switzerland in World War II (positive: the preservation of the German language and German thought and culture during the war period; negative: an intransigent immigration policy that was only modified in 1968 when larger numbers of non-Jews were allowed to enter Switzerland after the Soviet invasion of Czechoslovakia). Viewing the film *Das Boot ist voll* is, of course, de rigueur when reading Frisch, as are discussions of the Swiss banks' hoarding of *both* Nazi and Jewish gold, money, and valuables. Class discussion frequently centers on the disparity between the simultaneous Swiss rejection of Jews as human beings and acceptance of their valuables and funds. In many ways, this self-serving materialistic bent reflects the stereotypes used by the racists in *Andorra* to characterize the Jews. When I offer the course again, I would like to assign Jane Kramer's 1997 *New Yorker* article, "Manna from Hell."

Discussions concerning *Des Teufels General* deal with the realism of the *Neue Sachlichkeit* movement of the 1920s and 1930s as well as the immediate overwhelming success the play enjoyed in post-World War II Central Europe. I particularly direct student attention to Harras's celebration of humanity in contrast to the Nazi propaganda spouted by those characters who are members of the National Socialist Party. The students find Oderbruch's role in the third act fascinating, and much of class discussion deals with his form of "active" resistance as opposed to Harras's barbed language and suicide.

I have frequently chosen *Biedermann und die Brandstifter* as a concluding text in the comparative literature class in order to discuss what Frisch says about individual responsibility, existential choice, and deeply personal decision making in the face of genocidal evil. Though this play has been mounted throughout much of its performance history in North America as a statement against racism in the South, it clearly could never have been written had the Holocaust not taken place. Its very imagery dealing with conflagration and its helpless chorus of bystanders who begin life anew in the Epilogue as if no catastrophe had ever occurred resonate with the events of the Holocaust. Therefore, I would like to conclude with this short play the next time I teach my course in German as well.

Although there are no examinations, there are significant written assignments in the course. I require three six- to nine-page papers, each dealing with a different genre. For the first paper, students might wish to write about a scene, theme, or character in one of the plays previously assigned or about an entire drama not discussed in the course at all (for example, Bertolt Brecht's *Der aufhaltsame Aufstieg des Arturo Ui*, Peter Weiss's *Die Ermittlung*, Rolf Hochhuth's *Der Stellvertreter*, etc.). These are not research papers, but should be interpretative thesis papers that reveal close literary analysis. In their course evaluations, students state that the topic of the Holocaust lends itself better to contemplative and analytical papers than to in-class examinations. They also find it helpful that the instructor reads and comments on drafts of their papers before they submit a final version.

Poetry

The week-long discussion of the poetry by Paul Celan and Nelly Sachs first deals with examples of verse by each of these poets and then proceeds to a comparison of Celan's "Todesfuge" and Sachs's "Chor der Geretteten," a mutually illuminating pair of poems. We compare imagery from texts previously read in the class—either from the memoirs or the dramas—with imagery in the lyrics of these two poets. A recent enlightening discussion of Celan's life and work written by critic John Felstiner is useful for helping students come to a preliminary understanding of Celan's great poetry. Furthermore, I show illustrations of abstract paintings by the contemporary German artist Anselm Kiefer to point to the resonance Celan's work has found in a post-Holocaust German-language society. We also discuss the role of crematoria poetry vis-à-vis the views of such writers as Jean Paul Sartre, Theodor Adorno, and George Steiner, who emphatically questioned whether one could ever again create imaginative writing after Auschwitz.

During this middle section of the course I draw upon two other creative arenas, music and film, for the insights they can offer. I present lectures on Holocaust-related scores by musicians such as Schoenberg, Weill, Shostakovich, Ullmann, Eisler, and Dessau. As for film, after four evening showings of all $9\frac{1}{2}$ hours of the film *Shoah* (both the English and the German scenarios are on reserve), the class discusses the role of the oppressors (for example, Franz Suchomel, the surreptitiously interviewed Nazi officer from Treblinka), the Polish bystanders outside of the camps, and the survivors. For their second paper, students must analyze a poem, deal with a musical/operatic work, or analyze a segment from *Shoah* or any other Holocaust-related film.

I incorporate a film series into both the German-language course and the comparative literature class. Attendance at the showings has been generally high, as I have integrated the films shown with the readings. Furthermore, with the advent of videotape, students can view the films as often as they wish in the language laboratory. Certain films, such as the aforementioned *Anne Frank Remembered*, *Triumph des Willens* (shown when reading *Furcht und Elend des Dritten Reiches*), *Das Boot ist voll*, *Shoah*, and *Jakob der Lügner* (Jacob the Liar), are so closely paired with the readings in the course that regular attendance at the films becomes almost second nature to the students. As to the actual screenings, I hand out duplicated material just prior to a viewing. These handouts—short, to the point, and often based on material from Annette Insdorf's second edition of *Indelible Shadows*—provide basic information that the students will find useful in understanding the film. I never show films in class unless specific frames or segments are under discussion, but rather schedule films in the middle of the week, often on a Wednesday, so that they are fresh in the students' minds and discussions the following day can be most effective. The importance of film in undergraduate courses on the Holocaust cannot be overestimated: when one is discussing facts that boggle the mind, a picture is literally worth a thousand words.

These weekly out-of-class film showings are crucial for my course. At the beginning of the semester, *Triumph des Willens* helps students to comprehend the enormous importance attached by the Nazis to mass psychology. *Die Wannsee-Konferenz* and *Die weiße Rose* illustrate, respectively, the calculated planning of the Holocaust and a major example of courageous German resistance to the Nazi dictatorship. For the drama section of the course, *Das Boot ist voll* reveals the wholesale Swiss abandonment of the Jewish refugees. *Shoah*, with its unique direct representation of perpetrators speaking and singing in German, offers a glimpse into the minds of the executioners operating the death camps, and at the end of the course, the viewing of *Anne Frank in Maine* is most helpful by drawing direct connections to racial problems in the U.S. today.

The Novel

As a start, we read two novellas: Thomas Mann's prescient "Mario und der Zauberer" and Stefan Zweig's psychological *Schachnovelle*. Both immediately show the epic power of descriptive detail and provide insight into the minds of both persecutor and victim. We study the three novels—Jurek Becker's *Jakob der Lügner*, Grete Weil's *Meine Schwester Antigone*, and Gregor von Rezzori's *Memoiren eines Antisemiten*—in very different ways, although I emphasize *one* theme: the humanistic, antiheroic, yet all-too-realistic character portrayals versus the unrealistically heroic Nazi notion of triumphalism.

The Becker novel provides the course with an introduction to East German literature. Also, as so much of the work's energy focuses on the narrator's quest to learn what actually transpired in the Lodz Ghetto, the students discuss the motivation for the narrator's post-Holocaust search. Two other matters that we pursue are: (1) the alternative endings to the work, which illustrate what Bruno Bettelheim, as a reaction to the emphasis by Terrence Des Pres on the survivors' skills for endurance (27–31), has perceived as the role of chance in surviving (274–314), and (2) the crucial role of the humor surrounding Jakob and his friends, a Schlemiel-like, Woody Allenesque, humanizing humor that pervades the work. Finally, the class discusses the critical role of the child in Holocaust literature and the specific function of fairy tales in this novel. As the instructor, I provide background information as to why so much Holocaust literature—from Leslie Epstein's *King of the Jews* to Harold and Edith Lieberman's *Throne of Straw* and from Shimon Wincelberg's *Resort 76* to the clandestinely written *Chronicle of the Łódź Ghetto*—takes place in the Lodz Ghetto.

The Weil novel permits the class to examine Holocaust literature from a feminist perspective. We consider a variety of questions: why is Antigone's story of taking a firm moral stand and surrendering her life for this idealism at the center of this largely factual work? In what ways is Weil's heroine a survivor, and how is she able to pass on her "story" to her younger spiritual sister? How is "Petrikau," the Friedrich Hellmund manuscript about the *Einsatz-Gruppen,* which is incorporated into the novel, crucial in understanding the role of the German soldier in World War II, and in what ways does this manuscript help to underscore Daniel J. Goldhagen's major theories regarding German eliminationist antisemitism in his recent history, *Hitler's Willing Executioners*?

Since the *Memoiren eines Antisemiten* consists of five more or less equally weighted and intricate novellas, we all analyze the first one in class, and the students usually choose one of the remaining four for their final paper. We begin our discussion of this work by reading Franz Fühmann's brilliantly troubling "Das Judenauto," which also takes place in the hinterlands and illustrates how easily children can learn to hate. The triangulation within Rezzori's novel; the narrator's tragic blindness throughout his "story"; the repeated victimization of Jews, all falsely accused of "crimes" that their persecutors actually committed; and the relationship between nineteenth-century antisemitism and twentieth-century Nazi eliminationist antisemitism—these are some of the main facets of this remarkably self-revelatory, post–World War II Austrian text that the class discusses. I find it useful to end the novel section by considering the fact that the Weil and Rezzori novels, two essentially nonfictional works, are structured and presented as fictional accounts, in much the same way as is Thomas Keneally's *Schindler's List.*

Having started the novel section with two novellas, I conclude it and the course by using four shorter prose texts (three of which are nonfiction) to stimulate synthetic, contemplative discussions: Robert H. Jackson's closing argument at the Nuremberg Trials (it contains many crucial literary allusions), the pioneering 1985 "Weizsäcker Rede" (with a videotape and in an annotated edition provided by the AATG), Christa Wolf's autobiographical "Blickwechsel," and Timothy W. Ryback's 1992 *New Yorker* article, "Report from Dachau." These works raise critical issues concerning, respectively, individual guilt, *Vergangenheitsbewältigung,* German displacement, and official German reluctance even today to memorialize the past. Addressing such questions and issues does not provide closure, but does, I hope, give the students intellectual fuel for further thought and contemplation beyond the confines of the course.

Conclusion

Aside from the healthy enrollment patterns that the Holocaust courses have provided the German Department, these courses have also exposed the stronger students to a broad range of possible topics for term or year-long senior honors projects. In the last few years alone, as a direct result of the course offerings I have directed honors projects on "The Theme of the Holocaust in Wolfgang Hildesheimer's Fiction," "The Role of the Physician in Imaginative Writing on the Holocaust," "The Representation of Gays in Holocaust Literature," and "Framing the Post-War Landscape: Literary Form and the Holocaust in the Work of Max Frisch."

My experience with teaching these Holocaust courses has led me to suggest some "Do's and Don't's" that may help colleagues contemplating offering such courses. On the positive side, be at the out-of-class film showings to talk informally with the students both before and afterwards; have regular and frequent office hours so that if students become disturbed by the high-affect material encountered in the class, they may talk with you in private; carefully go over drafts of papers with students to help them think clearly and analytically about their writing; bring in current newspaper articles (not necessarily Holocaust-related) about human rights, racial conflicts, and ongoing questions concerning race relations, particularly those dealing with North American issues.

On the other hand, do not categorically equate all Germans between 1933 and 1945 with the Nazis; do not limit yourself to discussing the persecution of the Jews (gays, Sinti and Roma, the mentally retarded, etc., were also persecuted); do not view a wallowing in collective guilt as a viable form of understanding past misdeeds, especially because so much of Holocaust imaginative writing deals with *individual* complicity and guilt; don't assume anything. So much that teachers and scholars take for granted, such as the root causes of World War II, has become "ancient history" for our students.

The fact that so many of the titles of the memoirs, dramas, poems, and novels contain the names of the protagonists portrayed shows the unalloyed significance of individuals and their particular personhood as representatives of human life and human dignity. If as an *Auslandsgermanist* I am at least partially successful in drawing my students' attention to *both* the specifics of the Holocaust and the significant universal concerns about combating racism, I will be grateful.

Bowdoin College	Prof. Steven R. Cerf

DEUTSCH 398, DER HOLOCAUST UND DIE LITERATUR

Woche 1
  Einleitung: Resnais' Film, *Night and Fog*
  Wiesel, *Night*
  Film: Interview mit Wiesel*
  Wiesel, *Night*

Woche 2
  Frank, *Tagebuch*
  Frank, *Tagebuch*
  Film: *Anne Frank Remembered**
  Frank, *Tagebuch*

Woche 3
  Brecht, *Furcht und Elend des Dritten Reiches*
  Brecht, *Furcht und Elend des Dritten Reiches*
  Film: *Triumph des Willens**
  Frisch, *Andorra*

Woche 4
  Frisch, *Andorra*
  Frisch, *Andorra*
  Filme: *Die weiße Rose* und *Das Boot ist voll**
  Zuckmayer, *Des Teufels General*

Woche 5
  Zuckmayer, *Des Teufels General*
  Zuckmayer, *Des Teufels General*
  Lyrik, Paul Celan—erste Arbeit fällig

Woche 6
  Lyrik, Nelly Sachs
  Vergleiche zwischen Celan und Sachs
  Film: *Shoah*, Erster Teil*
  "Entartete Musik und Kunst" im Dritten Reich—Gastvortrag

Woche 7
  Wagner im Dritten Reich—Gastvortrag
  Mann, "Mario und der Zauberer"
  Film: *Shoah*, Zweiter Teil*
  Mann, "Mario und der Zauberer"

Woche 8
    Mann, "Mario und der Zauberer"
    Zweig, *Schachnovelle*
    Film: *Shoah*, Dritter Teil*
    Zweig, *Schachnovelle*

Woche 9
    Zweig, *Schachnovelle*—zweite Arbeit fällig
    Shoah: Die Verfolger
    Film: *Shoah*, Vierter Teil*
    Shoah: Die Verfolgten

Woche 10
    Shoah: Die Zuschauer
    Becker, *Jakob der Lügner*
    Film: *Die Wannsee-Konferenz**
    Becker, *Jakob der Lügner*

Woche 11
    Becker, *Jakob der Lügner*
    Becker, *Jakob der Lügner*
    Film: *Jakob der Lügner**
    Weil, *Meine Schwester Antigone*

Woche 12
    Weil, *Meine Schwester Antigone*
    Weil, *Meine Schwester Antigone*
    Film: *Europa Europa**
    Hellmund, "Petrikau"

Woche 13
    Fühmann, "Das Judenauto"
    von Rezzori, "Skutschno"
    Film: *Anne Frank in Maine**
    Jackson, "Closing Address" der Nürnberger Prozesse, und "Die Weizsäcker Rede"

Woche 14
    Wolf, "Blickwechsel," und Ryback, "Report from Dachau"
    Schlußdiskussion: Rassismus heute (Frisch, *Biedermann und die Brandstifter*)
    Schlußarbeit fällig

*Diese Filme werden abends gezeigt.

Works Cited

Print Sources

Adorno, Theodor W. *Noten zur Literatur.* Frankfurt am Main: Suhrkamp, 1974.

Becker, Jurek. *Jakob der Lügner.* 1969. Frankfurt am Main: Suhrkamp, 1982.

Bettelheim, Bruno. *Surviving and Other Essays.* New York: Knopf, 1979.

Brecht, Bertolt. *Der aufhaltsame Aufstieg des Arturo Ui.* 1941. Frankfurt am Main: Suhrkamp, 1981.

———. *Furcht und Elend des Dritten Reiches.* 1938. Frankfurt am Main: Suhrkamp, 1981.

Celan, Paul. *Ausgewählte Gedichte.* Frankfurt am Main: Suhrkamp, 1972.

Dawidowicz, Lucy S. *The War Against the Jews: 1933–1945.* New York: Holt, Rinehart and Winston, 1975.

Des Pres, Terrence. *The Survivor: An Anatomy of Life in the Death Camps.* New York: Oxford University Press, 1976.

Dobroszycki, Lucjan, ed. *The Chronicle of the Łódź Ghetto, 1941–1944.* Trans. Richard Lourie et al. New Haven: Yale University Press, 1984.

Eliach, Yaffa. *Hasidic Tales of the Holocaust.* New York: Avon Books, 1982.

Epstein, Leslie. *King of the Jews.* New York: Coward, McCann & Geoghegan, 1979.

Felstiner, John. *Paul Celan: Poet, Survivor, Jew.* New Haven: Yale University Press, 1995.

Frank, Anne. *Das Tagebuch der Anne Frank.* 1947. Frankfurt am Main: S. Fischer, 1985.

Frisch, Max. *Andorra. Stücke 2.* 1961. Frankfurt am Main: Suhrkamp, 1973. 185–285.

———. *Biedermann und die Brandstifter. Stücke 2.* 1961. Frankfurt am Main: Suhrkamp, 1973. 81–145.

Fühmann, Franz. "Das Judenauto." 1962. *Das Judenauto. Vierzehn Tage aus zwei Jahrzehnten.* Zurich: Diogenes, 1968. 7–18.

Gies, Miep, and Alison Leslie Gold. *Anne Frank Remembered.* New York: Simon and Schuster, 1987.

Goldhagen, Daniel J. *Hitler's Willing Executioners: Ordinary Germans and the Holocaust.* New York: Knopf, 1996.

Hochhuth, Rolf. *Der Stellvertreter.* 1963. Hamburg: Rowohlt, 1991.

Insdorf, Annette. *Indelible Shadows.* 1983. 2nd ed. New York: Cambridge University Press, 1989.

Jackson, Robert H. "Closing Address in the Nuremberg Trial." *The Law as Literature.* Ed. Ephraim London. New York: Simon and Schuster, 1960. 467–506.

Keneally, Thomas. *Schindler's List*. New York: Simon and Schuster, 1982.
Klemperer, Viktor. *LTI*. 1957. Leipzig: Reclam, 1991.
Kramer, Jane. "Manna from Hell." *The New Yorker* 28 April and 5 May 1997: 74, 76–78, 83–86, 88–89.
Lanzmann, Claude. *Shoah: The Complete Text of the Acclaimed Holocaust Film*. 1985. English ed. translated from the French. New York: Da Capo, 1995.
_____. *Shoah*. Trans. Nina Börnsen and Anna Kamp. 1st German ed. Düsseldorf: Claassen, 1986.
Lieberman, Harold and Edith. *Throne of Straw*. 1972. Skloot 113–96.
Mann, Thomas. "Mario und der Zauberer." 1930. *Tonio Kröger und Mario und der Zauberer*. Frankfurt am Main: S. Fischer, 1996. 75–126.
Rezzori, Gregor von. *Memoiren eines Antisemiten*. Munich: Steinhausen, 1979.
Rosenthal, Nan. *Anselm Kiefer: Works on Paper in the Metropolitan Museum of Art*. New York: The Museum; [distributor] H. N. Abrams, 1998.
Ryback, Timothy W. "Report from Dachau." *The New Yorker* 3 August 1992: 43–61.
Sachs, Nelly. *Ausgewählte Gedichte*. New York: Harcourt, Brace & World, 1968.
Sartre, Jean Paul. *"What Is Literature?" and Other Essays*. Cambridge: Harvard University Press, 1988.
Skloot, Robert, ed. *The Theatre of the Holocaust: Four Plays*. Madison, WI: University of Wisconsin Press, 1982.
Steiner, George. *After Babel: Aspects of Language and Translation*. New York: Oxford University Press, 1975.
Weil, Grete. *Meine Schwester Antigone*. Zurich: Benziger Verlag, 1980.
Weiss, Peter. *Die Ermittlung*. Frankfurt am Main: Suhrkamp, 1965.
Weizsäcker, Richard von. *Zum 40. Jahrestag der Beendigung des Krieges in Europa und der nationalsozialistischen Gewaltherrschaft*. Ed. Thomas O. Beebee, Steven R. Cerf, and James L. Hodge. Cherry Hill, NJ: AATG, 1987.
Wiesel, Elie. *All Rivers Run to the Sea: Memoirs*. New York: Alfred A. Knopf, 1995.
_____. *Night*. Trans. Stella Rodway. 1960. New York: Bantam Books, 1982.
Wincelberg, Shimon. *Resort 76*. 1981 [originally *The Windows of Heaven*. 1962]. Skloot 39–112.
Wolf, Christa. "Blickwechsel." 1971. *Gesammelte Erzählungen*. Darmstadt: Luchterhand, 1982. 5–23.

Zuckmayer, Carl. *Des Teufels General.* 1946. Frankfurt am Main: S. Fischer, 1992.
Zweig, Stefan. *Schachnovelle.* 1942. Ed. Harry Zohn. London: Methuen & Company, 1962.

Films/Videotapes

Anne Frank in Maine. Dir. Burrill Crohn. 1979. Video. New York: Anti-Defamation League of B'nai B'rith, 1981.
Anne Frank Remembered. Dir. Jon Blair. 1995. Video. Columbia TriStar Home Video, 1996.
Das Boot ist voll. Dir. Markus Imhoof. 1981. Video. Embassy Home Entertainment, 1985.
Europa Europa. Dir. Agnieszka Holland. 1990. Video. Orion Home Video, 1992.
Facing Hate. Interview of Elie Wiesel with Bill Moyers. Prod. and dir. Catherine Tatge and Dominique Lasseur. PBS. Nov. 1991. Video. Films for the Humanities, 1997.
Jakob der Lügner (Jacob the Liar). Dir. Frank Beyer. East German Television, 1976. Rental film. National Center for Jewish Film, Brandeis University.
Night and Fog. Dir. Alain Resnais. 1955. Video. Video Images, 1981.
Die Rede des Bundespräsidenten [Richard von Weizsäcker]. Dir. Irmgard von zur Mühlen. Video. Inter Nationes, 1987.
Shoah. Dir. Claude Lanzmann. Video. Paramount Video, New Yorker Films, 1985.
Triumph des Willens. Dir. Leni Riefenstahl. 1935. Video. Embassy Home Entertainment, Janus Collection, 1975.
Die Wannsee-Konferenz. Dir. Heinz Schirk. 1984. Video. Films Incorporated, 1986.
Die weiße Rose. Dir. Michael Verhoeven. 1982. Video. MGM/UA Home Video, 1983.

Chapter 7

THE HOLOCAUST AND RESISTANCE IN GERMAN LITERATURE

Gisela Brude-Firnau

The general aim of this course is to foster an understanding of the Holocaust through works of fiction. The underlying assumption is that the humanist discourse of the post-Holocaust age has to focus on human negative potential and ask how it might be integrated into the Western cultural tradition. The epistemological aim of the course is the comprehension of the specific contribution of the literary text to our understanding of this bleak period of German history.

Teaching the Holocaust mainly through works of literature begins with the admission that no literary work can do justice to the historical events. All the texts read have evoked controversy. But despite these drawbacks, they offer unique insights and do contribute to our understanding of the humanness of the Holocaust. I chose literary texts in which the theme of resistance is an important aspect. The discussion of the various forms of resistance to a totalitarian regime helps both to counteract a sense of despair among students and to sharpen their sense of social responsibility.

It seemed particularly important to teach a course on the Holocaust at the University of Waterloo located in the Kitchener-Waterloo area, a community with a large population of German origin and two vital Jewish congregations. Survivors and some alleged perpetrators live close together, and court proceedings at the Canadian national level provoke intense public debates. The concerns and values of the strong Mennonite population of the area, an important component of the cultural and religious life of Kitchener-Waterloo, are reflected in the Peace and Conflict Studies Program based at one of the affiliated colleges of the university. The Holocaust course is cross-listed as one of that program's content courses.

In preparing to teach this course I had to identify and work through several important issues. I realized that I was motivated by a sense of existential responsibility characteristic of many of my generation who have childhood memories of the catastrophic end of the war and started reading newspapers when the reports on the concentration camps appeared. I do not share a feeling of collective guilt, but neither can I view the Holocaust as a purely academic subject, and I wish I had the "professional ability to distance oneself," which a younger colleague once identified as an indispensable asset in this context. I often feel as if I were learning about the atrocities for the first time and may never "get used" to what I teach in this course. The students' awareness that an existential element is present for their instructor helps to create an atmosphere of seriousness and solidarity between instructor and students, as well as among the students themselves.

The Holocaust and Resistance in German Literature is a third-year, one-semester undergraduate course offered by the Department of Germanic and Slavic Languages and Literatures of the University of Waterloo. It is open to students of all disciplines. The texts must therefore be available in English translation, and this limits the selection of titles. So far I have taught the course twice with an average enrollment of fifteen students. Eventually it will also be part of the offerings of the planned Jewish Studies Program in the Faculty of Arts. I teach the course in two weekly sessions. We devote the two-hour meetings to the analysis and discussion of literary texts and reserve most of the one-hour sessions for students' questions, guest speakers, and discussion of films. In our first session I ask the students how they became interested in the subject and what it means to them, and I share the reasons for my own involvement. Or students interview one another and report back to the class. This technique creates an atmosphere of familiarity as well as seriousness.

I then give a historical overview, stressing that the Holocaust is by no means a closed chapter of history. I explain that there was no monocausal historical development leading to the events of 1933 to 1945. Of the numerous causes that led to German fascism, I emphasize the development of ideological racism and antisemitism, but I also point out that National Socialism arose in a state with a democratic constitution, and that the Third Reich was neither predestined nor preordained. To counteract any impression of inevitability, the historical overview ends with the discussion of a statement by the historian Michael Marrus: "For the pre-Hitler period, it is difficult to make the case that Germany was an anti-semitic country par excellence ..." ("'Good History' and Teaching the Holocaust" 10).

I begin our discussion of the literary texts of the course by asking the basic question: why teach the Holocaust through literary texts if there are more credible testimonies and an abundance of scientific historiography? The preliminary answer, elaborated throughout the course, is that historiography and literature reflect different aspects of reality and do not compete. The events themselves are primarily the subject of historiographic analysis; the individual encounter with the events, the human experience, is that of artistic, especially literary, interpretation. In reading a fictional text, the reader oscillates between imaginative involvement and critical reflection, and this leads to a different and more complex kind of understanding than a purely factual account.

I discuss with students Adorno's concern about whether it is appropriate to make the Holocaust the subject of art, and whether the depiction of the suffering of the victims might not give the reader a type of aesthetic pleasure. To appreciate this predicament, the class reads Hermann Broch's poem "The Ones Who in the Cold Sweat of Execution," which addresses the obligation and inability to convey the suffering of the victims. I repeatedly stress to students that there is no inherent moral effect in a literary work; art does not necessarily humanize its readers and was one of the Nazis' best propaganda tools. Rather, a literary text provides an opportunity for interactive discourse, and each text gives a somewhat different answer to these concerns.

Anna Seghers's *The Seventh Cross* (1942) is the first work we read, and I outline its background and origin. With this preparation, from the four groups of people (the prisoners in the concentration camp, the seven escapees, the Nazi perpetrators, the people outside the camp), each student chooses one of the more developed characters and prepares an oral account, taking into consideration the character's biography, his or her development and attitude toward the National Socialist regime, whether he or she has a conflict to solve or a decision to make, and whether he or she could have decided in a different way. These reports start the general discussion and allow for individual assessments. They also lead to a better understanding of the social, economic, and, to a lesser degree, the political situation of prewar Germany, the mentality and the dominant reasons for cooperation, as well as the obstacles and risks of resistance. Most students react quite positively to this novel, which reminds them of a *Kriminalroman*; they can easily identify with some of the characters.

I summarize the class discussion of *The Seventh Cross* by raising several critical objections. For instance, the novel acquaints its reader with the outlook of "little people," but lacks political context. It has only a few Jewish characters and does not acknowledge the uniqueness of the Jewish fate in Germany despite the Nuremberg Laws, which had already been in effect for several years. Furthermore, the fact that some of the actions of resistance in the novel are unrealistic, e.g., the description of written messages being secretly circulated in the factory, betrays that the narrator's optimism is unwarranted.

From Edgar Hilsenrath's *The Nazi and the Barber* (1977) I select the fictitious, satirical, and partly surrealistic depiction of Hitler as an orator and his psychological effect on the mass audience (50–77), an excerpt which helps the reader to understand the Führer's demagogical skills as well as his manipulation of the masses to hatred and antisemitism. I guide the discussion of Hilsenrath's intricate text by posing questions: why do the crowds expect a charismatic speaker? Why does Hitler quote from the Bible, especially from the Sermon on the Mount? How does he surreptitiously change the evangelical code to a message of hatred and violence? How does he manipulate people's hopes and resentments? Which promise gives rise to mass euphoria? Which traditional and which more recent antisemitic prejudices does the speech activate? By which stylistic devices does the narrator indicate his own critical and satirical point of view? To differentiate between the unexpectedly high factual content and its literary interpretation, I have found it useful to compare this excerpt from *The Nazi and the Barber* to an eyewitness account of Hitler as an orator (*Facing History* 139–40).

The international "Storm over *The Deputy*" (Bentley) in 1963 to 1965, as well as the problems which arose between 1987 and 1989, when there were threats of censure and protests against performances in both Vienna and Bavaria ("Hochhuth: Die Wiederkehr"), demonstrate that Hochhuth's 1963 drama *The Deputy* is highly provocative. For a course on the Holocaust and resistance in literature, the value of the play transcends its indisputable aesthetic flaws. Lively discussions in my classes have attested to the ongoing validity of Karl Jaspers's statement that the work has "summoned great numbers of people to reflection" (99). Because of the controversial nature of Hochhuth's criticism of the Pope, I invite a Catholic colleague to present the opposing point of view and answer questions about the role of the Vatican during World War II.

A major assignment for students is to choose a fictitious character and, using Hochhuth's appendix containing historical documentation, to compare this character with the corresponding historical figure. This assignment helps students to grasp the play's ambiguous position between documentary and traditional theater, and for some students also provides the basis for their major term essay. Students are able to understand a range of then contemporary attitudes toward the destruction of the Jews, since most of the characters are mouthpieces of their particular organization—church, SS, or industry.

We then deal with the question of factual accuracy, which we examine, in part, by the manner in which historical statements, such as that of the Pope to the *Osservatore Romano*, are integrated into the dialogues of Hochhuth's text. To help the class gain a more objective understanding of the role of the Catholic Church, I prepare a handout taken from Marrus's *The Holocaust in History* (179–83) and compare this with Hochhuth's criticism of Pius XII. This allows students to comprehend the respective characteristics and differences of the dramatic and historiographic genres.

The question of civil and moral responsibility is central to the play and elicits lively responses from young people. On the basis of their more intimate knowledge of at least one character, the students can address the questions of individual responsibility and guilt. The discussion considers the questions: to what extent are the characters determined by their social circumstances? Does the traditional value system of their corporation or their profession conflict with the Nazi ideology? Does their education enable them to reflect critically on this ideology? What determines why some of them speak out and act? Where does the assumption of responsibility lead them? The students see that Hochhuth propounds the ethics of resistance no matter what the outcome. However, the class realizes that it was almost impossible to keep one's moral integrity in a totalitarian regime, as demonstrated, for example, by the political duplicity to which Kurt Gerstein must resort despite his strong ethical convictions.

The play's subtitle, "A Christian Tragedy," omitted in the English translation, reveals the central argument: Christianity does not provide an answer to the Holocaust. For Hochhuth the Holocaust is devoid of transcendental meaning. However, by using Elaine Murdaugh's perceptive analysis to retrace the stages of development that Riccardo goes through, I show my students how the existential challenge of life in the camps brought out very individual human responses.

To sum up, I point out some aspects of aesthetic criticism, for instance, that Holocaust discourse repeatedly shows, particularly in Germany, that works of lesser artistic value trigger the most intense debates. Flawed art and public success are not mutually exclusive, as Hochhuth's play and the TV series *Holocaust* demonstrate. After discussing briefly the concept of *Kitsch* or pseudo-art and its often quite questionable application, I point out the most blatant weaknesses of the play—the sometimes oversimplified, naive, and stereotypical characters; the tasteless juxtaposition of the erotic and the horrible; or the cumulation of effects in Act V. Once one alerts their attention to certain artistic weaknesses, such as the play's verbosity, students readily identify examples. I devote more time to the figure of the Doctor, who is aggrandized to mythical proportions as a Satan against whom humans are powerless. As such, this figure diminishes individual responsibility and thus contradicts the existentialist statement made by the figure of Riccardo. However, despite its flaws, Hochhuth's play attempts to take a moral stance, for it grapples with questions that other German authors had mostly ignored until the late 1960s.

Peter Weiss's *The Investigation* (1965) adds a new dimension to German literature. This documentary play seems to lead the reader progressively and relentlessly to the horrific centers of Auschwitz and allows the most sobering look at the rather average people who became perpetrators. As this is the most emotionally trying work in the course, we first discuss individual reading experiences so that students can understand their sometimes quite contradictory reactions to a text which seems to some of them almost impossible to absorb. Others talk about the difference between just "knowing" the facts and actually "seeing" the victims in Weiss's play. This introductory exchange may also help them to appreciate the play's concerns, for as the reader is horrified or grows numb and has the feeling of not being able to go on reading, these reactions contrast with the laughter, cynicism, and moral insensitivity of the accused on stage.

In order to enable students to understand Weiss's sociopolitical convictions and their importance for the play, I explain the social trends and attitudes in Germany at the time of the Auschwitz Trials (1963–65), which the dramatist attended for several months and which provided the documentary basis of his work. We move on to the Marxist point of view—that is to say, the ideological blind spots in the play—which completely disregards certain elements of National Socialist ideology, primarily its murderous antisemitism.

We then identify the features of the play that remain problematic issues for us today: the claim of ignorance, a leitmotif in the play, still serves many as an excuse. The survivors, their memories and nightmares, are a part of our time, as are the perpetrators, some of whom still await trial. The concepts of following orders and of duty, as well as the question of the role of ideological indoctrination, continue to be troubling.

Not until now do I give students a handout listing the relevant characteristics of the two genres of fiction and historiography, based on the astute observations of Karlheinz Stierle. In order to apply these concepts, the class undertakes a comparative analysis of one scene from *The Investigation* ("The Song of the Camp" 75–76) and the corresponding passage from Bernd Naumann's *Auschwitz* (133, 138; also in Langer 32), a collection of newspaper reports on the court proceedings in Frankfurt, which served as one of Weiss's sources. Students have the initial impression that both texts are very much the same. However, with close reading they become aware of the literary transformation that has taken place. All students discover the author's essential omission: instead of the "Jewish children" in the original source, Weiss mentions only "children." According to his ideological orientation, there are only "political prisoners, criminal prisoners and racial prisoners" (142). To sum up, I stress that both categories of texts are linguistic constructs created by an individual consciousness and are thus an interpretation of reality. They do not compete and are not different in rank, since they describe different aspects of reality. The historian provides information and knowledge about collective experiences. The literary text helps us understand the individual experience and individual conflicts.

A handout summarizing the formal critical analyses of Erika Salloch and Peter Demetz allows students to prepare for a discussion of the aesthetic form of *The Investigation*. The students identify many examples in the text to corroborate Salloch's observation that the play's form can be considered as the "anti-model" to Dante's *Divina Commedia*, and thus as a literary depiction of the decay of the Western value system (13). We also devote considerable time to finding examples of perverted, degrading, or inadequate language. At the conclusion of our discussion, my students generally agree that Peter Weiss has transfigured the factual reports of the Frankfurt court proceedings into a literary creation, an "oratorio of human degradation" (Salloch 11).

When we then turn to Jurek Becker's novel *Jacob the Liar* (1969), its theme of emotional and mental resistance (Becker, "Resistance") seems to allow students to regain a guarded humanistic belief. I base our class discussion on Adi Ophir's assumption that the novel attempts to "demythologize" or "desacralize" the victims in order to humanize them and to show them as everyday characters (qtd. by Marrus, "The Use and Misuse" 116). Thus the reader can more easily understand and, perhaps, identify with them. I ask students to choose one character and report to the class by answering some of the following questions: does the victim remain humane under inhumane conditions? Which side of the victim's personality gains the upper hand? Does the character as an inhabitant of the ghetto develop characteristics that nobody noticed before? To what extent does he or she keep his or her personal integrity?

We then discuss the theme of resistance in *Jacob the Liar*. The novel seems intended to show the absurdity of the postwar idea that the majority of victims died a heroic death. It even parodies violent resistance in the plans of two young boys to blow up the German headquarters. However, it also contains many forms of nonheroic or passive and moral resistance, as shown in the behavior of characters such as Professor Kirschbaum and his sister, Herschel Schtamm, and Kowalski. We discuss the value of these forms of resistance and then focus on the role of storytelling. Gradually, students understand that Becker's novel explores both the potential and the limits of storytelling. On the one hand, Jacob's fictional radio and his creative storytelling are a major form of resistance that sustains life and hope in the ghetto. However, in the final analysis, storytelling cannot solve the problems of persecution and death.

Students must come to terms with the fact that, contrary to their expectations, morality is neither the concern of the novel nor a literary concept in general. By discussing the novel's two endings, we address the reader's desire to see the wicked punished. Predictably, all students prefer the first ending, which shows an almost heroic Jacob, who dies shortly before the Russians liberate the ghetto. With the second ending the narrator yields to historical reality and forces the reader to face the horrors of the Holocaust. Students thus become aware of the discrepancy between their expectations as readers and their knowledge of the cruel historical facts.

The discussion of Becker's novel and historical truth then turns to the question of whether the narrator's rather lighthearted tone is compatible with the conditions experienced in the ghettos and whether the criticism of the work by survivors, especially by Becker's father (Becker, "Answering Questions" 288), is justified. Becker's paradoxical concern with and neglect of historical facts further underscores this problem. To reach a conclusion we juxtapose excerpts from the novel with the correlated paragraphs from *Lodz Ghetto: Inside a Community under Siege* and *The Chronicle of the Łódź Ghetto, 1941–1944*. These historical texts make clear how well Becker portrayed some aspects of the ghetto's atmosphere, for instance, the general uncertainty and the immense importance of information, aspects which illuminate the value and risk of owning a radio. The students also look at photographs in *The Chronicle of the Łódź Ghetto* and try to determine whether any episodes from the novel or comments by the narrator enhance their understanding of these pictures. Since the editor of the *Chronicle* himself acknowledges the verisimilitude of Becker's novel (xxv), *Jacob the Liar* is thus a major contribution to the literary reception of the Holocaust.

Holocaust denial is the topic of one of the last sessions. *Holocaust Denial*, a report by the Simon Wiesenthal Center (1994), offers up-to-date material for preparation of a class on this subject. I remind students that only knowledge of facts, documents, and laws, not the literary works, equips one for a confrontation with antisemitic revisionists or Holocaust deniers. We briefly discuss the notorious Canadian deniers, as well as German and Canadian neo-Nazi groups and their strategies.

Each time I offered the course, I invited three or four guest speakers. The testimony of the survivors Eve Bergstein and Mania Kay produced the most intense experience. When Mrs. Kay pushed up her sleeve and showed the Auschwitz number on her arm, students gasped. Everything we had discussed so far appeared to be more real. History had been transformed into presence; it had become a part of our own lives. Colleagues from other departments addressed a wide range of topics: Professor Robert van Pelt spoke about documents and construction drawings from the camps Auschwitz and Birkenau, which have recently become accessible in Moscow archives; Professor Geoffrey Winthrop-Young elaborated on the projects and plans of architects and artists during the Third Reich; Professor Rem Kooistra described his project "Oral History of the Holocaust," for which he had interviewed survivors in the Kitchener-Waterloo area; Professor Aubrey Diem discussed a novel on World War II that he had just completed; Professor John Whiton defended the position of the Pope during the war; and Professor Erwin Biener recalled the tribulations and persecutions of his childhood years in Hungary.

I treated the films and videotapes as an enrichment activity and showed them outside of class. During classes I briefly tried to outline the temporal context of each film and discussed questions raised by students. Fred Zinnemann's version of the *Seventh Cross,* however, lends itself well to introducing aspects of hermeneutics: students not only realize the obvious differences between the novel and the film, they are also fascinated by the way the film reflects the political and commercial interests of its era. We compare Zinnemann's own retrospective evaluation—the picture was "nothing to be ashamed of" (51)—with critic Manfred George's condemnation of the film for having perpetrated "'a gross crime ... because of what it neglects to show'" (qtd. in Horak 127). Jan-Christopher Horak's insightful analysis of the "genre strategies" developed by Hollywood for its anti-Nazi films of the 1940s (127–28) facilitates our understanding of the reasons for the divergent views of Zinnemann and his critics.

The students' reactions to the course were very positive, as the results of the evaluations showed. One student wrote: "It is a very touchy subject, and we were eased into it and in that way we gained a truer understanding because we were not overwhelmed with numbers and killings." Another saw as the strength of the course "that a German instructor has presented this very important historical event." Several students thought "more time should be allotted to this topic," and that "it is an important course which needs to be offered." Another student wrote: "I wish everyone had to take it—I think quite a few of them would change some of their opinions." Some students thought that the guest speakers were the most valuable aspect of the course. Several students felt that the amount of reading, a total of 1,250 pages, presented a problem, and that it was "difficult to stay current for each class and be prepared for discussions."

My own evaluations and concerns refer to the choice of texts: Max Frisch's *Andorra*, which I taught the first time, seemed to be rather abstract, so I have replaced it with excerpts from Hilsenrath's novel. Since the amount of reading is considerable, I may decide to omit the excerpts as well. The amount of historical information given in class seemed to be a problem: while some students felt that the outline at the beginning sufficed, others asked for more details. In order not to take more time away from the discussions of the literary texts, I have compromised by expanding my lecture notes, adding military events of World War II primarily, and distributing the copies. Finally, as in other courses, there is the didactic dilemma of striking the right balance between general class discussions, which may at times stray from the subject proper, and the more formal textual analysis.

Colleagues who teach courses on the Holocaust at other universities confirm my experience that teaching this subject creates a certain emotional stress and saddens the instructor as much as the students. This reaction, however, is greatly offset by the open-mindedness and new awareness of most of the students, as demonstrated by their essays. Teaching the Holocaust through literature also generates new awareness in the instructor and a deepened understanding of this "Zäsur und unheilbarer Bruch der Zivilisationsgeschichte" (Grass [paraphrasing Adorno] 14), which in turn influences the teaching of other subjects. It has become impossible for me to teach a course on German Classicism, for example, without discussing how the Holocaust has modified our reading of the great classical works. The ongoing interdisciplinary Holocaust discourse in numerous publications represents a constant intellectual challenge and in turn modifies my teaching: class discussions of *The Deputy*, for example, have become very topical due to recent publications and admissions of the Roman Catholic Church about its own anti-Judaism and the theological roots of antisemitism. Further, many discussions with friends and colleagues about the teaching of the Holocaust, in particular during a two-week Institute for the Study of Holocaust and Jewish Civilization held by the Holocaust Educational Foundation at Northwestern University in June 1996, have been infinitely more rewarding than I could ever have expected.

The University of Waterloo — Prof. Gisela Brude-Firnau

GERMAN 381, THE HOLOCAUST AND RESISTANCE IN GERMAN LITERATURE

After a brief outline of the events leading to the reign of National Socialism, the course will focus on the literary rendering of the Holocaust experience by authors from the German-speaking countries such as Jurek Becker, Hermann Broch, Peter Weiss, and others. Literary motifs to be discussed include the inability of language to describe the unthinkable horrors, the world forsaken by God, the monstrosity of man, humaneness in an inhuman environment, as well as collective guilt and responsibility. There will also be a study of works that deal with various attempts at resistance (by individuals; political, Jewish, church, and youth groups) and the reasons for failure, as described, for example, by Rolf Hochhuth and Anna Seghers. A comparison between Holocaust testimonies (diaries, autobiographical reports) and the fictional rendering of analogous motifs leads to the question of whether the literary transfiguration of these extreme experiences is justifiable. There will be three or four guests speaking about their own Holocaust or war experiences.

Reading List

1. Anna Seghers: *The Seventh Cross* (1942)
2. Rolf Hochhuth: *The Deputy* (1963)
3. Peter Weiss: *The Investigation* (1965)
4. Jurek Becker: *Jacob the Liar* (1969)

Copies of other texts will be distributed in class.

Grading Scheme

Oral Assignments and Participation	20%
Midterm	20%
Final Examination	30%
Term Paper (ten to twelve pages)	30%

The following videos and films will supplement the class discussions (course participants should have seen a minimum of four):

The Seventh Cross (1944)
Blueprints of Genocide (1994)
The Wannsee Conference (1984), Eng. subtitles
The Architecture of Doom (1991)
The Nazi Concentration Camps (1945)

Week 1
    Introduction. Holocaust and Literature. Poem: H. Broch
    Historical Overview

Week 2
    Historical Overview. Anna Seghers: *The Seventh Cross*
    Anna Seghers: *The Seventh Cross*
    Film: *The Seventh Cross* (evening)

Week 3
    Anna Seghers: *The Seventh Cross*
    Edgar Hilsenrath: *The Nazi and the Barber* (excerpts)
    Video: *Blueprints of Genocide* (evening)

Week 4
    Guest speaker: Prof. R. van Pelt
    Rolf Hochhuth: *The Deputy*

Week 5
    Rolf Hochhuth: *The Deputy*
    Rolf Hochhuth: *The Deputy*

Week 6
    Rolf Hochhuth: *The Deputy*
    Guests: Mrs. Eve Bergstein and Mrs. Mania Kay
    Video: *The Wannsee Conference* (evening)

Week 7
    Peter Weiss: *The Investigation*
    Midterm Exam

Week 8
    Peter Weiss: *The Investigation*
    Guest speaker: Prof. G. Winthrop-Young
    Film: *The Architecture of Doom* (evening)

Week 9
    Peter Weiss: *The Investigation*. Poem: Leonard Cohen
    Guest speaker: Prof. Erwin Biener
    Film: *The Nazi Concentration Camps* (evening)

Week 10
    Jurek Becker: *Jacob the Liar*
    Jurek Becker: *Jacob the Liar*

Week 11
Jurek Becker: *Jacob the Liar*
Jurek Becker: *Jacob the Liar*

Week 12
Jurek Becker: *Jacob the Liar*. Holocaust Denial
Summing up

Works Cited

Print Sources

Adelson, Alan, and Robert Lapides, eds. *Lodz Ghetto: Inside a Community under Siege.* New York: Viking, 1989.

Adorno, Theodor W. "Commitment." *The Essential Frankfurt School Reader.* Ed. Andrew Arato and Eike Gebhard. New York: Urizen, 1978. 300–18.

Becker, Jurek. "Answering Questions about *Jakob der Lügner.*" *Seminar* 19 (1983): 282–92.

———. *Jacob the Liar.* Trans. Leila Vennewitz. New York: Arcade, 1996.

———. "Resistance in *Jakob der Lügner.*" *Seminar* 19 (1983): 269–73.

Bentley, Eric, ed. *The Storm over The Deputy: Essays and Articles about Hochhuth's Explosive Drama.* New York: Grove, 1964.

Broch, Hermann. "The Ones Who in the Cold Sweat of Execution." Unpublished trans. by Helmut Fischer. [German: "Diejenigen, die im kalten Schweiss. ..." *Gedichte. Kommentierte Werkausgabe.* Vol. 8. Ed. Paul Michael Lützeler. Frankfurt am Main: Suhrkamp, 1980. 49.]

Cohen, Leonhard. "All There Is to Know about Adolph Eichmann." *Stranger Music: Selected Poems and Songs.* Toronto: McClelland and Stewart, 1993. 53.

Cornwell, John. *Hitler's Pope: The Secret History of Pius XII.* London: Viking, 1999.

Demetz, Peter. *After the Fires: Recent Writing in the Germanies, Austria, and Switzerland.* San Diego: Harcourt, 1986.

Dobroszycki, Lucjan, ed. *The Chronicle of the Łódź Ghetto, 1941–1944.* Trans. Richard Lourie et al. New Haven: Yale University Press, 1984.

Facing History and Ourselves: Holocaust and Human Behavior. Brookline, MA: Facing History and Ourselves National Foundation, Inc., 1994.

Frances, Henry, and Carol Tator. *Holocaust Denial: Bigotry in the Guise of Scholarship.* Toronto: Simon Wiesenthal Center, 1994.

Frisch, Max. *Andorra: A Play in Twelve Scenes.* Trans. Michael Bullock. New York: Hill and Wang, 1964.

Grass, Günter. *Schreiben nach Auschwitz. Frankfurter Poetik-Vorlesung.* Frankfurt am Main: Luchterhand, 1990.

Hilsenrath, Edgar. *The Nazi and the Barber.* Trans. Andrew White. Garden City, NY: Doubleday, 1971. [Out of print.]

Hochhuth, Rolf. *The Deputy.* Trans. Richard and Clara Winston. New York: Grove Press, 1964.

"Hochhuth: Die Wiederkehr des '*Stellvertreters.*'" *Der Spiegel* 14 March 1988: 232–34.

Horak, Jan-Christopher. "The Other Germany in Zinnemann's *The Seventh Cross*." *German Film and Literature: Adaptations and Transformations.* Ed. Eric Rentschler. New York: Methuen, 1986. 117–31.

Jaspers, Karl. "On *The Deputy.*" Bentley 99–102.

Langer, Lawrence. *The Holocaust and the Literary Imagination.* New Haven: Yale University Press, 1975.

Marrus, Michael R. "'Good History' and Teaching the Holocaust." *Perspectives: American Historical Association Newsletter* 31 (May/June 1993): 1, 6–12.

———. *The Holocaust in History.* London: Penguin, 1989.

———. "The Use and Misuse of the Holocaust." *Lessons and Legacies: The Meaning of the Holocaust in a Changing World.* Ed. Peter Hayes. Evanston, IL: Northwestern University Press, 1991. 106–19.

Murdaugh, E. Elaine. "The Apostate Ethic: The Alternative to Faith in Hochhuth's *Der Stellvertreter.*" *Seminar* 4 (1979): 275–89.

Naumann, Bernd. *Auschwitz.* Trans. Jean Steinberg. London: Pall Mall, 1966.

Salloch, Erika. "The *Divina Commedia* as Model and Anti-model for the *Investigation* by Peter Weiss." *Modern Drama* 1 (1971): 1–12.

Seghers, Anna. *The Seventh Cross.* Trans. James A. Galston. 1942. New York: Monthly Review Press, 1987.

Stierle, Karlheinz. "Erfahrung und narrative Form. Bemerkungen zu ihrem Zusammenhang in Fiktion und Historiographie." *Theorie und Erzählung in der Geschichte.* Ed. Jürgen Kocka and Thomas Nipperdey. Munich: dtv, 1979. 85–118.

Weiss, Peter. *The Investigation: A Play.* Trans. Jon Swan and Ulu Grosbard. New York: Atheneum, 1966.

Zinnemann, Fred. *An Autobiography.* London: Bloomsbury, 1992.

Films/Videotapes

The Architecture of Doom. Dir. Peter Cohen. Video. First Run Features, Icarus Films, 1991.

Blueprints of Genocide. Dir. Robert van Pelt. Video. CBC, 1994.

Holocaust. Dir. Marvin Chomsky, Herbert Brodkin, and Robert Berger. Four-part television series. NBC. 16–19 April 1978. Video. Republic Entertainment, Inc., 1994.

The Nazi Concentration Camps. Documentary film. 1945. Video. International Historic Films, 1985.

The Seventh Cross. Dir. Fred Zinnemann. MGM, 1944.

The Wannsee Conference. Dir. Heinz Schirk. 1984. Video. Infafilm GmbH, 1987; Prism Entertainment, 1988.

Chapter 8

INSERTING A SHORT COURSE ON THE HOLOCAUST INTO GERMAN OFFERINGS AT A SMALL LIBERAL ARTS COLLEGE

Nancy M. Decker

Frankly, I had avoided teaching the Holocaust. I did not deny the Holocaust as a historical fact nor think I could not teach it, even though it is not my area of research. After all, as a Germanist at a small liberal arts college, I have to teach many things far outside my areas of specific training and expertise. I avoided teaching the Holocaust for two reasons: (1) I felt sure someone else was providing intensive instruction on the Holocaust and could most likely do it better than I; and (2) so many popular images of things German come out of the National Socialist period that I thought it was important that I offer an antidote by focusing my instruction on everything else but the Holocaust. Those were my thoughts ten years ago. Experience has convinced me I was wrong in both cases. While students indeed learn something of the Holocaust in courses on European history, religion, political science, sociology, and world literature, no one here was offering instruction that dealt extensively with the destruction of European Jewry and other population groups during World War II. Furthermore, by avoiding the National Socialist period in my presentation of things German, I was relinquishing the very subject that draws students not already attracted to this Central European culture and its "difficult" language. I was missing an opportunity to broaden the range of students I serve at this small private liberal arts college.

Notes for this section begin on page 118.

Pragmatism ultimately forced me to change my thinking. I wanted to offer a new course in English that would attract students with the hope that some few of them might then continue in the language. Even if they did not find learning German itself attractive, I would at least be doing something significant in confronting them with the disturbing issues bound up in the study of the Holocaust. Our academic calendar at that time facilitated just such experiments. Between the longer fall and spring semesters lay a shortened three to four-week "Winter Term," a time when Rollins College encouraged both students and faculty to experiment with courses not regularly offered during the fall and spring.

Organizing a new course on the Holocaust is no small task. The overwhelming amount of information available[1] means a first-time instructor needs to consider course objectives very carefully. The United States Holocaust Memorial Museum sets out guidelines for teaching about the Holocaust in its World Wide Web document to encourage teachers to reflect carefully on their individual objectives for approaching this subject and cites the following reasons "offered by educators who have incorporated a study of the Holocaust into their various courses and disciplines" as to why others should also do so:

- The Holocaust was a watershed event, not only in the twentieth century, but in the entire history of humanity.
- Study of the Holocaust assists students in developing understanding of the ramifications of prejudice, racism, and stereotyping in any society. It helps students develop an awareness of the value of pluralism, and encourages tolerance of diversity in a pluralistic society.
- The Holocaust provides a context for exploring the dangers of remaining silent, apathetic, and indifferent in the face of others' oppression.
- Holocaust history demonstrates how a modern nation can utilize its technological expertise and bureaucratic infrastructure to implement destructive policies ranging from social engineering to genocide.
- A study of the Holocaust helps students think about the use and abuse of power, and the role and responsibilities of individuals, organizations, and nations when confronted with civil rights violations and/or policies of genocide.
- As students gain insight into the many historical, social, religious, political, and economic factors which cumulatively resulted in the Holocaust, they gain a perspective on how history happens, and how a convergence of factors can contribute to the disintegration of civilized values. Part of one's responsibility as a citizen in a democracy is to learn to identify the danger signals, and to know when to react.[2]

At first glance, these points relate best to questions of sociological structure, civil rights and responsibilities, and the value of a diverse society, and would appear to favor relegating instruction on the Holocaust to colleagues in the social sciences or in minority studies. It may not be readily apparent what Germanists—traditionally trained in German language, literature, and culture—could expect to contribute to the discussion. However, closer inspection reveals that the above points speak to values and general abilities that all "liberal arts" courses should foster. Germanists, furthermore, can deny neither the significance the Holocaust continues to have for German thought and culture today nor the fascination that this historical event holds for students. Some students, in fact, who might not be attracted to the traditional German Studies curriculum find the idea of studying the Holocaust intriguing.

How can Germanists best include instruction on the Holocaust in an established curriculum? At small liberal arts colleges they can serve their institutions by offering courses on the Holocaust in English. Packaging instruction on the Holocaust into a short course has three distinct advantages: (1) It is difficult for both students and the instructor to sustain the level of intellectual and emotional energy necessary to investigate the horrors of the Holocaust over an entire fourteen to fifteen-week semester or a nine to ten-week quarter. (2) Dedicating an entire semester or quarter to the study of the Holocaust alone may be impossible for small departments. A short course may more easily fit into the staffing constraints of an established roster of teaching duties in a German Studies faculty. (3) Inserting a two-week component on the Holocaust into an existing course on Germany may pose fewer problems in terms of finding teaching staff. However, the attraction the Holocaust holds for students becomes diluted in the larger topic around which this kind of semester or quarter course is structured. Thus students not already involved in German Studies are less likely to take note.

An additional factor in my desire to develop a short course on the Holocaust has to do with the wealth of information easily at my disposal. Within a ten-minute drive from my college lies the Holocaust Memorial Resource and Education Center of Central Florida. At the Center I can make use of print and media resources as well as of pedagogical aids that have been developed for both elementary and secondary school pupils. Florida has mandated instruction on the Holocaust in its public schools. The Holocaust Memorial Center houses teaching tools developed for this audience, many of which I can tailor for use in my college short course. The resources and exhibits at the Holocaust Center parallel those at such centers throughout North America. Furthermore, the information now available through the Internet and through the United States Holocaust Memorial Museum makes it possible for those who are not near a resource center to draw on the experience and wisdom of others to organize such short courses.[3]

For an instructor who has decided to develop a course on the Holocaust, the United States Holocaust Memorial Museum sets out on its Web listing of teaching guidelines fourteen methodological considerations for further thought:

1. Define what you mean by "Holocaust."
2. Avoid comparisons of pain.
3. Avoid simple answers to complex history.
4. Just because it happened, doesn't mean it was inevitable.
5. Strive for precision of language.
6. Make careful distinctions about sources of information.
7. Try to avoid stereotypical descriptions.
8. Do not romanticize history to engage students' interest.
9. Contextualize the history you are teaching.
10. Translate statistics into people.
11. Be sensitive to appropriate written and audio-visual content.
12. Strive for balance in establishing whose perspective informs your study of the Holocaust.
13. Select appropriate learning activities.
14. Reinforce the objectives of your lesson plan. (USHMM home page)

I have found points 3, 8-11, and 13 to be particularly significant tasks. They serve as focal points for this investigation.

Point 3: Avoid simple answers to complex history.

To aid students in contemplating the variety of factors that scholars have identified as significant for an understanding of the Holocaust, and especially to help them in pondering the Holocaust from the viewpoint of German Studies, I have found it necessary to include a central historical text among the required readings. For my first attempt at teaching a course on the Holocaust, I assembled a sizable course packet of articles. Because of copyright difficulties as well as a better understanding of what my students already know and can be expected to digest in three to four weeks, I have since dispensed with the packet and choose instead a published volume. Other than Raul Hilberg's *The Destruction of the European Jews*, I have also used Joachim Fest's *Hitler* and Michael Berenbaum's *The World Must Know*. Since students in my short courses given in English need not have had any previous instruction in German or in history, they must gain some basic knowledge of the sequence of historical events from the turn of the century through the Holocaust. At midterm (approximately ten days to two weeks into the term) I test students on their ability to identify events, names, concepts, dates, and places central to an understanding of the Holocaust.

Point 8: Do not romanticize history to engage students' interest.

The most significant difference in the short course I offered in 1990 and subsequent courses involves the release of the film *Schindler's List* in the winter of 1993/94. Point 8 admonishes instructors to avoid too great an emphasis on a phenomenon underlined by the film, sometimes referred to as the "Americanization of the Holocaust."[4] This approach requires that students be left with some source of consolation, some reason for hope, some uplifting experience, some sense of the "saving power of individual moral conduct and collective deeds of redemption" in the face of the awesome destruction that is the Holocaust (Rosenfeld 37). *Schindler's List* clearly has redirected discussion about the Holocaust away from the victims and toward the survivors and particularly their rescuers. However, "even the highest estimate [of rescuers] ... represents less than one-half of 1 percent of the total population under Nazi occupation" (Oliner and Oliner 2). The challenge lies in maintaining a sense of the limited number of resisters while still offering young students something positive, a sense of hope.

The popularity of *Schindler's List* as both a film and a novel surely tempts Germanists to aggrandize the significance of Oskar Schindler. After so many negative images of Germans from the 1930s and 1940s, a German-Czech "hero" emerges who was willing to risk his personal wealth and well-being for the sake of those the Nazis labeled unfit to live. Yet even the label of "hero," let alone "Righteous Among the Nations,"[5] sits precariously on Schindler's shoulders. This Nazi Party member, abuser of alcohol, and philanderer hardly fits our usual image of a hero. Indeed, it is far more advantageous to problematize students' conceptions of what a hero is by making them confront Schindler's frailties than to let them lionize him and, by overlooking his shortcomings, see him as an extraordinary, superhuman figure.

Those few German rescuers and resistance groups about which we have documentation (White Rose, Kreisau Circle, von Stauffenberg's 20 July group, etc.) also enable the class to gain some understanding of the pervasive nature of the totalitarian state and the opportunities that remained to resist the state successfully. I use the films *The White Rose* and *The Plot to Kill Hitler* to provide information about some of these figures. Therefore, I do expose students to figures such as Oskar Schindler, Helmuth von Moltke, Claus von Stauffenberg, and Sophie Scholl, but I also point out the obstacles and fears that they failed to overcome. These discussions help students ponder what it takes to resist a totalitarian regime successfully.

Point 9: Contextualize the history you are teaching.

One of the most energizing and illuminating exercises I have found to provide students insights into the situation that produced the meteoric rise of the NSDAP involves the use of case studies.[6] The exercise divides the class into up to seven teams of three or four students. Each team receives a description of the party platforms of three political parties identified only as Party A, Party B, and Party C. Upon close examination of the platform planks but sometimes not until the end of the exercise, it becomes clear to the students that the descriptions apply to a Communist, a democratic, and a National Socialist party platform. Each team then reads the case history of one fictitious individual, decides how that individual would most likely have voted in the 1930 election in Germany, and reports the team's conclusions to the class.

Students found this activity very fruitful. It not only provided them with a sense of the political reality and the turmoil for individuals in the economic and political chaos in Germany in 1930, but also promoted a sense of teamwork within the class in that students had to pool their knowledge of the Weimar Republic in order to understand the party platforms and then to choose the most appropriate party for the team's fictitious voter.

Point 10: Translate statistics into people.

Numbers play an important role in understanding the need to study the Holocaust today. The Holocaust meant the destruction of six million European Jews. Whereas 500,000 Jews lived in Germany in 1933, today approximately 50,000 reside in the Federal Republic. In 1939 fifty-eight percent of all Jews lived in Europe, thirty-three percent in North and South America, and three percent in Palestine. Current statistics indicate that fifty percent of all Jews now live in North and South America, twenty-seven percent in Israel, and twenty-one percent in Europe. These statistics (Wolffsohn 144–45) give North American students additional impetus to study the Holocaust since it resulted in the redistribution of Jews away from Europe and into North America and Israel.

At the same time, one cannot reveal the story of the Holocaust without the "voices" of individuals and families that breathe life into these cold, mathematical figures. In a short course, focusing on the experiences of young people and women can provide students with accounts of life before, during, and after the Holocaust. These groups are of particular interest to many students in the traditional college age groups. Accounts by young people—young Jews in the 1930s and 1940s, young Auschwitz prisoners, members of the Hitler Jugend and Bund deutscher Mädel, young people of postwar generations—remain favorites since the historical distance the students feel toward the Holocaust period can be mitigated by the subjects' similarity in age. Since most survivors today were young people in the 1930s and 1940s, they add a sense of immediacy to the discussion of the Holocaust. The organization of young people into groups from the turn of the century onward—from Pathfinders to Boy Scouts; to Wandervögel; to Jungvolk, Hitler Jugend, and Bund deutscher Mädel; to Freie Deutsche Jugend; to modern gangs—never fails to captivate the students' attention. It is also useful to arrange to have young Germans who are not class members speak to the class about their knowledge of the Holocaust and their assessment of Germany's progress in dealing with the Nazi past. In this connection, one can use the films *Europa Europa* and *The Nasty Girl*, as well as the Peter Sichrovsky book *Schuldig geboren. Kinder aus Nazifamilien*.

The reasons for focusing on women may not immediately be as clear. After all, one need only contrast Leni Riefenstahl with Sophie Scholl to show how hard it is to make general statements about the reactions of females as a group. However, as Alison Owings writes in the introduction to her collection of interviews with German women who had lived through the Third Reich, women had one of the best vantage points from which to gain an understanding of how the Third Reich affected the home front, that place where the political and the personal converged. Men were more involved in the public and in the military spheres. Indeed as of 1939, most of them had to leave home to face the possibility of injury and death in the armed forces. Women confronted more directly how the Third Reich affected children, particularly since their role as childbearers became so central to Nazi policy (Owings xxiii–xxiv). Students also appreciate having Nazi *Frauenpolitik* placed into the context of developments regarding women in the first half of the twentieth century.[7] Good works to consult for more information on this subject include Claudia Koonz's *Mothers in the Fatherland* and Jill Stephenson's *Women in Nazi Society*.

Point 11: Be sensitive to appropriate written and audio-visual content.

Because the National Socialists exploited the power of visual images in order to convince German citizens of the necessity of some of their goals, the stockpile of moving pictures from this era is considerable and tempting. Furthermore, because the industrialized destruction of human life in the Holocaust continues to exert the power of horror and fascination, film adaptations of aspects of the story of the Holocaust fill the shelves at videotape rental shops. Yet without careful attention these filmic works may be incomprehensible to a young audience because the scenes of death, violence, filth, and degradation are so overwhelming that the audience relegates the images to the world of fantasy (British documentaries of Bergen-Belsen, some modern film adaptations); the mindset of viewers in the 1930s is foreign to the modern spectator. Students need to be made aware of the development of film editing and camera techniques in order for them to understand the significance of documentaries such as *Triumph of the Will*, *Olympia*, and *The Eternal Jew*; the critique of National Socialism is so subtle or academic that the intent is lost on the audience unless one prepares the class well for viewing *Beruf Neonazi* (Profession Neo-Nazi) and *The Wonderful, Horrible Life of Leni Riefenstahl*.

I have devoted more time to filmic texts in recent courses than I did originally. Although students are often visually oriented learners, they are not necessarily visually literate. Simply showing the movies does not usually suffice. Students need time to comment on the films either during or soon after each viewing. For this reason I have found it very effective to teach this course in the shortened term when I hold class for about three hours per day for three or four days per week during the four-week course. This schedule allows for time to show major films in their entirety. If there has to be any time lag between watching and discussing the films or if students have been asked to report on films that the class cannot watch together, one should prepare clips of important segments. Without having the possibility of reviewing scenes from the films, students often have trouble discussing them in any detail.

Point 13: Select appropriate learning activities.

With this point the United States Holocaust Memorial Museum staff emphasizes how counterproductive some activities may be to studying the Holocaust. Models of extermination camps, for instance, represent a huge investment of time, yet the knowledge gained relates only tangentially to the objectives of the course. Furthermore, while active learning situations do increase student engagement with the material, simulation activities may prove unsound (USHMM home page). Nor are those activities necessary, because discussion of the Holocaust lends itself to other extensions of the classroom that allow for student involvement, as the following examples show.

(1) Oral reports, approximately five to ten minutes in length, create a space in the classroom for student voices to be heard. Unlike discussions or orchestrated class activities, these reports place individual students at center stage to present prepared information to the class. Individual students or perhaps student pairs become the experts on their topics. In this manner, even those who seldom contribute voluntarily in open class discussions have an opportunity to speak. It is important to ensure that the class takes the information presented by student colleagues as seriously as that presented by the instructor. Thesis sheets or report summaries distributed by the presenters can act to focus class attention on the presentations as well as to remind students (and the instructor) of important points at test time. I generally give students the choice of summarizing a scholarly article the others have not been required to read, researching a specific topic (i.e., Hitler's *Mein Kampf*, Jim Crow laws in comparison to the Nuremberg Laws, Hitler Youth, leaflets from the White Rose, etc.), presenting a film that the rest of the class has not seen, or dramatizing a scene from a novel or memoir (Anne Frank's diary,[8] Cynthia Ozick's *The Shawl*). I see a distinction between acting out a portion of a book and building a camp model or dividing the class through the wearing of badges. Students understand in a dramatization that they are being provided only with a highlight of a text. A simulation activity attempts to convey a sense of the system as a whole. A scene from a memoir or work of fiction makes no such claim.

(2) Visitors to the class, particularly those who come once the students have sufficient historical background to feel confident in their questions, can provide classes with significant insights. Holocaust survivors and eyewitnesses dispel any lingering illusion that information on the Holocaust presented in class is a fabrication of the instructor's imagination. I also find it important for students to have the opportunity to talk to young

Germans about how the latter confront the Holocaust. Now at least two generations removed from direct responsibility for events of the 1930s and 1940s, young Germans have a different relationship to the Holocaust than did either their parents or their grandparents (see Schneider). A young German visited my class to report on a survey he had done of random passersby at the Dortmund train station concerning questions of nationality and pride. Students sat open-mouthed as they realized how the relationship between German young people and their country of birth remains greatly affected by the actions of their grandfathers' generation.

(3) Trips to Holocaust resource centers and museums also allow students to view another representation of the basic information they receive in class. Sometimes they note a difference in emphasis. For instance, the exhibit at the Holocaust Memorial Resource and Education Center in Maitland, Florida, ultimately links an understanding of the Holocaust with the fight against right-wing extremism and racial supremacists in the Central Florida area. The center works closely with the local courts to help change the lives of young people convicted of hate crimes by exposing them to the fates of those persecuted during the Holocaust. While that goal lies outside the scope of my course, it is nonetheless useful for students to see the ramifications that the subject they are studying have in the local community.

Readers may infer from my discussion of the points set forth in this essay that one need make plans for a short course on the Holocaust only once. It is my experience, however, that an instructor will find it impossible to teach exactly the same course twice. Since I last taught a course on the Holocaust two factors have contributed to changes in the way I will approach the subject next time. On the scholarly side, the publication of Daniel Goldhagen's *Hitler's Willing Executioners* has caught the attention of many.[9] While the book may not have had as wide an influence on the general population as was the case with Spielberg's film *Schindler's List*, the reaction among scholars on both sides of the Atlantic cannot go unmentioned. The question of the culpability of "ordinary" Germans for the destruction of millions of Jews and the question of the uniqueness of German history and society in that regard require attention in courses taught by North American Germanists.

The second factor that will change the way I will teach the Holocaust next time is my experience in taking part in the 1996 Fulbright Landeskunde Seminar. During the three weeks of the seminar marking the fiftieth anniversary of the founding of the Fulbright Commission, participants explored the academic programs in Jewish Studies available at German universities and inquired about the state of German Jewish communities today. The seminar brought me into contact with both German and American Holocaust scholars and provided me with an appreciation of contemporary issues that face Christians and Jews in the Federal Republic today. No longer stagnant, the number of individuals who identify themselves as Jews in Germany has nearly doubled to about 50,000 with the influx of Russian Jews coming into Germany from the former Soviet Union. The next time I teach a short course for undergraduates on the Holocaust, I intend to conclude the discussion with an account of what it might mean to be a Jewish schoolchild in present-day Germany.[10] In the past I have finished short courses with articles students have located on incidents of genocide around the world. However, this new conclusion will allow me to fulfill point 14 in the United States Holocaust Memorial Museum's list of guidelines. By ending my course with a look at the Jewish community in Germany today, I will reinforce my objective of outlining the significance that the Holocaust has had for Germany.

Notes

1. Over 40,000 documents register if one runs a World Wide Web search on the term "Holocaust" using Alta Vista.
2. *United States Holocaust Memorial Museum*, <http://www.ushmm.org/>. The passages of the guidelines (<http://www.ushmm.org/education/guidelines.html>) that I quote, here and elsewhere in this essay, from the home page with the Museum's permission, which I gratefully acknowledge, also appear in the USHMM publication *Teaching about the Holocaust: A Resource Book for Educators.*
3. Information about and from many Holocaust centers and museums can be found in the database of the Holocaust Memorial Resource and Education Center of Central Florida and at many Web sites. See, for example, those of Yad Vashem, <http://www.yad-vashem.org.il/>; Holocaust Memorial Center of Bloomfield, MI, <http://www.holocaustcenter.org/>; Cybrary of the Holocaust, <http://remember.org/>; The Mining Company, <http://holocaust.miningco.com/>; and the USHMM home page.
4. This term seems to have been coined in Henryk Broder's "Das Shoah-Business," 248. It is also quoted in Robert S. Leventhal's "Romancing the Holocaust or Hollywood and Horror: Steven Spielberg's *Schindler's List*" and in Alvin H. Rosenfeld's "The Americanization of the Holocaust."
5. See definition, <http://www.yad-vashem.org.il/RIGHT.HTM#who>.
6. *The Nazi Holocaust*, 60–62. Other curricula worth consulting include: Bolkowsky, Ellias, and Harris, *A Holocaust Curriculum: Life Unworthy of Life*; and Merti, *Understanding the Holocaust*. Germanists may also be interested in pedagogical materials on the Holocaust collected by the Bundeszentrale für politische Bildung: *Holocaust: Materialien zu einer amerikanischen Fernsehserie über die Judenverfolgung im "Dritten Reich"* and *Arbeitshilfen für die politische Bildung zum Film "Schindlers Liste."* Address: Bundeszentrale für politische Bildung, Frazis-Druck GmbH, Postfach 150740, 80045 München.
7. Women could not seek degrees at German universities until 1908; women's suffrage came to German women not as a matter of suffragettes marching on the streets, but rather from stipulations in the Treaty of Versailles, etc.
8. There is considerable information on the World Wide Web on Anne Frank. To place the Frank family in the context of German refugees in the Netherlands, see, for example, the transcript of a lecture given by Anthony E. Anderson, "Anne Frank Was Not Alone: Holland and the Holocaust," <http://www-lib.usc.edu/%7Eanthonya/holo.htm>.
9. Der Deutsche Akademische Austauschdienst and the Fernuniversität in Hagen have produced a collection of reactions to Goldhagen's book from German and some American newspapers through October 1996: Dieter Gutzen, ed., *Erinnern—Verdrängen—Vergessen. Die Goldhagen-Debatte in Deutschland.* For copies contact: Inter Nationes, Kennedyallee 91-103, 53175 Bonn.
10. See Brum et al., eds., *Ich bin, was ich bin, ein Jude.*

Rollins College   **Prof. Nancy M. Decker**

GMN 266 W, THE HOLOCAUST

Texts: Michael Berenbaum. *The World Must Know: The History of the Holocaust As Told in the United States Holocaust Memorial Museum.* New York: Little, Brown and Company, 1993.

Peter J. Haas. *Morality after Auschwitz: The Radical Challenge of the Nazi Ethic.* Philadelphia: Fortress Press, 1988.

Objectives: Holocaust—in Greek it means total burning. To the people of the twentieth century, the word is linked forever with the attempt by the German Nazis to annihilate Jews. We shall investigate the background to the "Final Solution," the process itself, and the significance those events still have for us today.

Requirements: Students with more than three unexcused absences cannot pass the class participation portion of the course. Every student will be asked to present a report to the class on one of the assigned readings. Each presenter should make a one-page typed summary of the important points for the class. Students should be prepared for a pop quiz at any time. Furthermore, there will be two larger tests in the course of the term.

Grades: Student grades will be determined according to the following formula:

Class participation and attendance	15%
Oral presentation	25%
Pop quizzes	10%
Tests	50%

Day 1
   Introduction   FILMS: *Memory of the Camps, Nazi Concentration Camps*

Day 2
   Text: Haas, 1–58;   FILM: *Nosferatu*
      Berenbaum, 1–16

Day 3
   Text: Haas, 59–110   FILM: *Triumph of the Will*

Day 4
   Text: Berenbaum, 16–65   FILM: *Olympia*

Day 5
    Text: Haas, 113–77   FILM: *The Eternal Jew*

Day 6
    Text: Berenbaum, 68–153   FILM: *The Wannsee Conference*

Day 7
    Review   FILM: *Lodz Ghetto*

Day 8
    Examination   Excursion to the Holocaust Memorial Center

Day 9
    Text: Haas, 179–229   FILM: *Weapons of the Spirit*

Day 10
    Text: Berenbaum, 156–223   FILM: *The White Rose*

Day 11
    Presentations   FILM: *Schindler's List*

Day 12
    Turn in final exam

Optional trip to Washington, DC
United States Holocaust Memorial Museum

Works Cited

Print Sources

Arbeitshilfen für die politische Bildung zum Film "Schindlers Liste." Munich: Bundeszentrale für politische Bildung, 1995.
Berenbaum, Michael. *The World Must Know: The History of the Holocaust As Told in the United States Holocaust Memorial Museum.* New York: Little, Brown and Company, 1993.
Bolkowsky, Sidney M., Betty Rotberg Ellias, and David Harris. *A Holocaust Curriculum: Life Unworthy of Life.* Farmington Hills, MI: Center for the Study of the Child, 1987.
Broder, Henryk. "Das Shoah-Business." *Der Spiegel* 19 April 1993: 248–56.
Brum, Elexa, et al., eds. *Ich bin, was ich bin, ein Jude.* Cologne: Kiepenheuer & Witsch, 1995.
Fest, Joachim C. *Hitler.* New York: Harcourt Brace Jovanovich, 1974.
Frank, Anne. *The Diary of a Young Girl: The Definitive Edition.* Trans. Arnold J. Pomerans. New York: Doubleday, 1995.
Goldhagen, Daniel. *Hitler's Willing Executioners: Ordinary Germans and the Holocaust.* New York: Alfred A. Knopf, 1996.
Gutzen, Dieter, ed. *"Erinnern—Verdrängen—Vergessen. Die Goldhagen-Debatte in Deutschland.* Bonn: Deutscher Akademischer Austauschdienst; Institut für neuere deutsche und europäische Literatur der Fernuniversität in Hagen; [printer and distributor] Inter Nationes, 1996.
Haas, Peter J. *Morality after Auschwitz: The Radical Challenge of the Nazi Ethic.* Philadelphia: Fortress Press, 1988.
Hilberg, Raul. *The Destruction of the European Jews.* 1961. New York: Holmes & Meier, 1985.
Hitler, Adolf. *Mein Kampf.* Trans. Ralph Manheim. 1943. Boston: Houghton Mifflin, 1971.
Holocaust: Materialien zu einer amerikanischen Fernsehserie über die Judenverfolgung im "Dritten Reich." Munich: Bundeszentrale für politische Bildung, Frazis-Druck GmbH, 1978.
Koonz, Claudia. *Mothers in the Fatherland.* New York: St. Martin's Press, 1987.
Merti, Betty. *Understanding the Holocaust.* Portland, ME: J. Weston Walch, Publisher, 1982.
The Nazi Holocaust. Albany, NY: University of the State of New York, State Education Department, Bureau of Curriculum Development, 1985. Unit III, vol. 2 of *Teaching about the Holocaust and Genocide.* The Human Rights Series. 3 vols. 1985–86.

Oliner, Pearl M., and Samuel P. Oliner. *The Altruistic Personality: Rescuers of Jews in Nazi Germany*. New York: Free Press, 1988.
Owings, Alison. *Frauen: German Women Recall the Third Reich*. New Brunswick, NJ: Rutgers University Press, 1994.
Ozick, Cynthia. *The Shawl*. New York: Alfred A. Knopf, 1989.
Rosenfeld, Alvin H. "The Americanization of the Holocaust." David H. Belin Lecture in American Jewish Affairs. University of Michigan, Ann Arbor. 20 March 1995. Revised version. *Commentary* (June 1995): 35–40.
Schneider, Peter. "The Sins of the Grandfathers: How German Teenagers Confront the Holocaust, and How They Don't." *New York Times Magazine* 3 December 1995: 74–80.
Sichrovsky, Peter. *Schuldig geboren. Kinder aus Nazifamilien*. Cologne: Kiepenheuer & Witsch, 1987.
Stephenson, Jill. *Women in Nazi Society*. London: Croon Helm, 1975.
Teaching about the Holocaust: A Resource Book for Educators. United States Holocaust Memorial Museum.
Wolffsohn, Michael. *Ewige Schuld? 40 Jahre deutsch-jüdisch-israelitische Beziehungen*. Munich: Piper, 1988.

Films/Videotapes

Beruf Neonazi (Profession Neo-Nazi). Dir. Winfried Bonengel. 1993. Video. Drift Releasing [last known distributor], 1995.
The Eternal Jew. Dir. Fritz Hippler. 1940. Video. International Historic Films, Inc., 1988.
Europa Europa. Dir. Agnieszka Holland. 1990. Video. Facets Video, 1991.
Lodz Ghetto. Dir. Alan Adelson and Kathryn Taverna. 1989. Video. Jewish Heritage Project, 1995.
Memory of the Camps. Dir. Sidney Bernstein. [1945.] Frontline. PBS. 1985. Video. PBS Educational Video, 1995.
The Nasty Girl. Dir. Michael Verhoeven. 1989. Video. Facets Video, 1991.
Nazi Concentration Camps: Witness to Genocide. Dir. U.S. Counsel for the Prosecution of Axis Criminality. 1946. Video. Zenger Media, [n.d.].
Nosferatu. Dir. Friedrich W. Murnau. 1922. Video. Republic Pictures Home Video, 1991.
Olympia. Dir. Leni Riefenstahl. 1936. Video. Home Vision Cinema, 1997.
The Plot to Kill Hitler. Dir. Lawrence Schiller. Video. Movies Unlimited, 1990.
Schindler's List. Dir. Steven Spielberg. 1993. Video. Baker & Taylor, 1994.

Triumph of the Will. Dir. Leni Riefenstahl. 1935. Video. Connoisseur Video Collection, Esicma Corp., 1993.
The Wannsee Conference. Dir. Heinz Schirk. 1984. Video. Facets Video, 1986.
Weapons of the Spirit. Dir. Pierre Sauvage. 1986. Video. Anti-Defamation League, 1989.
The White Rose. Dir. Michael Verhoeven. 1982. Video. Facets Video, 1983.
The Wonderful, Horrible Life of Leni Riefenstahl. Dir. Ray Muller. 1993. Video. Image Entertainment, Kino International Corp., 1995.

Electronic Sources

Anderson, Anthony E. "Anne Frank Was Not Alone: Holland and the Holocaust." Transcript of a lecture at the University of Southern California. 24 October 1995. July 1997 <http://www-lib.usc.edu/%7Eanthonya/holo.htm>.
Cybrary of the Holocaust. Dir. Michael Dunn. 25. April 1995. Cybrary of the Holocaust. January 1997 <http://remember.org/>.
Holocaust home page of The Mining Company. Guide Jennifer Rosenberg. About.com, Inc. July 1997 <http://holocaust.miningco.com/>.
Holocaust Memorial Center. Holocaust Memorial Center. January 1997 <http://www.holocaustcenter.org/>.
Leventhal, Robert S. "Romancing the Holocaust or Hollywood and Horror: Steven Spielberg's *Schindler's List.*" 1995. July 1997 <http://jefferson.village.virginia.edu/holocaust/schinlist.html>.
United States Holocaust Memorial Museum. United States Holocaust Memorial Museum. July 1997 <http://www.ushmm.org/>.
Yad Vashem: The Holocaust Martyrs' and Heroes' Remembrance Authority. Yad Vashem. January 1997 <http://www.yad-vashem.org.il/>.

Chapter 9

TEACHING THE SHOAH IN CONTEXT
A Course on Jewish German Relations

Karen Remmler

During a discussion about the meaning of interdisciplinarity in a German Studies senior seminar on Exile and Immigration, one student suggested that Jewish Studies and German Studies merge into one program: "We cannot understand contemporary German culture without a sound knowledge of Jewish culture."[1] Another student added that it was most appropriate for a German Studies major to take a course on the Shoah, but only after achieving a thorough knowledge of Jewish German relations before 1933.[2] These premises raise questions about the content and form of German Studies courses that focus on the killing of Jews and other victims of the Nazi genocide. Whose task is it to convey the complexity of Jewish German relations within German-speaking domains and the culmination of these relations in the killing of over six million Jews by Nazi Germans and their accomplices? In her article "Critical Performances," Angelika Bammer points out that "those of us who teach German culture" bear a particular responsibility to represent German culture with the Holocaust in mind: "How we teach German culture 'after Auschwitz,' then, has to do not only with how we position ourselves in relation to that history, but also with how we position ourselves in relation to our work as teachers" (1).

I believe it is my responsibility as a teacher of contemporary German culture not only to make reference to the Shoah and its consequences for

---

Notes for this section can be found on page 133.

present-day political, social, and cultural life in Germany, but also to provide students with tools to face the dilemma of trying to understand an event that cannot be fathomed. Students can indeed learn from the past, precisely because the past that constitutes the Shoah continues to determine Germany's present. Without knowledge of what came before the Shoah, a student would have a skewed view of what happened during and what came after the Third Reich. Therefore, an instructor would be remiss to teach a course on any aspect of contemporary German culture without a discussion of the changing presence of the Shoah and its effect on public spheres in Germany. A course on contemporary German culture that defines culture as a heterogeneous entity in flux, particularly since unification, would be deficient without analyses of the media events and public consciousness affecting and being shaped by Jewish German relations. Indeed, a focus on Jewish German relations can serve as a seismograph to measure the cultural and social tremors in the post-Wall German public sphere.

With these thoughts in mind, I developed a course on Jewish German relations from the Enlightenment to the present, with an emphasis on the postwar era. I based the course material on my own work during the year of memory (1995) in Berlin, where I had researched the representation of Jewish and German identities after unification in light of the many commemorative activities dedicated to remembering the end of World War II and those who were killed in concentration and work camps, in battle, and in bomb attacks. Despite my focus on contemporary relations between Germans and Jews, it became clear to me as I developed the course that any exploration of contemporary Jewish German relations required an understanding of the historical and cultural contexts preceding as well as during the Shoah.

Therefore, I designed the course not only to address contemporary issues of *Vergangenheitsbewältigung*, but also to engage students in an in-depth study of Jewish German relations from the Enlightenment to the present. The central theme of the course was not the Shoah, but rather Jewish German relations before, during, and after the Third Reich. By exploring the extent, depth, and nature of these relations, I intended to place the Shoah in a historical continuum of German and Jewish culture, instead of presenting it as an aberration thereof. Accordingly, the notion of a Jewish German symbiosis played a central role in our class discussion, since its feasibility was constantly called into question by the contradiction between the relative tolerance that Jews enjoyed in Prussia, for example, at the turn of the eighteenth to nineteenth centuries and the virulent political antisemitism that developed following the "birth" of the

German nation under Bismarck, a development instrumentalized by the Nazis for the destruction of European Jewry. Although the main focus was on gaining insight into the historical and cultural contexts during this time period, the course also explored issues of representation. Any course that addresses the presence of the Shoah and the forms of its remembrance in the present must, in my opinion, cross disciplines and incorporate not only historical contextualization but also the transmission and representation of history, memory, and experience into its syllabus.

Accordingly, class discussion of the course materials not only dwelled on descriptions of Jewish German relations per se, but above all on the self-representation of Jews in German culture as well as on projections of "Jewishness" or "non-Germanness" upon self-identified Jews by non-Jews. I encouraged students to analyze and synthesize both written and visual texts from the perspective of their second major, and I anticipated that they would gain insight into the multifaceted identities and experiences both within "Jewish" and "German" communities and in the portrayals of the lives and interactions of people who identified with these designations.

Although I originally conceived and taught the course on Jewish German relations in German to third- and fourth-year German majors at Mount Holyoke College, I also had the opportunity to teach the course in English to predominantly non-German majors for the German Studies Department at Amherst College. The contrast between the two teaching experiences is the subject of this essay.

By comparing the two courses, I will show that the language in which one teaches about the Shoah and the cultural background of the students make a major difference in how students grasp the unknowability of the Shoah, as well as place it in a larger context of significance for both contemporary Jewish and German culture. I will refer to the course taught in German as German 315 and to the course in English as German 43. In the first instance, eleven of the twelve students in the seminar identified themselves as Americans. One student had one Jewish parent; one regarded herself as Jewish and had had a very positive experience as an exchange student in Freiburg; and a third, a student from Germany, had converted to Judaism. The last was one of the most vocal students in the class and often contributed her knowledge of Jewish religion to the class discussions. Most of the students had spent their junior year abroad and were therefore able to converse in German at a level that corresponded to their intellectual level in their mother tongue. Because of the relative lack of knowledge about Jewish culture and religion, we spent a great deal of class time covering background material on this subject. Accordingly, the focus on any given day often shifted from a study of Jewish German relations to a study of Jewish culture within Germany or even in the United States. Most of the students had had little contact with Jewish culture. Though fairly well versed in the German classics, few students had realized that Heine, for example, was born a Jew.

Initially, the students reacted with curiosity to the emphasis on Jewish writers and thinkers within German culture, a culture they had studied for three years. Then a period of dismay and worry set in, in which students began to wonder out loud about their previous uncritical embrace of German society and culture. This became especially acute during the unit on the Shoah, which focused on the diary of Hertha Nathorff, a Jewish German doctor who recorded the events of her everyday life in the Third Reich before her escape to the United States, and the Nazis' propagandistic rendition of *Jud Süß*.

Eventually, however, students began to welcome a more differentiated view of Germany and the opportunity to learn about Jewish German culture. They expressed a desire to know more about Jewish American culture as well. Thus, the German majors in the course revised their previous image of Germany, deepened their understanding of the relation between the past and present as it affected Jewish German relations in contemporary Germany, and became interested in expanding their knowledge of and interaction with Jews in the United States.

The experience of the students in German 43 at Amherst College was similar, but in the reverse. By the end of the semester, the students, many from a Jewish background, expressed an interest in traveling to Germany and in meeting their German contemporaries. Whereas their image of Germany had been mixed, if not negative, at the beginning of the course, by the close of the semester this image had been transformed in a positive direction. The students were predominantly from a Jewish secular background, while one student identified himself as a German American. The course included one older native speaker of German, who was an auditor of the course. Whereas the German majors in German 315 approached the material more neutrally, the decision to take the course was anything but neutral for the students in German 43. From the very beginning, they expressed their apprehension about engaging in discussion about Jewish German relations, because it would inevitably involve reading and talking about the Shoah. Some came to class with strong anti-German sentiments, but were interested in reexamining their prejudices and learning more about contemporary Germany. Like the students in German 315, they wanted to know more about Jewish culture in Germany prior to 1933 and to explore family roots. Two of the students had had the opportunity to participate in a three-week tour of Germany for young Jewish

Americans sponsored by Hillel and wanted to enhance their initial impressions with "facts and figures."

Given the different backgrounds of the students in the two seminars, the presentation of the class materials differed in the respective courses. When I chose the material for the German course, availability played a major role, as did level of difficulty, and, most of all, relevance and importance to the subject at hand. Given the survey nature of the course, each text had to elicit a deeper understanding of a particular context and to become a red thread to which we could refer often throughout the course. The readings included works that provided an overview of Jewish German relations both historically and culturally, such as Erica Burgauer's overview of Jews in Germany after 1945, Rürup's edition on *Jüdische Geschichte in Berlin*, and the collection of essays *Zerbrochene Geschichte*, as well as primary literature by Jewish German writers and three films (*Jud Süß*, *Architektur des Untergangs* [Architecture of Doom], and *Sojourners*), which focused on the period of the Third Reich and the postwar era. A course reader, which I handed out at the beginning of the semester, contained many of the texts except for the two main literary works of the course, Jurek Becker's *Bronsteins Kinder* and Esther Dischereit's *Joëmis Tisch*. In addition, I chose well-known Jewish German authors (Heinrich Heine, Hannah Arendt, Franz Kafka, etc.); a firsthand account by a Jewish German doctor, Hertha Nathorff; interviews with GDR citizens of Jewish background that the editors, John Borneman and Jeffrey Peck, had compiled to accompany their film of the same name *(Sojourners);* and texts that embodied a particular time and space from which students could develop a better grasp of the more theoretical and philosophical considerations of Jewish German relations.

Students gave class presentations to provide background for the readings and to initiate class discussion. Despite the heavy amount of reading and the various discourses to which the course reader introduced them, the students made exceptional progress. Whereas the students in German 315 read materials in German, the students in German 43, except for three with a command of German, relied on English sources. The structure of the courses was similar, but the readings differed substantially. For German 43 the amount of reading increased; I incorporated the English translation of the texts used in German 315 when possible, but relied on more recent texts, such as Sander L. Gilman and Karen Remmler's *Reemerging Jewish Culture in Germany: Life and Literature since 1989* and essays by George Mosse and Enzo Traverso. Thanks to the two collections of contemporary Jewish German writers by Susan Stern and Elena Lappin, I could introduce students to recent essays and literature by Jewish authors writing in German. In addition, we read Hilsenrath's *The Nazi and the Barber* and Greta Weil's *The Bride Price*, both of which sparked the most lively class discussions.

In response to student evaluations, I would reduce the number of readings in both courses in the future in order to allow more time for in-depth discussion—in this case, less is better. In order to take advantage of the most comprehensive and well-written works on the subject of Jewish German relations as well as primary texts by contemporary Jewish writers, I would recommend combining English and German texts in a German Studies seminar, rather than limiting the readings to German. Whereas improvement of target language skills remains a major focus in German Studies seminars at the undergraduate level, a course in English allows for more in-depth analysis of content. In the German class, students wrote and rewrote extensive essays and prepared discussion questions. Rather than concentrating on form per se, discussion of language centered on the meaning of words in context. The connotation of the word "Jude" in German, for example, sparked a heated debate about the meaning of the term "Jew" in American culture, thus allowing students to respond to cultural differences that language both shapes and expresses. Students who had learned Yiddish words in German without knowing their Yiddish origins became more sensitive about the painful absence of Yiddish speakers in Germany and, indeed, the world.

Whether one teaches such a course in English or German, the first class day is probably the most crucial. Given the sensitive nature of the material and the background of some of the students as descendants of victims, perpetrators, or bystanders, I addressed students' concerns immediately by requesting them to write and speak about their reasons for taking the course, their expectations, and their previous experience with the subject matter. In German 315 students wanted to know more about why the Shoah happened or to understand why Germans today were "obsessed" with things Jewish. In German 43, students expressed a desire to overcome their prejudices against Germany and to learn about the history of their Jewish European ancestors, some of whom had immigrated from Germany or been killed by the Nazis. It took a few class periods for the students in this course to achieve a comfortable rapport with one another—some Jewish students decided they were not ready to face the subject matter, at which point an emotional Jewish German dialogue ensued in response to tensions between the self-identified German American and a few of the Jewish students. Before we could engage with the material itself, we needed to find a basis for mutual respect across differences and to acknowledge the emotional impact some of our discussions about Jewish German experience might have upon one another. Without allowing for emotion, students may not be able to commit themselves to the intellectual rigor that the course material demands. Without acknowledging and articulating the emotion, the course would fail to achieve one of its main goals: to raise the level of discomfort in a safe environment in order to help students become witnesses to the deep wound that the Shoah has left in German and Jewish cultures.

The most successful class sessions required students to engage with a text in context—discussing the representation of Jewish identities in Heine's "The Rabbi of Bacherach," for example, would have been incomplete without a prior discussion of Jewish life in the Frankfurt ghetto at the historical time portrayed in the story or without an overview of Heine's relationship to Judaism and the circumstances under which he wrote the story. A critical reading of Arendt's biography of Rahel Varnhagen likewise necessitated mention of Arendt's own experience of exile and her stance on Jewish religion and culture. For the most part, student presentations and my introductory lectures provided the context for the readings in the two courses. Every student gave at least one twenty- to thirty-minute presentation on an author, social movement, historical event, or topic that pertained to the class assignments. This exercise encouraged students to do firsthand research and to assess secondary material. In German 315, I also required students to write a final research paper on a topic related to the contemporary relationship between Germans and Jews in Germany. I intended this project to be a culmination of the seminar's work—an essay grounded historically that expressed each student's own interpretation of the implications of past history on present-day Jewish German relations and her assessment of the probable future progress. In German 43, I opted for an essay exam designed to encourage students to place the topics of the seminar in context and to speculate upon the present situation of Jews in Germany based on the readings of related material.

Throughout the courses, I encouraged students to bring in newspaper or magazine articles that pertained to the subject matter and to place the content of these pieces into the context of the course. When German 43 was in progress, Daniel Goldhagen published *Hitler's Willing Executioners*. As soon as the reviews started appearing, students began bringing in the clippings and reporting on conversations with their parents about the reviews. Although none of us had had time to read the book and I decided not to include it formally in the course, the central question that was raised in the media—about the extent of the German people's culpability in committing and condoning atrocities—became a focal point of discussion for a number of weeks. Thus, a course on Jewish German relations will inevitably need to respond to current events, particularly as they pertain to German unification; debates about citizenship; and xenophobia in Germany, Europe, and the U.S. Consequently, even though the Shoah was not the main focus, but rather a constant presence in the courses, I tried to remain sensitive to the students' need to express rage, pain, or sadness, while helping them maintain a level of intellectual rigor without objectifying the experience of the Shoah. It became clear that a melding of both approaches is most appropriate and productive. Two students who engaged in a joint analysis of *Hitler's Willing Executioners* as their seminar project, summed up the course accomplishments most eloquently:

> We felt that creating our own interpretations of Goldhagen's work, as well as drawing our own conclusions, would also be a fitting way to end the semester. ... It is therefore appropriate to end a course by using a semester's worth of knowledge to distill and analyze a new work of literature in the field—in the end, such original critical thinking doesn't end with graduation since we will (hopefully) continue to familiarize ourselves with new scholarly material as it becomes available. We seized a further opportunity to engage in the complex interplay of a dialogical format because as students, original critique can only be enhanced by constantly having one's presuppositions and conclusions questioned. ... It is fittingly ironic that we find ourselves, as a German and a Jew respectively, in a position of engaging in a dialogue on the nature of the Holocaust. ... It is perhaps from these attempts at dialogue, and not necessarily from their conclusions themselves, that we begin to come to terms with that component of the Holocaust's legacy which affects not only Germans and Jews, but the global community at large. While it might be presumptuous of us to imply that we are contributing to the "legendary" German-Jewish symbiosis, it is nevertheless noteworthy that we are engaged in a "not-so-illusory" mutually beneficial relationship, each becoming richer for the other's contributions.[3]

Several issues stand out in examining this commentary. First, a course on Jewish German relations within a German Studies department cannot hope to be all-encompassing, but rather to provide substantial historical and cultural background and to raise provocative questions about the subject itself so that students develop an interest in critically assessing what they read, experience, and feel in this connection. Secondly, any course that focuses on Jewish German relations becomes a dialogue across differences, a method characteristic of good pedagogy in general, but perhaps more crucial when the subject matter has personal significance for the students. Thirdly, regardless of the students' background, one cannot expect them to represent a particular group perspective, that is, to be experts on their respective cultures, but one can ask them to make honest and fair judgments about the material they read and the comments they hear from both the teacher and other students.

This brings me back to the initial concern of this essay. Although the courses did not focus on the Shoah per se, the presence and centrality of how it is remembered and its continued effects on contemporary German and Jewish experience had a strong impact. With hindsight, students were quick to analyze, for example, Heine's description of the pogrom in "The Rabbi of Bacherach" as a premonition of the Shoah, a phenomenon that occurred in their reading of Kafka's work as well. We often debated whether a Jewish German symbiosis had actually existed—some students claimed that such a symbiosis could not have been "real" given the willingness of the majority of the German people to participate in the antisemitic policies of the Nazis.

Despite the similar structure and content of the two courses, they emerged as two different entities. In their course evaluations, students in German 315 wished they knew more about Jewish culture in general and the representation of Jews by Germans. In German 43, students expressed a desire to know more about German everyday culture and about German sentiment toward Jews today. It became clear to me while assessing the two courses that a responsible presentation of the historical material can and should include discussions about representation and about theoretical approaches to identity formation, cultural assimilation, and alienation.

Although I would be cautious about modeling an academic course as a Jewish German dialogue with all the trappings of the prevalent therapeutic rhetoric about conflict resolution, healing, and reconciliation, the ability of students to engage empathetically with one another across differences was particularly moving. At a discussion with the filmmaker Lisa Lewenz, for example, one of the participants, a German woman, responded tearfully by recalling her childhood at the end of the Third Reich, her family's flight from the eastern German states, and the contradictory stance of her father, who hid a Jewish friend, yet belonged to the Nazi Party. One of the Jewish students consoled her by saying that he did not judge her father or her. "I am Jewish, but if I were not, I am not sure what I would have done in Nazi Germany." Anecdotes like this exemplify the impact of the seminar upon the lives of students. They speak to the students' ability to delve into topics fraught with emotion that, at the same time, require their deepest and most rigorous intellectual attention.

Notes

1. This article is dedicated to the students who attended my seminars on Jewish German relations at Mount Holyoke and Amherst Colleges in 1995/96. I thank them for their curiosity, open minds, courage, and insightful suggestions.
2. I use the grammatically unusual and less prevalent term "Jewish German" in place of the more typical "German-Jewish" to question the positioning and hyphenating of supposed homogeneous depictions of collective identities such as "German" and "Jewish." Although style manuals assert that hyphens help to prevent a misunderstanding and misreading of the relation between words, it is exactly the ambiguity of the relation between and within these markers of identity and culture that I seek to inject into the discussion by omitting the hyphen. Similarly, placing "Jewish" first in the pair suggests a rethinking of the emphasis on the one or the other marker.
3. Klebe and Sahlein 2–3. I gratefully acknowledge permission to quote this passage from their seminar paper.

Amherst College   **Prof. Karen Remmler**

GERMAN 43, JEWISH GERMAN RELATIONS IN 20TH CENTURY GERMANY

Course Description: This course will examine the relationship between Jews and Germans in twentieth-century Germany with special emphasis on the sociocultural situation of Jews in Berlin, the center of Jewish German life from the Enlightenment until the Third Reich. A central focus of the course will also be the reemergence of Jewish culture in Berlin from the 1980s to the present. In order to provide an in-depth overview of the development of a Jewish German consciousness and its representation in German society, the course will explore such issues as: the self-representation of Jews in German society; changing definitions of "Jewishness" and "Germanness" in the works of Jewish German thinkers and writers; the transformation from a religious to a cultural Jewish identity in the nineteenth and early twentieth centuries and its representation in the works of Jewish writers and thinkers; German national identity and the "Jewish Question"; the marginalization, exclusion, and killing of Jews during the Third Reich; the remembrance and representation of the Shoah by survivors who returned to Germany after liberation; the coming of age of second-generation Jews in both East and West Germany in the late 1970s and 1980s; and the effects of unification on the development of Jewish communities in unified Berlin.

Course Goal: The goal of this course is to explore the intersection between history and culture as you learn about the relations between Jews and Germans in twentieth-century Germany. By combining literary texts, firsthand accounts, philosophical and historical essays, as well as films, the course will encourage you to develop new ways of approaching a topic in an interdisciplinary manner. In addition to providing knowledge about the historical situation of Jews in Germany, the course will also explore how images of Jewish and German identity have been transformed over time and how these images continue to affect Jewish German relations in present-day Germany.

Overview of Syllabus:

Week 1–3
Introduction to the cultural relationship between Germans and Jews from the Enlightenment to World War I. Readings by Jewish and German thinkers prior to the twentieth century will provide background on the development of a Jewish German consciousness and the changing position of Jews in the cultural life of Berlin during this period. Excerpts from

Moses Mendelssohn's essays, Hannah Arendt's biography of Rahel Varnhagen, and Heinrich Heine's story "The Rabbi of Bacherach" will establish the basis for exploring the transformation of religious identity to cultural conceptions of Jewishness. Topics include Judeo-Christian relations, the Berlin salons, the Jewish Reform movement, Zionism, and the relation between ideologies of racism and antisemitism.

Week 3–6
The further development of a Jewish secular culture after World War I up until 1933. Topics include Jewish women and social reform, the contributions of Jewish writers to German culture of the Weimar Republic, and representation of Jewishness in German culture. Readings include essays by George Mosse, Zipes's edition of *The Operated Jew*, Kafka's short story "A Report to the Academy," and essays from the collection *When Biology Became Destiny*.

Week 7–8
The destruction of Jewish culture by the Nazis and their active and passive accomplices and the experience of Jews living in the Third Reich as depicted by firsthand accounts of Jews in Berlin. Two films, *Jud Süß* and *Jacob the Liar*, and a collection of Nazi propaganda films will illustrate the relationship between the cultural politics of the Nazis and the exclusion and killing of Jews under the Third Reich.

Week 9 to end of semester
The relations of Jews and Germans after 1945 up to the present. Includes issues of *Vergangenheitsbewältigung* (coming to terms with the past) and the development of a Jewish German consciousness among second-generation Jews living in Germany. This unit will concentrate on the cultural and political events that continue to shape Jewish German relations today, such as the showing of the television film *Holocaust* (1978), the controversy about the Fassbinder play "Garbage, the City and Death" (1981), the Bitburg affair (1985), the Historians' Debate (1986), the controversial speech by Philipp Jenninger to commemorate the fiftieth anniversary of the November Pogrom Night (*Kristallnacht*) (1988), and finally German unification. Also of importance will be the debates about recent plans to build a Holocaust memorial in the center of Berlin and the makeup of Jewish communities after the fall of the Berlin Wall. In addition to the novels by Hilsenrath and Weil, readings include essays by Gilman and Remmler, excerpts from Stern and Lappin, short stories by Rafael Seeligmann and Barbara Honigmann, and poetry by Nelly Sachs and Paul Celan. The documentary film and text *Sojourners* will provide insight into the situation of Jews in the former East Germany.

Course Requirements:

1. Active class participation, regular attendance, and completion of assignments on time. Reading assignments are assigned on Thursdays and constitute the subsequent week's discussion material. **You are required to hand in two discussion questions on each reading assignment or film via e-mail by Sunday evening at 10:00 pm.** The questions may be informational, analytical, or elaborative in nature.

2. One class presentation on background material for class discussion. The purpose of the presentation is to provide an overview of the historical context and a critical reading of the text or film and to raise questions for class discussion. **Be sure to discuss your topic with me before your presentation so I can provide you with bibliographical and thematic material.**

3. Two five- to eight-page essays on a topic related to the subject matter of the course. **One essay should be based on your class presentation and is to be handed in one week after your class presentation.** The papers may be a critical reading of a text, a comparative study of two or more works, an analysis of a literary text or film, or the development of a theme covered in class using supplementary material. Suggested topics will be provided.

4. Final exam: This exam will give students the opportunity to choose from a number of essay questions.

Required Texts:
Becker, Jurek. *Jacob the Liar.*
Borneman, John, and Jeffrey M. Peck. *Sojourners.*
Gilman, Sander L., and Karen Remmler, eds. *Reemerging Jewish Culture in Germany.*
Hilsenrath, Edgar. *The Nazi and the Barber.*
Mosse, George L. *German Jews beyond Judaism.*
Traverso, Enzo. *The Jews and Germany.*
Weil, Grete. *The Bride Price.*
Zipes, Jack, trans. and commentator. *The Operated Jew.*

Course Reader: Readings will include essays, literary texts, and poetry from Jewish writers and thinkers, such as Moses Mendelssohn, Heinrich Heine, Franz Kafka, Nelly Sachs, Paul Celan, and Barbara Honigmann, as well as excerpts from the volumes listed below.

Arendt, Hannah. *Rahel Varnhagen.*
Bridenthal, Renate, Atina Grossmann, and Marion Kaplan, eds. *When Biology Became Destiny.*
Gilman, Sander L. *Jews in Today's German Culture.*
Kahn, Lothar. *Between Two Worlds.*
Lappin, Elena, ed. *Jewish Voices, German Words.*
Stern, Susan, ed. *Speaking Out.*

Films: *Jud Süß*, *Jacob the Liar*, *Sojourners*, and documentary films on the image of Jews in German society.

Works Cited

Print Sources

Arendt, Hannah. *Rahel Varnhagen. Lebensgeschichte einer deutschen Jüdin aus der Romantik.* Munich: Piper, 1991.

Bammer, Angelika. "Critical Performances." *Unterrichtspraxis* 25.1 (Spring 1992): 1–9.

Becker, Jurek. *Bronsteins Kinder.* Frankfurt am Main: Suhrkamp, 1986.

———. *Jacob the Liar.* Trans. Leila Vennewitz. New York: Arcade, 1996.

Blasius, Dirk, and Dan Diner, eds. *Zerbrochene Geschichte. Leben und Selbstverständnis der Juden in Deutschland.* Frankfurt am Main: Fischer, 1991.

Borneman, John, and Jeffrey M. Peck. *Sojourners: The Return of German Jews and the Question of Identity.* Lincoln: University of Nebraska Press, 1995.

Bridenthal, Renate, Atina Grossmann, and Marion Kaplan, eds. *When Biology Became Destiny: Women in Weimar and Nazi Germany.* New York: Monthly Review Press, 1984.

Burgauer, Erica. *Zwischen Erinnerung und Verdrängung. Juden in Deutschland nach 1945.* Reinbek bei Hamburg: Rowohlt, 1993.

Dischereit, Esther. *Joëmis Tisch. Eine jüdische Geschichte.* Frankfurt am Main: Suhrkamp, 1988.

Fassbinder, Rainer Werner. "Garbage, the City and Death." *Plays.* Edited, translated, and with an introduction by Denis Calandra. New York: PAJ Publications, 1985. 161–89.

Gilman, Sander L. *Jews in Today's German Culture.* Bloomington: Indiana University Press, 1995.

Gilman, Sander L., and Karen Remmler, eds. *Reemerging Jewish Culture in Germany: Life and Literature since 1989.* New York: New York University Press, 1994.

Goldhagen, Daniel Jonah. *Hitler's Willing Executioners: Ordinary Germans and the Holocaust.* New York: Knopf, 1996.

Heine, Heinrich. "The Rabbi of Bacherach: A Fragment." *Jewish Stories and Hebrew Melodies.* Trans. Charles Godfrey Leland. 1906. Updated and with a new introduction by Elizabeth Petuchowski. New York: Markus Wiener Publishing, 1987. 19–80.

Hilsenrath, Edgar. *The Nazi and the Barber.* Trans. Andrew White. Garden City, NY: Doubleday, 1971. [Out of print.]

Kafka, Franz. "A Report to the Academy." *The Complete Stories.* Ed. N. Glatzer. New York: Schocken Books, 1971. 250–59.

Kahn, Lothar. *Between Two Worlds: A Cultural History of German-Jewish Writers*. Ames: Iowa State University Press, 1993.

Klebe, Marcus, and Daniel Sahlein. Seminar Paper for German 43. Amherst College. Spring 1996.

Lappin, Elena, ed. *Jewish Voices, German Words: Growing Up Jewish in Postwar Germany and Austria*. Trans. Krishna Winston. North Haven, CT: Catbird Press, 1994.

Mosse, George L. *German Jews beyond Judaism*. Bloomington: Indiana University Press, 1985.

Nathorff, Hertha. *Das Tagebuch der Hertha Nathorff. Berlin–New York Aufzeichnungen 1933–1945*. Ed. Wolfgang Benz. Frankfurt am Main: Fischer, 1989.

Rürup, Reinhard, ed. *Jüdische Geschichte in Berlin. Essays und Studien*. Berlin: Hentrich Edition, 1995.

Stern, Susan, ed. *Speaking Out: Jewish Voices from United Germany*. Chicago: edition q, 1995.

Traverso, Enzo. *The Jews and Germany: From the "Judeo-German Symbiosis" to the Memory of Auschwitz*. Trans. Daniel Weissbrot. Lincoln: University of Nebraska Press, 1995.

Weil, Greta. *The Bride Price*. Trans. John Barrett. Boston: Godine, 1992.

Zipes, Jack, trans. and commentator. *The Operated Jew: Tales of Anti-Semitism*. New York: Routledge, 1991.

Films/Videotapes

Architektur des Untergangs (Architecture of Doom). Dir. Peter Cohen. Video. First Run Features, 1989.

Holocaust. Dir. Marvin Chomsky, Herbert Brodkin, and Robert Berger. Four-part television series. NBC. 16–19 April 1978. Video. Republic Entertainment, Inc., 1994.

Jakob der Lügner (Jacob the Liar). Dir. Frank Beyer. East German Television, 1976. Rental film. The National Center for Jewish Film, Brandeis University.

Jud Süß. Dir. Veit Harlan. 1940. Video. International Historic Films, 1983.

Sojourners. Dir. John Borneman and Jeffrey Peck. Video. 1992. [Documentary available from Jeffrey Peck, Canadian Centre for German and European Studies at the Université de Montréal and York University, Toronto, Ontario.]

Chapter 10

GERMAN MYTHS AND JEWISH TRAUMAS
Teaching Postwar Cultural History 1945–1995

Florentine Strzelczyk

At first glance, it might seem peculiar to find an essay on German cultural history from 1945 to 1995 in a volume dedicated to shedding light on the Holocaust. After all, postwar German history is presently discussed in terms of a closed era marked by two decisive ruptures: the break with the Nazi past as the "Zero Hour" of 1945, and the 1990 reunification of Germany, often proclaimed as the end of German postwar history and its legacies (Gilman and Remmler 1). In this essay, however, I will emphasize the continuities rather than the discontinuities of postwar Germany and reflect on the theoretical and pedagogical implications of this perspective for the teaching of cultural history.

The course entitled East Meets West in the New Germany: History, Politics, and Culture 1945–1995 was taught as a fourth-year undergraduate seminar in the winter term of 1996 at Queen's University in Ontario. Administered by the Department of German, it was cross-listed with History and Political Studies and open to film majors. Queen's University has a strong academic profile attracting students from all over Canada and abroad. Undergraduates enrolled in German courses are primarily German majors or other humanities majors.

During the first class of this newly established course, I conducted a mini-survey about associations with Germany after World War II among the fifteen participating third- and fourth-year students, a few of whom

---

Notes for this section can be found on page 150.

shared a very general background in European history. Responses like "1945," "economic powerhouse," "dominating European politics," "from totalitarianism to stable democracy," "separated and finally unified nation" were among the most common answers. Specific references to Germany's past, however, were absent from the responses.[1] To a certain extent, these answers echo the dominant features of Germany's self-representation since 1945, i.e., the concentration on postwar reconstruction and economic expansion as a means of evading confrontation with its past (Glaser 59–62).

It is no coincidence that this postwar success story has found its way into the teaching of German cultural history at many Canadian universities at the undergraduate level. When shrinking enrollment numbers threaten the existence of many German programs,[2] the urgent question arises: in what light should German culture be presented in order to maintain and foster students' interest? Because of the pressures of "marketability," teachers often feel compelled to emphasize the abovementioned achievements of post-1945 Germany over its struggle to face the past (Roche 23). Besides pressures of enrollment, however, there exist both methodological and pedagogical constraints with regard to presenting German postwar history in the classroom. We tend to think about history in terms of compartmentalized phases that lend themselves to "digestible" and "teachable" units, thereby often reinforcing notions of historical eras as coherent entities in themselves.

The course I will describe attempts to counter these problems by rendering visible the interconnections between the Holocaust and the construction of postwar German identity. From a methodological, pedagogical, and historical perspective, I will argue for teaching postwar German culture as a contested cultural arena in which past legacies intersect constantly with current concerns, an approach that allows students to engage in, reflect about, and re-address cultural material in an open dialogue with German culture and their own.

Theoretical Reflections: Postwar German Culture and German Cultural Studies

The seminar aimed at exploring postwar German culture from a multidisciplinary perspective. One of the objectives of the course was to explore how deeply the Holocaust has become enmeshed in postwar German history and identity. While in the former GDR a forced antifascism subsumed Jewish victims and German resistance under the demand for a new national identity (Burgauer 199–200), West Germans merely *staged* the Holocaust as a *spectacle* that provided a moral and ethical yardstick against which they displayed their "normalcy" as a postwar nation (Bodemann 13–14). The numerous attempts to redefine German identity in the postwar era were all sparked by debates about confronting or suppressing the past and including or excluding its memory from the present (Stern, "*Jewish Question*" 160). The fall of the Wall in 1989, thus, symbolized to many Germans the erasure of postwar guilt and the end of the German *Sonderweg* that led to Auschwitz (Verheyen 13–45).

While it is true that all nations tell their stories by molding discontinuous shreds of historical experiences into a continuous story, thereby suppressing or excluding alternate histories and marginal identities (Anderson 199–203), it is the perseverance of these dominant patterns in traditional civilization courses that is challenged by recent developments in the area of cultural studies. Teachers and scholars working in this heterogeneous field are committed to "interrogating the cultural practices that sustain or suppress contestations over inclusion and expulsion" (Grossberg, Nelson, and Treichler 12). If, further, the "concret[izat]ion of [cultural] identity" takes place in "figures of memory" (Assmann 128–29), the analysis of inclusion and exclusion in cultural processes will also have to take the form of critically mediating "between past and present at those crucial moments in German history when the two seem to move apart" (Geyer 112). Both the repeated reflections on the legacies of German history and the thematization of marginal perspectives throughout the course (different sessions foreground Jewish as well as other minorities in Germany today) are meant to question a history of postwar Germany in which the silencing of certain cultural issues and the suppression of historical legacies are closely intertwined with the formation of a dominant postwar German identity (Diner 18). German postwar history is thus understood as a process of contesting inclusions and exclusions of cultural identities as much as of suppressing and uncovering historical legacies.

Pedagogical Considerations: Teaching German Culture

These theoretical reflections about the conceptualization of cultural history consequently require a rethinking of pedagogical goals in teaching cultural history. First of all, such a perspective effectively counters the teleological "success story" that my students had sketched out at the beginning of the course. Secondly, the course productively utilizes the position of the students as outsiders to German culture, thus replacing an "affirmative concept of culture" with a more critical comparative one (Seeba 147). Instead of privileging a rather passive reading of canonical histories and texts, I present students with the opportunity to engage in deciphering, discussing, and evaluating German culture. In such an approach, students are no longer the passive recipients in a one-sided transmission of knowledge but are placed into an active position vis-à-vis German culture, which allows them to take part in and simultaneously reflect on the construction of German history (Berman 10). "Rather than the reproduction of a particular skill, body of knowledge, or set of values," the approach understands pedagogy to be what Henry Giroux calls another "form of cultural production" (202).

These reflections on cultural studies and pedagogy also determined the selection and presentation of course materials. I included a variety of diverse texts—historical, journalistic, political, legal, filmic, and literary— which were organized around the juxtaposition of dominant versus peripheral positions. Azade Seyhan proposes such a "dialogization" of culturally marginal with canonical texts on the one hand, and of different genres on the other, and regards the tensions resulting from this dialogue as a productive way for students to engage critically with the materials (8). The conflicts that have existed around the Holocaust in German society since 1945 not only raise students' awareness of the constructedness of historical narratives and the powerful acts of ordering these, but encourage them "to recognize the multilayered ideologies that construct their own identities" (Giroux 209).

German Tales and Jewish Traumas: History and Culture in Germany 1945–1995

The underlying premises for the following description are threefold: (1) The issues concerning both memory and suppression of the Holocaust play an integral role in the shaping of German postwar identity. (2) These issues have contributed to the continuing problematic relationship between Germans and Jews in postwar Germany. (3) Reunification has not resulted in the closure of the past many Germans had longed for, but rather it has exposed the Germans' unresolved difficulties with their past. These problematic intersections of Holocaust past and German present are highlighted throughout the weekly three-hour sessions of the twelve-week course. This essay uses five sessions to illustrate my approach. While sections C, D, and E describe individual three-hour sessions, A and B discuss subunits within weekly sessions. The sometimes heavy reading assignments of up to one hundred pages a week are common for a fourth-year course in most departments at Queen's University. A total of seven films were viewed during this twelve-week course. Students were required to watch the films outside of class by reserving a time slot in the departmental video viewing room.

A. The Question of German Guilt (Subunit)

Week two dealt with the early postwar decades between 1945 and 1963. We explored aspects of guilt and responsibility within the context of the Allies' reeducation and denazification attempts and German responses to these. Excerpts from Karl Jaspers's in-depth analysis of German accountability against the background of the Nuremberg trials, *The Question of German Guilt*, served as a means to explore dimensions of guilt by utilizing the dialogic question-and-answer pattern of the text. After a brief student report on the trials, I asked students to form groups and discuss possible responses to Jaspers's questions. We then read his responses and compared them to the students' replies. Reflecting on the differences between their own and his answers to the issue, students became more aware of their own positionalities and biases, but also recognized the way he becomes entangled in legalistic arguments in which the question of the "lost war" takes precedence over "crimes against humanity." Discussions reached an impasse when some students insisted on Jaspers's concept of individual guilt, while others pointed out that individual guilt assigned to a few prominent Nazis in the course of the trials also served to exonerate the majority of Germans and could lend itself to strategies of displacement and avoidance, a danger that Jaspers himself realized (74).

B. The Inability to Mourn (Subunit)

The strategies of displacement and avoidance were one of the topics raised in week three during which we discussed West German society during the 1960s and 1970s, the student protests, and the radicalization of the German Left. The most stirring and still controversial outcome of the intellectual debate at the time is Alexander and Margarethe Mitscherlich's *The Inability to Mourn* (1967) in which the two psychoanalysts, quite contrary to Jaspers's emphasis on individual guilt, scrutinize collective German defense mechanisms against responsibility and guilt.

In-class activities focused on how these mechanisms manifested themselves in individual life stories. Peter Sichrovsky's *Born Guilty* (1987), a collection of stories based on interviews with children of Nazi parents, served as the textual source for in-class work. Students had to prepare at least two of four different interviews; in class, each group decided on one story and first discussed and then reported on how Nazi parents communicated their involvement in the Third Reich and how it affected their children's lives. Students identified the parents' "inability to mourn" in their silence about their personal involvement, perceptions of themselves as victims, a distortion and banalization of the past, and a continuation of fascist attitudes within the family. While this aspect of the assignment consisted merely of applying the concepts developed by the Mitscherlichs to the stories, the more eye-opening task was the latter part of the report focusing on the children's generation. Though students had earlier expressed views such as "the past is the past" or "let sleeping dogs lie," their class reports sensitized them to the fact that it is exactly this attitude toward the past which causes the identity crisis that children of Nazis experience as extreme guilt and self-hatred, a revived fascination with fascism, or feelings of victimization. Students realized during the session not only that a suppressed past had a profound impact on the identity formation of the next generation of Germans, but also that the issues of guilt and responsibility surrounding the Holocaust cannot be resolved by the mere passage of time.

C. The Historikerstreit and the Normalization of the German Past (Full Session)

Week five addressed a number of political and cultural events in Germany during the 1980s that not only triggered intense international debates, but also indicated yet another turn in the formation of German postwar identity to which the meaning of the Holocaust became central. Through presentations and discussions, this session aimed at connecting three seemingly unrelated events—the reception of Edgar Reitz's controversial film epic *Heimat* in 1984, Helmut Kohl and Ronald Reagan's 1985 visit to the military cemetery at Bitburg to commemorate the fortieth anniversary of the end of World War II, and the *Historikerstreit* of 1986—by showing them as attempts to relativize the German past and thereby normalize the German present.

(1) Reitz's eleven-part TV series and media event in 1984 became the presentation project of a group of film majors. They described how the film was initially celebrated as a rehabilitation of German postwar identity in Germany, yet soon provoked criticism from American intellectuals (Hansen). With my assistance, the students—all of whom were familiar with the series from previous courses—selected a number of clips that they presented in class for discussion. The clips focused on (a) Reitz's mode of unfolding "the myth of *Heimat*" (Koch 13) as authentic stories of the everyday and (b) the consequences of such an approach that tends to ignore the political forces that invisibly influence individual life stories and results in the film's silence about the Holocaust (Kaes 173–74).

(2) Kohl and Reagan's visit to Bitburg, Reagan's infamous equation of the German war dead with concentration camp victims, and the public outcry about both these events were the presentation topic of another student group. I encouraged in-class discussions by showing the clip from German TV that provided the only images transmitted to TV stations in Germany and North America (Rentschler 87). The images focused exclusively on the two heads of state honoring the war dead, while at the same time ignoring local demonstrators, and denying the existence of forty-nine Waffen-SS soldiers' graves situated among those of the 1887 German soldiers (Ehrenstein 36). This visualization of the controversy enabled students to analyze Bitburg as an attempt to rewrite German history by removing the connection between Germany and Nazism and stimulated a lively discussion about North American investment in the German past.

(3) This segment on the 1986 *Historikerstreit* was based on assigned readings. Short student reports summarized the main arguments of two texts central to the debate. While the historian Ernst Nolte reassessed the Nazi period in ways that questioned the uniqueness of the Holocaust, the philosopher Jürgen Habermas accused Nolte of revisionism with the purpose of neutralizing German responsibility for Auschwitz. I organized class discussions around a list of questions about the (mis)use of history as an instrument of political debate from a letter accompanying the detailed documentation of the *Historikerstreit* sent to all German embassies by the Auswärtiges Amt in November 1986 (Piper 273–74).

(4) I concluded the session with a brief lecture on Michael Verhoeven's 1989 film *Das schreckliche Mädchen* (The Nasty Girl), followed by a class discussion. The film is based on the experiences of the lay historian Anna Rosmus who, in the early 1980s, was driven out of her hometown of Passau for exposing its Nazi legacy. It visualized and contextualized both the widespread reluctance of the postwar generation to face its responsibility and the normalizing tendencies in German society. To structure the discussion of the film, I used segments from an interview with Anna Rosmus broadcast by CBC Radio in 1992, which students enjoyed relating to different parts of the film.

D. Jews in Contemporary Germany (Full Session)

Week nine addressed the relationship between Jews and Germans in contemporary Germany. The Germans' unresolved entanglement in their past fostered philosemitic attitudes toward Jews living in Germany today (Stern, *Im Anfang* 11), which have led to a renewed German infatuation with the Jewish past in the last decade (Ochse). On the one hand, this has given rise to speculation about a reemerging Jewish culture in Germany

(Gilman and Remmler 1–12). On the other, the renewed German interest in things Jewish has not affected the widespread ignorance about real Jews living in contemporary German society (Fisher 206–13). In the last ten years, however, a new literature in the German language written by and about the generation of sons and daughters of Holocaust survivors has appeared. It can be characterized by three main aspects that I thematized during the session: (1) the ongoing "negative symbiosis" between Germans and Jews of the next generation (Diner), (2) a deep contradiction between feeling at home and homeless in Germany, and (3) a mode of writing that centers on the Holocaust, for which Thomas Nolden has coined the term "konzentrisches Schreiben" (10–11).

The first half of the session concentrated on the question of what it means for young Jews to grow up and live in Germany today. Drawing on the method used in session B, I assigned selected interviews from Peter Sichrovsky's *Strangers in Their Own Land* (1985). Class discussions revealed how strongly the young generation's hopes and doubts are affected by the horrors of the Holocaust its parents experienced. What one interviewee calls "the conflict of head and heart" (19) applies to most of the young Jews: the decision to make Germany one's home conflicts with the feeling of not belonging, resulting in a state of perpetual unsettlement. The class compared the accounts of the persecutors' children, as discussed in session B, with those of the victims' children and realized that the children of both groups, in fundamentally diverse ways, struggled to cope with a past engraved in their parents' memory but inaccessible to them.

In the second half of the session we further explored conflicts of identity and belonging as portrayed in two stories by young Jewish writers, Katja Behrens's "Perfectly Normal" (1993) and Chaim Noll's "A Country, a Child, but Not the Country's Child" (1992). "Perfectly Normal" describes how the daughter of a Holocaust survivor discovers her own Jewish identity as a result of the clash between the scarcely hidden antisemitism of the early postwar years and her mother's unchanged hope for assimilation into the German nation. Chaim Noll's text thematizes Jewish identity in the GDR. The career of the narrator's father as a high functionary attests to both the attraction of communism for the Jews in the early GDR (Nolden 34–36) and the state's construction of Jews as "anti-fascist monuments" in order to gain international acceptance (Ostow, "Agents" 233). The son's encounter with antisemitic stereotypes not only accelerates his own growing distance from the socialist ideology but also points to a widely unconfronted past beneath the surface of socialism (Burgauer 201).

Students worked in groups on either of the two stories, discussing them according to (a) the German environment in which the protagonists grow up, (b) the differences between the parents' and the childrens' attitude toward both their Jewish identity and German society, and (c) the stages of the childrens' identity formation. I incorporated the findings reported by the groups into a plenum discussion on the different norms regulating the relationship to the Nazi past in East and West Germany. To steer the discussion into a more intercultural direction, I used a quote from Behrens's story ("We were the ones who weren't normal, in our normal town, on our normal street, inhabited by normal people." 39–40) that rendered the stories' minority viewpoint productive in a Canadian cultural setting. The issues of norms and normalcy triggered an intense discussion in class precisely because of Canada's self-representation as a multicultural society in which, however, Anglo-Canadian Christian norms dominate cultural and social values. Students discussed attempts to "normalize" their nation's history not only in respect to the possibilities and limits of multiculturalism in contemporary Canada, but also in terms of Canada's past, for example, the refusal to grant asylum to Jewish refugees from Germany and its silencing in Canada today.

E. Antisemitism, Xenophobia, and the New Right (Full Session)

When the motto of the *Wende* changed from "We are the people" to "We are one people," it evoked the idea of a unified body, of a *Volk,* from which variously perceived others once more could be excluded. In the aftermath of unification, a wave of xenophobia swept through both parts of the united country, targeting not only foreigners and asylum seekers, but also Jewish cemeteries and Holocaust memorial sites, in an attempt to physically destroy the signifiers of Germany's extermination of the Jews. In week eleven we addressed this reemergence of the past at the proclaimed end of the postwar era. While background readings provided insight into activities and motivations of the Far Right (Childs, Husbands), students gained access to this topic through a discussion of Benjamin Korn's chilling essay "Witching Hour: Images of Germany—Sixty Years Later" (1993). Student opinion was split as to how important the unification of Germany has been for the reemergence of suppressed xenophobic and racist undercurrents in German society.

The second part of the session focused on translated excerpts from *Die Abrechnung. Ein Neonazi steigt aus* (1994), an autobiographical account by former East German neo-Nazi Ingo Hasselbach, coauthored with filmmaker Winfried Bonengel. Students majoring in German had the opportunity to translate and annotate a section from Hasselbach's life story, and introduce and comment on their work in class. The translations had been distributed a week earlier with the other reading assignments. Discussions concentrated on three main aspects: (1) the self-proclaimed status of the GDR as an antifascist state in which disillusioned GDR youths like Hasselbach employed symbols of Nazism to challenge the authoritarian structures of the state, (2) the influence on and even sponsorship of East German neo-Nazis by the political Right in the West, and (3) the interface of antisemitism and xenophobia in neofascist groups.

One student presentation introduced the heated public debate about the Canadian resident Ernst Zündel, who was under investigation in 1997 to 1998 for alleged violation of the Canadian Human Rights Act as one of the world's leading distributors of neo-Nazi materials. Another presentation addressed the tumultuous controversy that Winfried Bonengel's 1993 documentary *Beruf Neonazi* (Profession Neo-Nazi) triggered in Germany, during the course of which first the filmmaker and then his main subject, Bela Ewald Althans, faced charges of denying the Holocaust; the film itself was banned and subsequently re-released (Bathrick). I steered the class discussion toward: (1) cross-cultural and (2) thematic and formal aspects of the film.

(1) Describing the activities of Zündel in Toronto and then moving to those of Althans in Germany, students recognized a new type of right-wing activist featured in the film. Rather than the common caricature of the prototypical neo-Nazi as a jobless, uneducated skinhead, it shows the eloquent multinational profile of a new Right that not only knows how to manipulate the new media to disseminate its ideas, but also how to win over middle-class Canadian supporters. Students were shocked by their discovery that the issue of neo-Nazism was not just a "German problem," but an issue that also forces Canadians to both reexamine racism in a multicultural society and reevaluate freedom of expression and its limitations in a democracy.

(2) Discussion of the thematic and formal aspects concentrated mainly on the most hotly contested scene of the film, which depicts Althans denying, in a verbal exchange with a young American at Auschwitz, that the Holocaust had ever taken place. The debate split students into opposing groups, very much along the lines of the critiques the film received in Germany. While some students asserted that the complete lack of commentary in the Auschwitz scene came dangerously close to inviting viewers to identify with Althans's views, those students experienced in film studies argued that Bonengel's camera angles and the selection of footage were part of his aesthetic strategy to expose Althans through the latter's own contradictions. Students took from this session some rather disquieting insights into problematic questions of censorship and freedom of expression, the multifaceted meaning of cultural products, and how they themselves as

Canadians are challenged by the larger issues surrounding the Holocaust—and the realization that "the Nazi past is not only not overcome, but is not even past" (Bathrick 144).

Closing Remarks

The relatively small teaching units I have described are easily applicable to a number of possible courses including, but not restricted to, those pertaining to the Holocaust. Units are structured in a way that requires a minimum of lectures, preferring instead strategies of focused group work, carefully guided discussions, and the visualization and concretization of issues whenever possible. This kind of discovery approach enables students to express a North American perspective on German culture, in other words, to develop a critical intercultural competency that allows them not only to critically examine conflicts in postwar German society in relation to the country's past legacies, but also to draw conclusions about the mechanisms of remembering and forgetting as part of the construction of national narratives in both Germany and Canada. Yet there remains the question of why students should study cultural history at all. Michael Geyer has responded to this question in a way that applies directly to the course I taught: "It is not simply that the past proves to be an invaluable arsenal and, indeed, the determining resource for working out issues of sense-security and identity. Rather, it is the labor of history to separate what becomes past from what is present so we neither forget nor go 'back to the future'" (114).

Notes

1. These student responses agree with the observations of political scientist Andrej Markovits, who states that the evocation of the Holocaust is very much an academic perception of Germans and Germany in North America, whereas among popular beliefs the economic and political aspects prevail ("Germany").
2. For example, the University of Ottawa cut all third- and fourth-year courses as of the beginning of the academic year 1997/98, the University of Guelph reduced its German program to an Honors Minor, and at the University of Saskatchewan German was no longer taught beginning in 1999.

Queen's University	Prof. Florentine Strzelczyk

GERMAN 496 (ABBREVIATED SYLLABUS)
EAST MEETS WEST IN THE NEW GERMANY: HISTORY, POLITICS,
AND CULTURE 1945–1995

A. The Question of German Guilt

Preparation: Burns, Rob. *German Cultural Studies.* 209–56; Jaspers, Karl. *The Question of German Guilt.* 31–46 (excerpts).

In-Class Activities: Report on the Allies' denazification and reeducation policies; Jaspers, Karl. *The Question of German Guilt* (rearranged and slightly shortened excerpts from 51–60); report on the Marshall Plan and discussion of the Economic Miracle; mini-guest lecture: The Group 47.

B. The Inability to Mourn

Preparation: Burns, Rob. *German Cultural Studies.* 257–83; Markovits, Andrej S., and Philip S. Gorski. *The German Left: Red, Green and Beyond.* 46–78; Mitscherlich, Alexander and Margarethe. *The Inability to Mourn.* Ch. I, subchapters 1, 3, 4, 9, and 10; Sichrovsky, Peter. *Born Guilty: Children of Nazi Families.* Chs. 2, 3, 7, 9 (students choose two of the four stories); movie: *The Lost Honor of Katharina Blum.*

In-Class Activities: Discussion of *The Inability to Mourn*; group work on selected interviews by Sichrovsky.

C. The *Historikerstreit* and the Normalization of the German Past

Preparation: Burns, Rob. *German Cultural Studies.* 284–324; Habermas, Jürgen. "A Kind of Settlement of Damages: The Apologetic Tendencies in German History Writing." *Forever in the Shadow of Hitler?* 34–44; Nolte, Ernst. "The Past That Will Not Pass. A Speech That Could Be Written but Not Delivered." *Forever in the Shadow of Hitler?* 18–23; movie: *The Nasty Girl.*

In-Class Activities: Presentation on Edgar Reitz's *Heimat*; presentation on the Bitburg Affair; discussion of the *Historikerstreit*; discussion of *The Nasty Girl*; Anna Rosmus interviewed by Eleanor Wachtel on CBC Radio, 9 October 1992.

D. Jews in Germany Today

Preparation: Kugelmann, Cilly. "Tell Them in America We're Still Alive: The Jewish Community in the Federal Republic." 129–40; Ostow, Robin. "Becoming Strangers: Jews in Germany's Five New Provinces." 62–74; Sichrovsky, Peter. *Strangers in Their Own Land: Young Jews in Germany and Austria Today*. Chs. 1, 3, 8, 12 (students had to decide on two out of four stories); Behrens, Katja. "Perfectly Normal." *Jewish Voices, German Words*. 38–43; Noll, Chaim. "A Country, a Child, but Not the Country's Child." *Jewish Voices, German Words*. 44–64.

In-Class Activities: Group work on selected interviews by Sichrovsky; discussion of texts by Behrens and Noll.

E. Antisemitism, Xenophobia, and the New Right

Preparation: Documentary: Bonengel, Winfried. *Profession Neo-Nazi*; Childs, David. "The Far Right in Germany Since 1945." 290–307; Husbands, Christopher T. "Militant Neo-Nazism in the Federal Republic of Germany in the 1990s." 327–53; translation assignments: Hasselbach, Ingo, and Winfried Bonengel. *Die Abrechnung. Ein Neonazi steigt aus* (excerpts).

In-Class Activities: Discussion of *Die Abrechnung*; presentation on Ernst Zündel; presentation on the controversy surrounding *Profession Neo-Nazi*; discussion of *Profession Neo-Nazi*.

[A subunit on "Fears of a United Germany" is not included in this abbreviated syllabus nor in the essay, because it is less directly related to the focus on the Holocaust and Jewish topics than the other segments despite its significance to the course as a whole.]

Works Cited

Print Sources

Anderson, Benedict. *Imagined Communities: Reflections on the Origins and Spread of Nationalism.* 1983. London: Verso, 1991.

Assmann, Jan. "Collective Memory and Cultural Identity." Trans. John Czaplicka. *New German Critique: Cultural History/Cultural Studies* 65 (1995): 125–34.

Bathrick, David. "Anti-Neonazism as Cinematic Practice: Bonengel's *Beruf Neonazi.*" *New German Critique: Legacies of Anti-Fascism* 67 (1996): 133–46.

Behrens, Katja. "Perfectly Normal." Lappin 38–43.

Berman, Russell. "Global Thinking, Local Teaching: Departments, Curricula, and Culture." *ADFL Bulletin* 26.1 (1994): 6–11.

Bodemann, Y. Michal. *Gedächtnistheater. Deutsche, Juden und der Holocaust.* Hamburg: Rotbuch, 1996.

Burgauer, Erika. *Zwischen Erinnerung und Verdrängung. Juden in Deutschland nach 1945.* Reinbek bei Hamburg: Rowohlt, 1993.

Burns, Rob, ed. *German Cultural Studies.* Oxford: Oxford University Press, 1995.

Cheles, Luciano, Ronnie Ferguson, and Michalina Vaughan, eds. *The Far Right in Western and Eastern Europe.* 2nd ed. New York: Longman, 1995.

Childs, David. "The Far Right in Germany Since 1945." Cheles, Ferguson, and Vaughan 290–307.

Diner, Dan. "Negative Symbiose." *Babylon* 1 (1986): 3–21.

Ehrenstein, David. "Bitburg: A Film by Reagan." *On Film* 14 (Spring 1985): 36.

Fisher, Marc. *After the Wall: Germany, the Germans and the Burdens of History.* New York: Simon & Schuster, 1995.

Forever in the Shadow of Hitler? Trans. James Knowlton and Truett Cates. Atlantic Highlands, NJ: Humanities Press, 1993.

Geyer, Michael. "Why Cultural History? What Future? Which Germany?" *New German Critique: Cultural History/Cultural Studies* 65 (1995): 97–114.

Gilman, Sander L., and Karen Remmler, eds. *Reemerging Jewish Culture in Germany: Life and Literature since 1989.* Introduction by Gilman and Remmler. New York: New York University Press, 1994.

Giroux, Henry. "Resisting Difference: Cultural Studies and the Discourse of Critical Pedagogy." *Cultural Studies.* Ed. Lawrence Grossberg, Cary Nelson, and Paula Treichler. New York: Routledge, 1992. 199–212.

Glaser, Hermann. *Zwischen Grundgesetz and großer Koalition 1949–1967.* 1986. Frankfurt am Main: Fischer, 1990.
Grossberg, Lawrence, Cary Nelson, and Paula Treichler, eds. "Cultural Studies: An Introduction." *Cultural Studies.* New York: Routledge, 1992. 1–16.
Habermas, Jürgen. "A Kind of Settlement of Damages: The Apologetic Tendencies in German History Writing." *Forever in the Shadow of Hitler?* Trans. Knowlton and Cates. 34–44.
Hansen, Miriam. "Dossier on *Heimat.*" *New German Critique: Special Issue on Heimat* 36 (Fall 1985): 3–24.
Hasselbach, Ingo, and Winfried Bonengel. *Die Abrechnung. Ein Neonazi steigt aus.* Berlin: Aufbau, 1994.
Husbands, Christopher T. "Militant Neo-Nazism in the Federal Republic of Germany in the 1990s." Cheles, Ferguson, and Vaughan 327–53.
Jaspers, Karl. *The Question of German Guilt.* Trans. E. B. Ashton. 1947. New York: Capricorn Books, 1961.
Kaes, Anton. *From Hitler to Heimat: The Return of History as Film.* Cambridge, MA: Harvard University Press, 1989.
Koch, Gertrud. "How Much Naiveté Can We Afford? The New *Heimat* Feeling." *New German Critique: Special Issue on Heimat* 36 (Fall 1985): 13–16.
Korn, Benjamin. "Witching Hour: Images of Germany—Sixty Years Later." Lappin 297–301.
Kugelmann, Cilly. "Tell Them in America We're Still Alive: The Jewish Community in the Federal Republic." *New German Critique: Special Issue on Minorities in German Culture* 46 (Winter 1989): 129–40.
Lappin, Elena, ed. *Jewish Voices, German Words: Growing Up Jewish in Postwar Germany and Austria.* Trans. Krishna Winston. North Haven, CT: Catbird Press, 1994.
Markovits, Andrej S. "Germany and the Germans: A View from the United States." *German Politics and Society* 13.3 (1995): 142–64.
Markovits, Andrej S., and Philip S. Gorski. *The German Left: Red, Green and Beyond.* Cambridge: Polity Press, 1993.
Mitscherlich, Alexander, and Margarethe Mitscherlich. *The Inability to Mourn.* Trans. Beverley R. Placzek. New York: Grove, 1975.
Nolden, Thomas. *Junge jüdische Literatur. Konzentrisches Schreiben in der Gegenwart.* Würzburg: Königshausen & Neumann, 1995.
Noll, Chaim. "A Country, a Child, but Not the Country's Child." Lappin 44–64.

Nolte, Ernst. "The Past That Will Not Pass: A Speech That Could Be Written but Not Delivered." *Forever in the Shadow of Hitler?* Trans. Knowlton and Cates. 18–23.

Ochse, Katharina. "What Could Be More Fruitful, More Healing, More Purifying? Representations of Jews in the German Media after 1989." Gilman and Remmler 113–29.

Ostow, Robin. "Becoming Strangers: Jews in Germany's Five New Provinces." Gilman and Remmler 62–74.

──────. "Imperialist Agents, Anti-Fascist Monuments, Eastern Refugees, Property Claims: Jews as Incorporations of East German Social Trauma, 1945–94." *Jews, Germans, Memory: Reconstructions of Jewish Life in Germany*. Ed. Y. Michal Bodemann. Ann Arbor: University of Michigan Press, 1993. 227–42.

Piper, Ernst. "Afterword to the 'Historikerstreit.'" *Forever in the Shadow of Hitler?* Trans. Knowlton and Cates. 272–75.

Rentschler, Eric. "New German Film and the Discourse of Bitburg." *New German Critique: Special Issue on Heimat* 36 (Fall 1985): 67–90.

Roche, Jörg. "Zum Thema Nationalsozialismus in nordamerikanischen DaF-Lehrwerken. Widerstände und Möglichkeiten." *Zum Thema Nationalsozialismus im DaF-Lehrwerk und -Unterricht*. Ed. Joachim Warmbold, E.-Anette Koeppel, and Hans Simon-Pelanda. Munich: iudicium, 1994. 22–39.

Seeba, Hinrich. "Critique of Identity Formation: Toward an Intercultural Model of German Studies." *German Quarterly* 62.2 (1989): 144–54.

Seyhan, Azade. "Language and Literary Study as Cultural Criticism." *ADFL Bulletin* 26.2 (1995): 7–11.

Sichrovsky, Peter. *Born Guilty: Children of Nazi Families*. Trans. Jean Steinberg. New York: Basic Books, 1988.

──────. *Strangers in Their Own Land: Young Jews in Germany and Austria Today*. Trans. Jean Steinberg. New York: Basic Books, 1986.

Stern, Frank. *Im Anfang war Auschwitz. Antisemitismus und Philosemitismus im deutschen Nachkrieg*. Gerlingen: Bleicher, 1991.

──────. "The *Jewish Question* and the *German Question*, 1945–1990: Reflections in Light of November 9th, 1989." *New German Critique: Special Issue on German Unification* 52 (Winter 1991): 155–72.

Verheyen, Dirk. *The German Question: A Cultural, Historical, and Geopolitical Exploration*. Boulder, CO: Westview Press, 1991.

Audio/Visual Sources

Beruf Neonazi (Profession Neo-Nazi). Dir. Winfried Bonengel. 1993. Video. Drift Releasing [last known distributor], 1995.

Heimat: A Chronicle. Dir. Edgar Reitz. 1984. Video. 9 cassettes and guide. Facets Video, 1996.

Das schreckliche Mädchen (The Nasty Girl). Dir. Michael Verhoeven. 1989. Video. Facets Video, 1991.

Die verlorene Ehre der Katharina Blum (The Lost Honor of Katharina Blum). Dir. Volker Schlöndorff and Margarethe von Trotta. 1975. Video. Embassy Home Entertainment, 1983.

Voices from a New Europe, Part IV: Anna Rosmus Interviewed by Eleanor Wachtel. Writers & Company. CBC Radio. 9 October 1992.

Chapter 11

WITNESS GRETE WEIL
An Intensive Summer Graduate Seminar

Laureen Nussbaum

Including a graduate seminar on Grete Weil in a volume devoted to the teaching of the Holocaust introduces a touch of irony since Weil takes issue with the use of that Greek term to designate the Nazi genocide against the Jews. In her autobiographical novel *Generationen* (1983), she bristles: "Holocaust, die unerträglich falsche Bezeichnung, die den Gedanken an eine Naturkatastrophe aufzwingt. ... Nicht an langsam Gewordenes, von Menschen ausgeführt, die jahrhundertelang zu Gehorsam, Ordnung, Stillschweigen gedrillt waren" (12).[1] Yet I deemed the work of Grete Weil an ideal vehicle for teaching my students about the persecution and mass murder of the Jews during the Nazi era, and for exploring with them how a surviving Jewish intellectual can live in Germany with the knowledge of Auschwitz constantly on her mind.

The overall theme of the 1993 Deutsche Sommerschule am Pazifik, "Das neue Deutschland: Heute und Zukunft," quite obviously focused on the problems and prospects of the newly united country. It seemed to me that within this framework there was a need for a seminar dealing with the Nazi genocide. For however visible the sutures of the Germany that had recently been stitched together and however high that country's hopes for the future, one cannot escape the fact that the emerging new Germany is built on the ruins of Hitler's Third Reich, both in a literal and a figurative, psychological sense.

Notes for this section can be found on page 170.

Many of us who survived Hitler but who lost close relatives and friends in his gas chambers felt that their charge emanating with the smoke and ashes from the chimneys was: "Be a witness for us, tell the world, make sure this outrage will never be repeated!" This is how Grete Weil conceived her task as a writer throughout the postwar era, and hence I felt that a close study of her work would be a worthwhile endeavor for a graduate seminar.

In order to teach the course under a regular Portland State University graduate course number (German 553, reserved for 20th Century Prose), I had to win the approval of my colleagues. One of them doubted the wisdom of devoting a graduate seminar to the writings of a single author whose name did not appear on our "Reading List for MA Program in German" since her work was as yet not part of the canon. However, others pointed out that we had always allowed our graduate students to substitute texts they had studied for books on the reading list. Moreover, since I had twice directed the Deutsche Sommerschule am Pazifik, the new director trusted my judgment.

In recent years, the Deutsche Sommerschule am Pazifik has had an enrollment of forty-five to sixty upper-division and Master's students. It is a five-week, intensive, total immersion program that includes a two-week teacher training session taught in cooperation with the Goethe Institute. All classes are conducted in German, and students pledge to read and speak only in the target language for the duration of the program. My three-credit-hour seminar was scheduled to meet five days a week for seventy-five minutes daily. Six graduate students enrolled. However, since several of these students would have a conflict between my seminar and some of the teachers' courses at the end of the session, they persuaded me to teach the whole seminar within less than three weeks, sometimes meeting twice a day. That compression within an already very compact program was unfortunate and did not do justice to the subject matter. For reasons unrelated to scheduling and course content, one of the six students left for Germany before the term was half over. The remaining five, two of whom were teachers and one a University teaching assistant, followed through with the seminar and evinced great dedication. While none of these students came from Jewish families, one woman had converted to Judaism before she married her Jewish husband, and another was engaged to a Jew. My students were between approximately twenty-five and forty-five years of age; two of them were native speakers of German.

The body of Grete Weil's work is slim—one novella, four novels, and two collections of short stories—and on average her books are no more than 140 pages in length. Weil's prose is, however, dense and requires close reading. For non-native students who were only just beginning their graduate studies, the average reading assignments of almost sixty pages a day proved grueling. All of the students had some historical knowledge, but while they were aware of the wholesale extermination of European Jewry, none of them had ever heard of Grete Weil.

Hence, after discussing the course schedule, I talked about Grete Weil, née Dispeker, born in southern Bavaria in 1906 into a well-assimilated professional family with many intellectual and artistic contacts in Jewish as well as non-Jewish circles and strongly influenced by the German Enlightenment. My students were somewhat familiar with the tenets of this movement, and most had heard of Gotthold Ephraim Lessing, one of its guiding spirits and author of the seminal "philosemitic" play *Nathan der Weise*. I explained that the Dispekers, like many similar families at the time, felt so well integrated into German society that they did not think of themselves as German Jews, but as Germans of Jewish extraction, "German" being the common category. That made sense to my students since we always use "American" as the common denominator in the U.S., speaking of "Irish Americans," "Japanese Americans," and now of "African Americans."

I sketched Grete's education; her marriage in 1932 to Edgar Weil, a dramaturge with the progressive Munich Kammerspiele; the arrest of the upper echelon of this theater shortly after Hitler came to power. While all the other staff members were soon set free, Edgar Weil, the only Jew among them, was kept behind bars for almost two weeks. Since that experience led to the young couple's decision to leave Germany and go to the Netherlands for the duration, I asked my students what might have motivated this choice of refuge. Some knew that the Netherlands had remained neutral during World War I, and the one Dutch woman in the class told about her country's tradition of hospitality and tolerance and about the fact that the Jews were well integrated into all strata of society, especially in Amsterdam, the Weils' destination. I had to discuss the difference between exile and emigration so that everyone would realize that the Weils were "waiting it out" there, rather than trying to sink roots into the heavy Dutch soil, because like many refugees, they expected that National Socialism would not last in Germany.

After noting Grete's father's "timely" death in 1937, her mother's arrival in Amsterdam, and her brother's relocation to England, we began to discuss the wartime experiences of the family: Grete and Edgar's vain attempt to flee to England by boat when German troops invaded the Netherlands in May 1940; the occupation of Holland; the enactment of discriminatory laws to marginalize the Jews; the general strike in Amsterdam, February 1941, in solidarity with the city's Jewish population after the authorities had rounded up hundreds of young Jewish men who would soon meet their death in the notorious Mauthausen concentration camp. This account sparked many questions from the class: "Why did the Amsterdam population react so differently from non-Jews elsewhere?" "Was Mauthausen an extermination camp like Auschwitz? If so, how was this possible since the infamous Wannsee Conference did not take place until a year later?" With little time left that first day, I said that Grete Weil's books would answer many of these questions, adding that the horrors of Mauthausen were central to her writing because Edgar was sent there after his "accidental" arrest in June 1941. I dwelt briefly on her grief when learning of his death the following September, telling my students that Grete was ready to commit suicide but abstained to take care of her mother. Eventually, she obtained a job with the Jewish Council, which provided both women with much coveted deferment stamps on their identification papers.

For the next class meeting I assigned the first twenty-seven pages of Weil's novella, *Ans Ende der Welt* (1949), set in wartime Amsterdam in May 1943. It deals with the arrest of a law professor and his cousin, a diamond cutter, both rounded up with their respective families. They are among hundreds of other Jews crammed into the "Jewish Theater," by 1943 a notorious place whence people were sent East to their deaths. From her work as a reception clerk in the Jewish Theater, Grete Weil knew well what she was describing. We devoted two class sessions to this eighty-six-page novella, because it led so well into our subject.

It astounded my students to read about the gradual yet efficient way the class differences between the Jewish prisoners were annulled as they were stripped of their rights. In addition, the students responded emotionally to the unexpected love between the scions of the two families, the professor's spoiled daughter Annabeth and the beaten-up underground resistance worker Ben. When it is clear that he will be deported to Poland, she foregoes a chance at freedom, and the book ends with both of them, as well as her parents, going through selection "at the end of the world"—the notorious Auschwitz ramp.

In order to check both my students' understanding of the text and the level of their written German, I asked for a one- to two-page informal essay on an aspect of *Ans Ende der Welt* that they deemed important. Most focused on the total collapse of the two families' world, but one woman wrote about Annabeth, "Nicht Jüdin sondern Mensch," and admired the character's courage in rejecting a demeaning offer of freedom in the face of death. The enormity of the events described in Weil's novella gave all of the students pause.

The short papers were due for the fourth class meeting, while the students also had to read the first thirty-three pages of the novel *Tramhalte Beethovenstraat* (1963), Weil's next book, a somewhat longer, more complex, and hence more demanding text that caused the non-native speakers to read very late into the night. They were, however, fascinated by what appeared to be a firsthand account of the roundup of Jews in Amsterdam. Indeed, from her Beethoven Street apartment in the small hours of each morning during the second part of 1942, Weil had seen four hundred Jews of all ages herded into streetcars at the stop just below her window. My students realized that the Nazis had deliberately chosen the time to avoid protests from the population at large against the deportation of Jewish neighbors to the dreaded concentration camps. The traumatic experience kept haunting Weil. Decades later, she said: "Ich hatte nie bei etwas so sehr wie bei der *Tramhalte* das Gefühl, daß ich es schreiben muß, weil niemand auf der Welt es schreiben kann außer mir" ("Ich habe Auschwitz" 26).[2]

In the novel Weil transfers her compulsion to bear witness to the main character, the young writer Andreas, stationed in occupied Amsterdam as a reporter for a Munich newspaper. Immediately the question arose: "Why a German reporter?" The students quickly recognized that Weil creates the naive and unpolitical Andreas, who is drawn into the fate of his Jewish neighbors after witnessing the nightly roundup at the streetcar stop, to bridge the gap between her own experiences and those of her German readers of the early 1960s. We discussed how Weil repeatedly explores two important questions: "How could Germany, a nation so proud of its culture, have brought forth the murderous Nazis?" and "How did ordinary Germans of the postwar era live with the knowledge of the genocide committed in their name?" Although she does not answer these questions, the students understood that Weil forces her readers to ponder them and to follow Andreas on his postwar visits to Amsterdam and Mauthausen in his compulsive attempt to bear witness. Andreas comes to the conclusion that someone who has not had to live in a concentration camp cannot really identify with the victims or comprehend their suffering. "Die Gemordeten hatten das Geheimnis und das ihrer Mörder mit sich genommen,"[3] one of the final statements in the book (144), gave rise to a class discussion as to whether there could be such a thing as a "literature of the concentration camps." Of course, the works of Elie Wiesel and Primo Levi exemplify such a literature. I pointed out, however, that neither their first autobiographical accounts nor Weil's *Tramhalte Beethovenstraat* found a wide readership in Adenauer's *Wirtschaftswunder* Germany of the 1960s.

Slowly, toward the end of the 1970s, a new generation of Germans tried to come to grips with their country's recent past; and over the following two decades, a growing number of bewildered individuals would pay attention to the writings of both witnesses and survivors.

Meanwhile, for lack of response, Grete Weil temporarily gave up testifying through novels and wrote short stories instead. Rather than having the whole class read Weil's first collection of short prose, I called for individual students to review one of the three stories each for their classmates. We arranged for an extra class meeting for that purpose on their next free day, 1½ weeks into the session.

Set in North America, the stories of *Happy, sagte der Onkel* (1968) deal with survivors' traumas. They are related by a first-person narrator who shares many autobiographical features with Weil herself. The student who reported on the title story was sensitive to the "Californian" uncle and aunt's frantic yet awkward attempts to project themselves as super Americans, irascible in their rejection of everything German. From beneath their unreflected, total repudiation, sentimental memories of their homeland before the Nazi era keep bubbling up. They are happy but not *glücklich*, have learned nothing from their experiences, and do not want to hear from their visiting niece how their closest kin were rounded up and murdered. Moreover, they fault that niece for having moved back to Germany shortly after the war.

Since I had mentioned that there were so many parallels between Weil's own story and that of the narrator, my students wanted to know whether the author had also moved back to Germany. I reported that, liberated after hiding out in Amsterdam during the last twenty months of the war, Weil had soon returned to Germany, where she had married a non-Jewish German, the opera stage director Walter Jockisch. An old friend of the Weil couple, he had, as a German soldier, looked up the grieving young widow in Amsterdam shortly after Edgar's murder. When my students asked how I felt about Weil's return, I confessed that for many years after the war it seemed inconceivable to me that any Jew would want to move back to Germany, but that gradually I had come to appreciate what motivated Weil and other fine people like the scholars Hans Mayer and Ernst Loewy to return to their "Mörderland," as Weil calls Germany in *Generationen* (12). Loewy had actually moved back from Israel in 1956. Several students found that hard to comprehend. As members of the post–World War II generation, they felt more comfortable with Jews in Israel than in Germany.

The class's discomfort echoed that of a character in Weil's next story, "Gloria Halleluja," discussed by my Dutch student. Here the narrator finds herself in New York at the end of her stay in the United States. Since her experiences under the Nazis have made her sensitive to the prevalent undercurrent of racism, she insists on visiting Harlem. Made welcome in a black home, she is eventually thrown out, because the family holds her, as a Jew, responsible for the crucifixion. She takes refuge in a Jewish pawnshop whose owner had barely survived the notorious "medical" experiments performed on her by Nazi doctors in one of the concentration camps. Upon learning that the narrator is a Jew who had voluntarily moved back to Germany after the war, the irate shopkeeper sends her guest packing. Rejected as a Jew and despised as a presumed Nazi-lover, the narrator tries to recover in a bar. Again she is thrown out, this time as a white person in an all-black saloon. Especially because of the U.S. context, the student giving the report tried to come to terms with the comparisons Weil makes in "Gloria Halleluja" first explicitly, then implicitly. Is the Shoah experience under the Nazis unique, or can the lessons learned there be transferred to other historical situations of discrimination and genocide? The class decided that lessons can be drawn but also that there are differences in degree of racism and persecution. Time constraints did not permit us to delve deeper into this important topic for, during that same class session, we still had to deal with the most demanding of the three short stories, "B sagen," which I had given my oldest and most mature student, a German woman in her forties, to review for the group.

She duly reported how the narrator in this story visits archaeological sites in Mexico and cannot help comparing the black wall of the Toltecs, where the skulls of their prehistoric human sacrifices are piled up, with the black wall of recent executions in Auschwitz. The suave tour guide reminds her of a high-ranking, supercilious SS officer at the Jewish Theater in Amsterdam. Obsessed by this supposed figure from her past, the narrator challenges him in an inner dialogue and calls him to account. How can he play the gentleman-guide after having participated in the Nazi mass murders? But then, how can she herself travel all over the world, hungry for new impressions? Do they not share survival strategies just as they share a pre-Nazi German past in which neither of them was politically active enough to help stem the tide of National Socialism? Are they not both compromised by their affirmation of life after Auschwitz? The woman who reviewed this story was visibly shaken by its impact since it takes the "Holocaust" out of its relatively safe niche of the "then and there" and probes the "here and now" of the perpetrators as well as of the victims, of their descendants, and even of the readers.

While the three students were preparing for their presentations, we ventured as a class into Weil's 1980 novel, *Meine Schwester Antigone*. My students could piece together the story of the Greek princess who had paid with her life for her decision to follow her own moral precepts. She had buried her slain brother rather than obey King Creon's decree to leave the corpse to the vultures. For Weil, who had felt compromised by her work for the Jewish Council in Amsterdam because this Council was instrumental in the deportation of the Jewish population, the Antigone figure had always been a challenge and a guiding star.

The class noticed how the writer spins the tale of the Greek princess as a foil for the narrator's autobiographical story, so similar to Weil's own. Among the parallels she draws are a close relationship with a beloved father and an elder brother, and an independent streak that marks not only the narrator and the figure of antiquity, but also Sophie Scholl, the courageous Munich student who paid with her life for distributing anti-Nazi leaflets in 1943. We discussed the "Weiße Rose" resistance briefly, before returning to the independent streak that is also manifest in the aging narrator's everyday life in Germany. Remembering her time of hiding in Amsterdam, she gives shelter to a young woman connected with the student rebellion of the early 1970s. As she watches over her charge, she reads the authentic manuscript of a German soldier who reported in July 1943 about the liquidation of the Petrikau ghetto in Poland, an event he reluctantly witnessed. This report, which constitutes one-seventh of Weil's novel; the flashbacks to the narrator's experiences during the Nazi persecution; the associations with Antigone and with the "here and now" of the writer—all interconnected in 150 pages of terse and lucid prose—made *Meine Schwester Antigone* an invaluable resource for my students. They agreed that this book, with which Weil finally reached a wider public, should be on every reading list of German literature dealing with the Shoah.

At this point our seminar had only one week left. In retrospect, it would have been wise simply to forego *Generationen*, Weil's next novel (1983). Covering the turbulent years during which the narrator was working on *Meine Schwester Antigone*, it is closely connected with that book. Yet I could not reconcile myself to omitting *Generationen* since it contains some of Weil's tersest pronouncements on her condition as a survivor of the Shoah. In order to make it possible for my students to complete the daily reading assignments and then have time to assimilate the material, we agreed that they could take all summer to write their ten-page term paper. Each of them signed a contract stating that they would get an "Incomplete" for German 553 on their summer transcripts, with the actual final grade to follow in the fall upon completion of their assignment. Quite frequently, teachers of Deutsche Sommerschule courses allow students to hand in their papers late. However, I was probably the first to suggest that all participants in a seminar avail themselves of this option.

That done, we looked for the terse statements mentioned above and found a frequently quoted one: "Meine Krankheit heißt Auschwitz, und die ist unheilbar. Ich habe Auschwitz, wie andere Tb oder Krebs haben. Bin genauso schwer zu ertragen wie alle Bresthaften" (7).[4] We discussed the fact that Auschwitz is a code word for Weil which subsumes her sensitivity to any kind of violence and her allergy to expressions of hypocrisy concerning that violence. When the narrator remarks a little later: "Bin fast normal, so normal wie ein Mensch sein kann, dem der Tod in den Gaskammern zugedacht war, der nur aus Zufall entkommen ist. … Und bin nach Deutschland zurückgegangen, in das Mörderland, ich gehöre dazu; die Auszeichnung, daß ich einmal den gelben Stern trug, ist vertan" (11–12),[5] I asked my students why Weil would refer to the yellow star as "a badge of honor." They were quick to recognize that the star had set the victims of the Nazis apart from the perpetrators and the cowed or indifferent bystanders.

Subsequently, the narrator raises a very sore point: while the Dutch have a natural way of mourning for victims of the Nazi era and talk freely to their children and grandchildren about the terrible years of 1940 to 1945, Germans and Jews, as of the early 1980s, cannot reflect on this period effectively. The former tend to blame Hitler alone for all the horrors, while the latter, especially the Israelis, simplify by calling the Germans and the Palestinians devils and by equating Arafat with Hitler. They see the Jews, of course, as good. Thus, there is no differentiation and no real memory. "Bei den Deutschen, bei den Juden verwehren die Eltern durch Schweigen den Kindern das Mitleid. So wird Leben erstickt" (12–13).[6]

Weil's breaking a tabu by condemning perpetrators and victims in one breath especially appalled the two native Germans in my class, so our discussion shifted from "the Holocaust" to "living with the memory of the event," a situation that has marked so many people of Weil's generation as well as of mine. Since "Bewältigung" is impossible (12), is there a constructive way of remembering, a kind of awareness that might help younger generations cope productively with the legacy of the Shoah? In our text we found a response in the narrator's proffer: "Ich biete an: meine Geschichte. Ich habe einen Geliebten durch Mord verloren, habe Tausende an mir vorbei in die Vernichtung ziehen sehen, bin alt geworden. Das ist alles. Mögen andere schweigen, ich muß reden. Nicht um der Toten willen, es geht mir um die Lebenden" (132).[7]

My students claimed it was important to them that they were reading about the destruction of European Jewry with a teacher who could help them connect through her personal experience. My own recollections and some of the memorabilia I brought to class provided a "reality check" for them: one of my father's yellow stars with the word "Jood" printed on it in Hebrew-like letters; my husband's two Dutch identification cards, one with his true name and a big black "J" on it, the other one with an alias and without a "J," which he carried while in hiding; the Dutch book with the photograph of the murderous death steps down the Mauthausen quarry (Presser, vol. I 89), a photograph mentioned by Weil in *Meine Schwester Antigone* (84). To what extent one can really learn from somebody else's experience is, of course, a very personal matter.

If awareness can be transferred, then Weil's last two books are invaluable. In the novel, *Der Brautpreis* (1988), the octogenarian pits the voice of one narrator: "Ich, Grete, mit den beiden deutschen, den beiden christlichen Namen Margarete Elisabeth" (7) against that of her other narrator: "Ich, Michal, Tochter von König Saul, zweimal Frau von König David und eine seiner Witwen" (13).[8] Beyond the author's attempt to give her Jewish roots a place in her life, the book serves to recapitulate the horrors of the Nazi persecution and her grief for her murdered husband, as she juxtaposes Grete's story with that of Michal. While Grete's feelings toward her great Biblical ancestor, King David, remain ambivalent, she envies him and Michal for the fact that they died without knowing what lay ahead for their people. "Ich, die Spätgeborene, muß mit dem Wissen um Auschwitz mein Leben zu Ende bringen, es wird mich quälen bis zum letzten Atemzug" (236–37).[9]

We had returned to one of the main themes of my introductory remarks. Despite her suffering at the hands of the Nazis, Weil's ties to German life and culture have remained strong, her connection to Judaism and Israel rather tentative. That amazed several of my students who were familiar with Jewish pride and the strong pro-Israel stance of the Jews they knew. There was, however, no time for further discussion. To enable us to complete the seminar before the start of the Teachers' Training Course, my students willingly gave up yet another free day to have the second half of the class do its oral reports on the stories of *Spätfolgen* (1992).

All of these very short stories deal again with survivors' traumas. It came almost as a relief that the student who reviewed Weil's "Guernica," himself a seasoned high school teacher, ignored the heartbreak of that story's narrator as she agrees to meet a former friend under that haunting Picasso picture in the Museum of Modern Art and finds him totally unable to reflect about events during the Hitler years and about his subsequent life as a refugee. Instead, my student went back to basics and spoke about the German air raids on the town of Guernica in 1937 during the Spanish Civil War, which led to Picasso's painting his awe-inspiring picture. I still have copies of this student's handouts. His two classmates stayed closer to Weil's texts in their reports. One was deeply moved by the six-page story "Don't touch me," in which a concentration camp survivor reluctantly returns from the United States to visit her cousin in Munich and gets badly hurt in a traffic accident. She will not allow any German doctor to touch her and dies after three days "an inneren Verletzungen" according to Weil's well-chosen double entendre (34). In "Das Schönste der Welt," the middle-aged man whose wife and child were murdered in a concentration camp many years ago can no longer cope and takes his own life. The student who reported on this terse short story was also profoundly affected by it. Sadly, there was no time left to discuss in depth Weil's brief personal testimony, "Und Ich? Zeugin des Schmerzes," with which the book closes. Thinking of other witnesses, Jean Améry, Primo Levi, Paul Celan, and lately Bruno Bettelheim, all of them concentration camp survivors who eventually committed suicide, Weil wonders whether she has lived to be so old because, as yet, her testimony has proven insufficient (102, 105). We had to leave this probing question open as we disbanded.

There was, alas, no opportunity for the students to give a spontaneous, oral course evaluation, and the secretary of the Deutsche Sommerschule am Pazifik has been unable to locate the written *Fragebögen* for the summer of 1993. In the composite of the questionnaires, however, the Grete Weil seminar scores 3.83 out of four possible points. When, in the early fall of 1993, the students sent me their papers, one wrote: "I very much treasured your seminar on Weil," and another: "… das Wissen um Grete Weil und die Differenzierung der jüdischen Erfahrung werde ich nie vergessen."[10] A third student's response to my recent request for a constructive critique of the seminar read: "It was a great learning experience. If only we had had more time!"

Fortunately, I was able to reach the high school teacher who had made the informative "Guernica" presentation. During a long telephone conversation (16 March 1997),[11] he corroborated my recollection that I had given very brief outlines of each of Weil's pieces of short prose and then asked the students to choose which text(s) they wanted to report on. This was the kind of assignment he liked best. He had opted for "Guernica" because he wished to delve into the historical background of Picasso's painting. I asked him whether I had assumed too much advance knowledge on the part of my students. He did not want to speak for others, but for him a short historical overview of antisemitism in Europe would have been helpful. In fact, at the Deutsche Sommerschule the following summer, he had heard my *Grundkurs* lecture entitled "Deutsche Juden oder jüdische Deutsche?" which offered a historical overview of how the Jews had fared in the German lands from Roman times to the present. He would have liked this kind of information at the beginning of the Weil seminar.

This same former student reminded me of the yellow star and the other memorabilia I had brought to the seminar. They were important to him, and he suggested that a younger teacher, who does not have access to these authentic mementos, should bring some illustrative materials to class. He also felt that we had tried to read too much. Because we were concentrating on the Shoah and because Weil's *Generationen* and *Der Brautpreis* have as an important second theme the problems of aging, he thought that possibly half the class should have read *Generationen* and the other half *Brautpreis*. If each group had had an appropriate worksheet, he felt, the class as a whole would have had more time to discuss the salient common issues. He would also have been interested in reading a German-language author who explains his or her decision to emigrate to and remain in Israel after World War II, as a counterexample to Weil's choice.

Of the papers my students wrote, one entitled "Antigone, Grete Weils Widerpart" and another "Kern des Holocaustschreckens" penetrated their topics most deeply, but the other three also gave ample evidence that their writers had benefited from studying the Shoah through Weil's work. This was also apparent when I gave a *Grundkurs* lecture to the Deutsche Sommerschule at large that summer of 1993 under the title "Grete Weil: unbequem, zum Denken zwingend." My seminar students served as resource persons, and I believe that it is partly due to their enthusiasm that a German judge on the faculty as well as a student who had heard that lecture read Grete Weil in order to learn more about Jewish suffering during the Nazi period and about the problems of survivors.

If asked to come out of retirement once again and teach a Weil course, I would be sorely tempted because I found the seminar such a meaningful experience. However, I would never again do it as a course compressed into less than three weeks, and I might try to structure it differently. The Germanist in me had insisted on focusing on the primary texts, which we followed in chronological order, looking closely at the author's terse style and her many associations, a product of her unique gift for connective, lateral thinking. I now wonder whether it might not be more productive to provide the students with historical background information, and then read only *Ans Ende der Welt* and *Meine Schwester Antigone* with the whole class. After a thorough group discussion of the most relevant topics in these two works, we would then list them: for example, Auschwitz/Mauthausen;

Exile and Hiding; the Jewish Council (i.e., cooperating with the oppressor versus resisting); Jews, Blacks, *Gastarbeiter*, and Other Despised Minorities; a Jew in Pre- and Post-World War II Germany; Genocide and Refugees Then and Now; the Need and the Inability to Witness; Nonviolence and Environmental Concerns; the Reception of Grete Weil's (and Similar) Books through the Postwar Decades (in Germany, the Netherlands, the U.S.); the Relationship of a Secularized Jewish Intellectual to Judaism; and the Societal Role and the Strength of Women. The Weil texts not read by everybody would each be assigned to one (or, in a larger group, to more) of the students, and they would read their text closely and repeatedly in connection with the topic(s) at hand and bring their insights to the class. This would involve the students more actively than I was able to do during that short summer session of 1993 and thus possibly have a more lasting effect on their ability to incorporate the Shoah experience into their approach to life.

Although that restructuring of the course sounds plausible, concerns remain. Since all of the above topics overlap, would the sum of the parts ever approximate the whole? Would a reductionist approach ever add up to what Grete Weil conveys so uniquely in her books: honest and often uncomfortable reflections about the life of a person who had been marked for murder; about a life suffused with pain, guilt, and rage; experiences offered to the reader as an invitation to draw lessons from them? Having been so close to what Weil went through, I may not be the best teacher for the analytical approach outlined above. A younger colleague might want to try the idea; it would be interesting to learn whether it is productive.

Notes

1. "Holocaust, the insufferable misnomer which forces one to think of a natural catastrophe. ... [n]ot of something that developed gradually and was executed by people who had been drilled for centuries to be obedient, to maintain order, and to keep silent." [The translations in these notes are by Laureen Nussbaum.]
2. "With no other work did I ever feel so strongly as with *Tramhalte* that I had to write it, since nobody in the world except me could write it."
3. "The murdered had taken the[ir] secret and that of their murderers with them."
4. "My disease is called Auschwitz, and it is incurable. I have Auschwitz as others have TB or cancer. I'm just as difficult to put up with as anyone with a serious infirmity."
5. "I'm almost normal, as normal as a person can be who was designated for death in the gas chambers [and] who only escaped by chance. ... And went back to Germany, to the land of the murderers, [for] I'm part of it: the mark of distinction, [the fact] that I once wore the yellow star, is superseded."
6. "Among the Germans and the Jews, the parents' silence prevents the children from [feeling] compassion. In this way life is suffocated."
7. "I offer: my story. I have lost my beloved to murder, have seen thousands pass by me into extermination, have grown old. That is all. Others may keep silent; I have to speak. Not for the sake of the dead—my concern is for the living."
8. "I, Grete, with the two German, the two Christian names Margaret Elizabeth"; "I, Michal, daughter of King Saul, twice wife of King David and one of his widows."
9. "I, who was born late, must [live] my life to its end with the knowledge of Auschwitz; it will torment me until my last breath."
10. "... I will never forget what I learned about Grete Weil and the differentiation of the Jewish experience."
11. I gratefully acknowledge permission to report here on this former student's comments in our telephone interview.

Portland State University   **Prof. Laureen Nussbaum**

GER 553, Das Werk der Grete Weil

Portland State University, School of Extended Studies, Summer Session Program in collaboration with Lewis and Clark College, Portland, OR, and the Goethe Institute, San Francisco. Deutsche Sommerschule am Pazifik.

Kursbeschreibung: Die eminente Schriftstellerin Grete Weil, Deutsche und Jüdin, Flüchtling und Remigrantin der ersten Stunde, wurde erst 1980 durch ihren preisgekrönten Roman, *Meine Schwester Antigone*, bekannt. Ihr kompaktes Werk umspannt die Jahre der Weimarer Republik bis zur bundesdeutschen Gegenwart, wobei die Themen Flucht und Verfolgung und die Ermordung ihres Mannes im Konzentrationslager zentral stehen. Auch das Altern beschäftigt sie sehr. Grete Weil legt Zeugnis ab, zwingt zum Nachdenken und zur Eigenständigkeit. Wir lesen ihre fünf äußerst kurzen Romane. KursteilnehmerInnen halten Referate über Weils Erzählungen (die ausgeteilt werden) und schreiben eine längere Seminararbeit.

Texte:
Grete Weil, *Ans Ende der Welt*,
    Novelle   (Fischer Taschenbuch, Nr. 9175)
___, *Tramhalte Beethovenstraat*,
    Roman   (Fischer Taschenbuch, Nr. 5301)
___, *Meine Schwester Antigone*,
    Roman   (Fischer Taschenbuch, Nr. 5270)
___, *Generationen*, Roman   (Fischer Taschenbuch, Nr. 5969)
___, *Der Brautpreis*, Roman   (Fischer Taschenbuch, Nr. 9543)
Erzählungen (Kauf nicht erforderlich):
Grete Weil, *Happy, sagte der Onkel*   (Fischer Taschenbuch, Nr. 5254)
___, *Spätfolgen*   (Zürich: Nagel & Kimche, 1992)

Die Professorin wird den StudentInnen mehrere Sekundärwerke, Artikel, Interviews und Zeitungsausschnitte zu Grete Weil zur Verfügung stellen.

Wochenplan
(Für den konzentrierten knapp dreiwöchigen Kurs revidiert)

Erste Woche: Einführung in Weils Leben und Werk, Diskussion von *Ans Ende der Welt* und kurzer Essay zu einem Aspekt dieses Werkes, Diskussion von *Tramhalte Beethovenstraat*

Zweite Woche: Fortsetzung der Diskussion von *Tramhalte Beethovenstraat*, Referate über die Erzählungen in *Happy, sagte der Onkel*, Diskussion von *Meine Schwester Antigone*

Dritte Woche: Diskussion von *Generationen* und *Der Brautpreis*, Referate über die Erzählungen in *Spätfolgen*

Im Frühherbst: Einreichung der zehnseitigen Seminararbeiten

Works Cited

Nussbaum, Laureen. "Grete Weil: unbequem, zum Denken zwingend." Lecture. Deutsche Sommerschule am Pazifik. Portland, OR. July 1993. Later published with coauthor Uwe Meyer in *Exilforschung. Ein internationales Jahrbuch*. 11, Frauen im Exil. Munich: Text + Kritik, 1993. 156–70.

Presser, Jacob. *De Ondergang*. 2 vols. 's Gravenhage: Staatsuitgeverij, 1965. [Trans. Arnold Pomerans under the title *Ashes in the Wind*. London: Souvenir Press, 1968.]

Weil, Grete. *Ans Ende der Welt*. 1949. Frankfurt am Main: Fischer, 1989.

———. *Der Brautpreis*. 1988. Frankfurt am Main: Fischer, 1991.

———. *Generationen*. 1983. Frankfurt am Main: Fischer, 1985.

———. *Happy, sagte der Onkel*. 1968. Frankfurt am Main: Fischer, 1982.

———. "Ich habe Auschwitz, wie andere Tb oder Krebs." Interview with Liz Wieskerstrauch. *Anschläge. Zeitschrift für Kunst und Literatur* (Jan./Feb. 1988): 22–26.

———. *Meine Schwester Antigone*. 1980. Frankfurt am Main: Fischer, 1988.

———. *Spätfolgen*. Zurich: Nagel & Kimche, 1992.

———. *Tramhalte Beethovenstraat*. 1963. Frankfurt am Main: Fischer, 1983.

Chapter 12

A GRADUATE SEMINAR ON THE HOLOCAUST AND THE THIRD REICH AS REFLECTED IN POSTWAR GERMAN LITERATURE

Nancy A. Lauckner

In winter 1981 and spring 1994 I offered a graduate seminar in the then Department of Germanic and Slavic Languages at the University of Tennessee entitled "Der Holocaust und das Dritte Reich in der deutschen Nachkriegsliteratur." This seminar developed out of a university honors course on Holocaust literature that I gave in English in 1980 and 1985. My essay will focus on the 1994 seminar, with some references to the first seminar and brief allusions to the honors course.

My Holocaust courses are predicated on the conviction that Germanists have a special responsibility and obligation to teach the Holocaust because we teach and research the language, literature, and culture of the people who produced it. If we were to discuss in our classes only the admirable aspects of that culture and to ignore or give short shrift to the darkest chapter of its history, we would be derelict in our duty as scholars to offer a balanced and accurate picture of our subject. Still more important than that duty is our moral obligation to victims and survivors of the Holocaust to present their story so that our students may better understand the past and try to prevent or resist future recurrences of genocide. This task is especially urgent now that there will soon be no more living survivors of the Holocaust to counter the deniers as well as the comfortable, who just want to forget. If we Germanists shirk our responsibility,

---

Notes for this section can be found on page 182.

we implicitly side with the deniers and forgetters and risk increasing their ranks among our students, to whom we must convey the disturbing yet essential knowledge about the Holocaust. Unlike our German colleagues, we North American Germanists, in most cases, come to the study of the Holocaust without the emotional, social, historical, and personal baggage of shame, guilt, demands for a *Schlußstrich*, and denial that often marks Holocaust discourse in Germany. Of course, the North American context also brings certain disadvantages, and this essay will reflect how I deal with some of these.

While I respect Germanists who choose to treat the Holocaust as a subtopic or subtext in one or more courses and I recognize the advantages and benefits of this approach, the method does not suit my purposes in Holocaust teaching. Although I always discuss and allude to the Holocaust and German-Jewish issues in any course or context in which they fit, I have found it necessary to develop a Holocaust-specific course in order to expose students to a large amount of information about the Holocaust and to ensure their ongoing, focused consideration of it over an entire semester. There are three reasons why I chose a literary approach that requires students to read and discuss selected works of postwar German literature that reflect the Holocaust and the Third Reich: (1) my academic specialty is postwar German literature, (2) this method proved very successful in my university honors courses on Holocaust literature in English translation, and (3) literary works provide much factual information about the Holocaust, while, at the same time, giving an awareness of the human dimensions of the tragedy that nonliterary readings often fail to convey. I developed a seminar because many graduate students become teachers, so a graduate course influences more students in the long run, even though it has a smaller enrollment than an undergraduate course. In the absence of special topics courses, a seminar enables an instructor to introduce a new graduate course without the long process involved in adding a new offering to the curriculum.

My seminar is open to graduate students of German as well as to other graduate students with the necessary linguistic and literary preparation. We read and discuss all the works in German. In 1994 the seminar had an enrollment of six students, which was large for my small department, and one of them had been urging me for months to offer a Holocaust course. There were four men and two women; two of the students were middle-aged, and four were in their twenties or slightly older. Five were students of German, and the other had a French major with a German minor. One was a native German, and one had a full-time job and commuted from a town some one hundred miles away to take the course.

Since I knew my students quite well before the seminar began, I was able to tailor it to their needs. Three of the course goals also informed my first Holocaust seminar: (1) to read and discuss a common core of German literary works on the topic, (2) to consider the ethical questions of this tragic period, and (3) to have my students research a Holocaust theme in an individually selected literary work and present the resultant seminar paper to the class. Because I regard these goals as essential to any literary seminar on the Holocaust, they will govern all such seminars I offer. However, I added another goal for this group: to provide the needed historical and religious knowledge to facilitate understanding historical and religious references in works on the period. The younger students in particular did not have the background necessary to deal with these works successfully. Since this lack of historical background will only worsen in future generations of North American students, we must deal with it creatively and effectively in Holocaust teaching. The need for Jewish religious knowledge was a factor intrinsic to the student population at my Southern university.

Several strategies provided the historical and religious information my students lacked. I postponed my usual introductory lecture on the history of antisemitism, National Socialism, and the main events of the Third Reich and the Holocaust in order to introduce Holocaust history in a way that would have more personal impact. Here I ask the readers' indulgence and understanding, for I undertook, with the best intentions, an experiment that some may find controversial. One student who had been a high school teacher urged me to adopt for the seminar some Holocaust educational materials he had used successfully,[1] and I did so because of my confidence in his integrity and in the seriousness and maturity of my students. I borrowed the materials—entitled *Gestapo: Learning Experience about the Holocaust*, published in 1973 by Alternatives in Religious Education, Inc. in Denver—from the Education Department of Heska Amuna synagogue in Knoxville and used them at the second meeting of the seminar.

The materials consist of information cards that contain historical mileposts in the Nazi persecution of the Jews, such as "The Nazis require the marking of all Jewish homes and apartments," and "Germans are not allowed to patronize Jewish doctors and lawyers"; as someone reads these aloud, participants remove markers from their "Value Boards" in the appropriate category, such as "Civil Liberties," "Religion," "Income/Job," etc. Although the participant who has markers left after all cards are read "succeeds," almost no neophyte can achieve this because the actions against the Jews escalate so quickly. Of course, the product aims to teach students some basic Holocaust history and to impress upon them that death was virtually inescapable then, and it fulfills these purposes quite effectively. Unfortunately, it has several drawbacks as well. I cautioned: "This is *not* a game. It is a learning tool, and we will approach the experience seriously and with respect for the memory of the victims." Although the students treated it appropriately, a lifetime of playing with boards and informational cards nevertheless signaled "game" to them, and they soon employed familiar game strategies to their advantage. My views on my experiment with this product are still very ambivalent: it did give a rapid introduction to Holocaust history with great personal impact, yet the students' subconscious association of the product with games and their use of game strategies somewhat diminished the benefits of the experience.

The second method for providing needed background was more satisfactory. I developed a list of eighty-eight historical and religious concepts, names, terms, etc., important for understanding works about the Holocaust—e.g., *Appelle, Ghettos, Kaddisch, Schtetl*—and assigned each student a segment. Students gave a brief oral report on one of their items at the beginning of each class meeting. Because they gained practice in Holocaust research, acquired the background knowledge they lacked, and shared their information with the class, in my view the only disadvantage was that they became so interested in their findings that the reports often far exceeded the recommended length. One student suggested that it would have saved class time and been more effective if I had provided a list of short definitions of all the items at the beginning of the semester so that they could have referred to it whenever they encountered any of the items in their reading. Of course, I had intentionally foregone the time saving because I knew they would learn and retain more by doing the work themselves.

Since my Bible Belt students, though quite devout, have little or no acquaintance with Judaism, and many have never met a Jew, I wanted them to experience contemporary Jews practicing a vibrant faith to complement the somber images of Jews presented in Holocaust literature. To achieve this, we attended a Sabbath morning service at Heska Amuna (conservative-orthodox) synagogue with the rabbi's permission. Although the activity had to be voluntary, most of the students took part. They could follow the readings and some of the hymns from the English translations, and the exposure to the sights and sounds of the service did much to dispel for them the aura of mystery and fear that Jewish religious practice has historically evoked in many Gentiles. The warm welcome from the rabbi, the kindness of congregation members during the service, and the *kiddush* gathering afterward also contributed to a most salutary experience for the students.

After the Holocaust "learning experience" and the historical lecture, we began discussing the core readings, eight works selected to expose students to a wide variety of perspectives on and literary approaches to the Holocaust and the Third Reich. Max Frisch's *Andorra* was the first reading because it treats the effects of prejudice as well as presenting specific antisemitic stereotypes of Jews and thus provides a stylized yet effective introduction to the mindset that produced the Holocaust. The only problem with the students' reception of the text was the conclusion reached by some that they should fight prejudice and its consequences lest the flames engulf them, i.e., Christians. While this argument may serve as an initial motive to combat prejudice, it is not the main lesson I sought to inculcate in my students. I assigned Johannes Bobrowski's *Levins Mühle* as the second reading because its setting in Poland in the 1870s offers a historical glimpse into the ethnic, religious, and economic strife that later fueled the Third Reich and the Holocaust. Despite the linguistic and stylistic difficulties of the text, even for native Germans, the students felt it gave them a differentiated view of pre-Holocaust history. Bertolt Brecht's *Furcht und Elend des Dritten Reiches* followed because its short, hard-hitting scenes provide an excellent overview of people, attitudes, and events in the early years of the Third Reich. Different scenes impacted different students especially strongly, but the understated pathos of "Die jüdische Frau" affected them all.

Not chosen for literary quality but for its important place in the history of German literary treatments of the Holocaust and the Third Reich, Rolf Hochhuth's *Der Stellvertreter* was the first reading that directly depicts the Holocaust. It led to many lively discussions about "representing the unrepresentable," the dangers inherent in demonizing Hitler and the Nazis, and the lessons—literary, ethical, and historical—that one can derive even from mediocre Holocaust works. Heinrich Böll's *Billard um halb zehn* followed, selected because it treats the lingering effects of the Third Reich in the postwar period from the perspective of one family's experience. Although the students found the symbolism and structural complexity of the work very difficult, the discussions of ethical issues it raises made their struggles worthwhile.

I chose Friedrich Dürrenmatt's *Der Verdacht* because this relatively short work contains the important but seldom treated theme of revenge by Holocaust survivors. It also facilitated consideration of both the medical experiments in the camps and the adaptation of the legend of the Wandering Jew, but the use of the grotesque proved a great hurdle for some of the more literal-minded students. Ruth Klüger's memoir *weiter leben* followed, chosen for its genre, its author—the only woman author of the seminar readings—its approach to the experience of the camps, and its clear demonstration of the long-term effects of the Holocaust on survivors. This book had great immediacy and authority for the students as a "true" rather than fictional account of events, but some found Klüger's pervasive feminism aggravating and the degree to which her unresolved relationship with her father still haunts her hard to understand.

The final core reading of the seminar is always Simon Wiesenthal's autobiographical text *Die Sonnenblume* with its "Kommentare," because its author, too, is a survivor, and because it readily stimulates penetrating discussions of some central ethical issues of the Holocaust. I place it last so that students will bring a strong background on the Holocaust to their consideration of this work, which raises the question of forgiveness, in order to short-circuit the tendency, prevalent among Christian students, to respond quickly and unthinkingly in favor of forgiveness, based on their religious tenets. They first read and discuss only the story so that exposure to the "Kommentare" does not bias their views, and then they read those selections. Although the general discussion of the varied views of the authors and the students on the ethical issues is always interesting, it is particularly useful to require each student to report on which selection he or she finds most and which least meaningful and to give a rationale. When a student realizes that his or her favorite selection is the one another student finds least convincing, this does more to counteract a rigid approach to ethical problems than anything an instructor or text can say. In 1994 my students responded to the Wiesenthal work as positively as they had in the past; their only regret was that there was too little time to devote to all of the important issues it raises.

Since discussion of the core readings exceeded the time allotted, we had to forego the brief reports on selected interviews from the two Sichrovsky texts. In the remaining time available, I showed the video *The Wannsee Conference*. It provided a needed change of pace and a dramatic illustration of the attitudes and decisions behind the Holocaust. Despite all of their experience by this point, my students were aghast at the film's revelations and the characters' callousness and brutality. Because movie theaters were showing Steven Spielberg's *Schindler's List* when my seminar was in progress, most of the students saw the film—some several times—and we also discussed it in class. Although they found it impressive, they did recognize and candidly analyze some of its drawbacks.

Each student read an additional literary work on the Holocaust or the Third Reich, wrote a research paper of fifteen to twenty pages on some topic related to it, and presented the paper orally to the class. Besides providing practice in research, writing, and critiquing, this requirement almost doubled the amount of Holocaust literature to which the students were exposed. Suggestions about which work to choose came from a reading list I provided and their own reading, and they selected their topics in consultation with me. The resultant papers were quite varied: a psychological interpretation of Eva Deutsch in Brigitte Schwaiger's and her *Die Galizianerin*, a case study of the protagonist in Jurek Becker's *Der Boxer*, an investigation into the use of humor in Edgar Hilsenrath's *Der Nazi und der Friseur*, a survey of the depiction of the Church's role in selected German Holocaust works, an analysis of the documentary aspect of Peter Weiss's *Die Ermittlung*, and a comparison of moral and spiritual issues in Franz Werfel's *Jakobowsky und der Oberst* and Carl Zuckmayer's *Der Gesang im Feuerofen*. Despite the expected range of quality, the papers well fulfilled my purposes in assigning them.

Late in the semester, the Simon Wiesenthal Center's traveling exhibit *The Courage to Remember* came to campus, and I urged my students to see it. One morning several students reported they had done so, with the comment, "Don't bother to go. It's just words and pictures on the wall." Their cavalier dismissal of this renowned exhibit shocked me, but it illustrated an important reality that Holocaust teaching must confront to reach the rising generations. If mature graduate students, already well versed in the Holocaust and intent on learning more, can reject a fine exhibit on this basis, the increasingly visually oriented and technologically expert students now in elementary and secondary schools will demand greater visual variety and technological sophistication in their university classes. Unless we find creative ways to incorporate these aspects into Holocaust teaching, students will drop our courses or simply not enroll in them. Although some professors are still "technologically challenged" and regard some of the information available through the new technologies as insufficiently scholarly, our mission of teaching future generations about the Holocaust is so vital that we must adapt our methodologies to interest and challenge those students.

Because my course fulfilled the goals I set for it and the student evaluations were very positive, I will retain many of the components when I teach the seminar again: the synagogue visit, the oral reports on historical and religious terms, the seminar papers, and a corpus of core readings. Although I vary some of the readings each time, especially if an important new work has appeared or a particular work proved unsuccessful, some are permanent fixtures of the course: *Die Sonnenblume* and, normally, Becker's *Jakob der Lügner*. However, I had used the latter the previous semester in a postwar literature course as a means of sparking interest in the 1994 seminar. I will certainly use *weiter leben* again and try to find ways to overcome the problems students had with it. Despite the effectiveness of the *Gestapo* materials in teaching basic Holocaust history quickly, I have decided not to utilize them again because of their "game" connotations.

The seminar will undergo some changes based on my conviction that the future poses two major challenges to Holocaust teachers: the problem of teaching the Holocaust when there are no more survivors and when denial thus increases,[2] and the abovementioned problem of meeting student demands for visual and technological sophistication. Since there would be a major Holocaust conference on campus not too long after my seminar, I did not include a visit from a survivor or much discussion about Holocaust denial, but I will do so when I offer the seminar again. Eventually videotaped survivor interviews from Yale's Fortunoff Archive or other sources will have to supplant a visit. To deal with the other challenge, I will reduce the core readings and introduce more visual and technological components. Indeed, the current decrease in student interest and facility in reading complex literature is already impacting text selection; thus, I chose *Der Verdacht* rather than Becker's *Bronsteins Kinder* to represent the theme of revenge because the former is shorter. Given the current application of the business and corporate model in higher education, it may even prove necessary to increase potential enrollment and make the seminar accessible to a broader student audience by assigning readings in English for those who cannot read German and by teaching the course in English, practices I had used in my university honors course. The next version of the seminar will include several videotapes and a project that requires students to find and evaluate Holocaust material in German on the Internet and the World Wide Web.[3] By adding media that they prefer, I hope to spur and retain their interest in Holocaust study, while providing an academically sound introduction to the subject matter and practice with using technology for Holocaust research. As Holocaust teaching moves ahead into the twenty-first century, teachers and students alike will have much to learn.

Notes

1. I acknowledge with thanks this suggestion and information from Terry A. Osborn (M.A., University of Tennessee, 1993; Ph.D., University of Connecticut, 1998).
2. At Holocaust conferences large and small, scholars regularly predict this increase, a danger they view as one of the greatest concerns for future teaching.
3. I credit this idea and my awareness of the importance and feasibility of integrating electronic sources into Holocaust study in German to my University of Tennessee colleague Professor Peter Höyng, who discussed with me in spring 1996 his plans to incorporate them into a unit on Holocaust poetry in one of his courses.

The University of Tennessee	Prof. Nancy A. Lauckner

DEUTSCH 622, DER HOLOCAUST UND DAS DRITTE REICH
IN DER DEUTSCHEN NACHKRIEGSLITERATUR

Woche 1
Einführung in das Seminar und zu den Texten
Gestapo: Learning Experience about the Holocaust

Woche 2
Vorlesung über den Antisemitismus, den Nationalsozialismus, und die wichtigsten Ereignisse des Dritten Reiches und des Holocausts
Max Frisch, *Andorra*

Woche 3
Andorra
Johannes Bobrowski, *Levins Mühle*

Woche 4
Levins Mühle
Bertolt Brecht, *Furcht und Elend des Dritten Reiches*

Woche 5
Furcht und Elend
Rolf Hochhuth, *Der Stellvertreter*

Woche 6
Der Stellvertreter
Der Stellvertreter

Woche 7
Heinrich Böll, *Billard um halb zehn*
Billard

Woche 8
Billard
Friedrich Dürrenmatt, *Der Verdacht*

Woche 9
Der Verdacht
Ruth Klüger, *weiter leben*

Woche 10
weiter leben
weiter leben

Woche 11
Simon Wiesenthal, *Die Sonnenblume* (nur die Erzählung)
Die Sonnenblume (die Kommentare)

Woche 12
Die Sonnenblume (die Kommentare)
Zusammenfassungen von Sichrovsky Interviews

Woche 13
Zusammenfassungen von Sichrovsky Interviews

Woche 14
Seminararbeiten
Seminararbeiten

Woche 15
Seminararbeiten

Lernziele des Seminars sind: (1) sich die notwendigen historischen und religiösen Kenntnisse anzueignen, um historische und religiöse Bezüge in literarischen Werken über die NS-Zeit verstehen zu können; (2) acht zentrale deutsche literarische Werke zu diesem Thema gemeinsam zu erarbeiten; (3) die ethische Problematik dieser tragischen Periode zu besprechen; (4) ein eigenes Thema zu erarbeiten, indem Sie ein neuntes literarisches Werk—für jeden Teilnehmer ein anderes—wählen, darüber eine Seminararbeit schreiben, und sie der Klasse vortragen.

Mündliche Teilnahme: Regelmäßige Teilnahme an den Diskussionen wird erwartet. Obwohl die Diskussion normalerweise auf deutsch geführt wird, wird bei der mündlichen Bewertung nicht Ihre Deutschfähigkeit, sondern Ihr inhaltlicher Beitrag berücksichtigt.

Mündliche Kurzreferate: Zu Beginn des Semesters wird eine Liste von achtundachtzig wichtigen Begriffen, Namen, Wörtern, usw. ausgeteilt. Zu jedem Stichwort, das Ihnen zugeteilt wird, müssen Sie kurz mündlich referieren. Am Anfang von jeder Stunde werden wir einige dieser Referate hören.

Seminararbeit: Jeder muß ein neuntes literarisches Werk lesen, das den Holocaust oder das Dritte Reich darstellt; ein im Werk behandeltes Thema wählen und erforschen; und eine Seminararbeit darüber schreiben und vortragen. Das Werk und Ihr Thema müssen Sie mit mir vereinbaren. Die von mir ausgeteilte Bibliographie enthält Vorschläge, aber auch andere Titel wären zu erwägen. Die doppelzeilig-getippten, fünfzehn bis zwanzig Seiten langen Arbeiten sind nach dem MLA-Stil anzufertigen.

Sofern Ihre Muttersprache nicht Deutsch ist, ist die Arbeit auf englisch zu schreiben.

Mündliche Zusammenfassung: Wenn uns genug Zeit bleibt, soll jeder eine Person aus den beiden Sichrovskybüchern wählen, und eine kurze mündliche Zusammenfassung von den zwei Interviews geben.

Sonderveranstaltungen: Ich hoffe, daß Sie folgende Sonderveranstaltungen besuchen werden. Obwohl Sie nicht dazu verpflichtet sind, erwarte ich Ihre aktive Unterstützung. Die Sonderveranstaltungen wären: (1) ein Gottesdienst am Sabbatvormittag in der Synagoge Heska Amuna; (2) einige Filme und Videos zum Thema Holocaust; (3) ein öffentlicher Vortrag von einer Professorin für Judaistik.

Benotung: Ihre Schlußnote für dieses Seminar wird folgendermaßen berechnet:

Mündliche Kurzreferate	10%
Zusammenfassung	10%
Mündliche Teilnahme	30%
Seminararbeit	50%

Wenn die Zusammenfassungen ausfallen, wird die mündliche Teilnahme 40% der Note ausmachen.

Works Cited

Print Sources

Becker, Jurek. *Der Boxer*. Frankfurt am Main: Suhrkamp, 1976.
———. *Bronsteins Kinder*. Frankfurt am Main: Suhrkamp, 1986.
———. *Jakob der Lügner*. 1969. Frankfurt am Main: Suhrkamp, 1978.
Bobrowski, Johannes. *Levins Mühle*. 1964. Frankfurt am Main: Fischer, 1991.
Böll, Heinrich. *Billard um halb zehn*. 1959. Munich: dtv, 1974.
Brecht, Bertolt. *Furcht und Elend des Dritten Reiches*. 1938. Berlin: Suhrkamp, 1975.
The Courage to Remember. Traveling exhibit of the Simon Wiesenthal Center. Los Angeles, CA. University of Tennessee, Knoxville. Spring 1994.
Dürrenmatt, Friedrich. *Der Verdacht*. 1953. Reinbek bei Hamburg: Rowohlt, 1991.
Frisch, Max. *Andorra. Stück in zwölf Bildern*. 1961. Frankfurt am Main: Suhrkamp, 1975.
Hilsenrath, Edgar. *Der Nazi und der Friseur*. Cologne: Literarischer Verlag Helmut Braun, 1977.
Hochhuth, Rolf. *Der Stellvertreter*. Reinbek bei Hamburg: Rowohlt, 1963.
Klüger, Ruth. *weiter leben. Eine Jugend*. Göttingen: Wallstein, 1992.
Schwaiger, Brigitte, and Eva Deutsch. *Die Galizianerin*. Vienna: P. Zsolnay, 1982.
Sichrovsky, Peter. *Schuldig geboren. Kinder aus Nazifamilien*. Cologne: Kiepenheuer & Witsch, 1987.
———. *Wir wissen nicht, was morgen wird. Wir wissen wohl, was gestern war*. Cologne: Kiepenheuer & Witsch, 1985.
Weiss, Peter. *Die Ermittlung. Oratorium in 11 Gesängen*. Frankfurt am Main: Suhrkamp, 1965.
Werfel, Franz. *Jakobowsky und der Oberst. Komödie einer Tragödie in drei Akten*. New York: F. S. Crofts & Co., 1945.
Wiesenthal, Simon. *Die Sonnenblume. Eine Erzählung mit Kommentaren*. 1969. Frankfurt am Main: Ullstein, 1990.
Zuckmayer, Carl. *Der Gesang im Feuerofen. Drama in drei Akten*. 1950. Frankfurt am Main: Fischer, 1956.
Zwerin, Rabbi Raymond A., Audrey Marcus, and Leonard Kramish. *Gestapo: Learning Experience about the Holocaust*. Educational materials. Denver: Alternatives in Religious Education, Inc., 1973.

Films/Videotapes

Schindler's List. Dir. Steven Spielberg. Video. Universal City Studios, Inc. and Amblin Entertainment, Inc., 1993.

The Wannsee Conference. Dir. Heinz Schirk. 1984. Video. Prism Entertainment, 1988.

Part II

Chapter 13

THE NAZI PERIOD, THE HOLOCAUST, AND GERMAN-JEWISH ISSUES AS INTEGRAL SUBJECTS IN A GERMAN LANGUAGE COURSE

Karin Doerr

Pedagogical Objectives

North American colleges and universities usually teach the Holocaust as a specialized and separate course rather than as part of the general curriculum of, for instance, history, sociology, or German literature and language. The Nazi period, the Holocaust, and German-Jewish issues should be integrated into German Studies programs because these subjects are part of German history and culture. Generally, our textbooks do not cover these historically important areas adequately and sometimes not at all. For this reason, throughout the semester I add supplementary course material to the basic course content, which is to enhance language skills and students' knowledge about German-speaking countries. I shall focus here on German Composition and Conversation, an intermediate, six-credit course taught over two semesters that is part of the German program of Concordia University in Montreal, Canada.

There are three main pedagogical objectives for including these historical, sociopolitical, and cultural issues in a regular German language and literature course. The first is to give students a more complete and more accurate picture of Germany and its past than is available from their textbooks. The second is to keep students informed about current events in

---

Notes for this section can be found on page 196.

Germany and the other German-speaking countries. The third and most far-reaching objective is to sensitize students to prejudice and discrimination against minorities and to demonstrate the pernicious effects of such attitudes and behavior. I use examples from Germany's Nazi period to alert students to signs of both particular and general political developments that may signal threats to civic rights or democratic processes.

Methodology and Content

In order to achieve these goals, one can adopt different pedagogical approaches in beginners' and in advanced German courses. For example, for the German Composition and Conversation course, I included texts relevant to German-Jewish issues during the course of the semester. There were biographical sketches, such as the ones contained in the *Kulturchronik*, published in Bonn by Inter Nationes. I also added short prose literature by Franz Kafka; poetry by Paul Celan, Heinrich Heine, or Gertrud Kolmar; as well as texts with historical and cultural information, particularly with reference to events that occurred during the Nazi period.

With regard to biographical materials on Holocaust survival, I found that one particular life story as the focal point was easier for students to assimilate and relate to than statistics enumerating the murder of anonymous millions. For example, students interested in the lives of women could concentrate on the biographies and works of the poet Gertrud Kolmar and the painter Charlotte Salomon. Of the eight essay topics in the two-semester course, I assigned one on the Third Reich. This motivated students to undertake research in this broad subject area on an aspect of their choice. In a previous college course, I linked such projects to university events, such as a Holocaust symposium, a Remembrance week, a genocide conference, and displays on the Holocaust. I included written and visual course projects in *Polyglot*, an annual Modern Languages publication for college students.

As another means of enhancing German Composition and Conversation, I distributed articles from newspapers and other publications about current events in Germany, Austria, and Switzerland. Each professor will have different sources available from which to select articles. The following provided me with useful texts for my class: *Deutschland: Zeitschrift für Politik, Kulturchronik, Wirtschaft und Wissenschaft, Der Spiegel, Die Zeit, Canadian Jewish News*, the *New York Times*, and the *New York Times Book Review*. In addition, I relied on local papers, various German newspapers and magazines, and Internet information, some brought to class by students who surfed the Net. I encouraged students to look for printed material of their choice and bring it to class for distribution. Due to the fact that such information becomes obsolete very fast, I do not provide specific bibliographical references here.

Throughout the semester, I circulated these texts among the students. The topics derived from many areas, including German culture, history, politics, economics, entertainment, sports, and tourism. The sources and texts varied from reports, interviews, book reviews, film synopses, and critiques, to Internet information. I started with city portraits of Berlin, Hamburg, Frankfurt, Jena, Vienna, Zurich, and the like. Then I moved to general information on culture and education, followed by current affairs topics often covering the contemporary issues of German unification; neo-Nazi violence; repatriation of *Auslandsdeutsche*, Germans from Eastern Europe and the former Soviet republics; the German language reform; and the Daniel Goldhagen debate. The North American papers contained a great deal of information on films concerning Germany's Nazi past, such as the German film *The Nasty Girl*, *Schindler's List*, the docudrama *The Wannsee Conference*, a report on the filmmaker Leni Riefenstahl, the 1995 award-winning documentary *Anne Frank Remembered*, and more. Topics related to Germany's past also appeared in book reviews and interviews. The latter were often conducted with Holocaust survivors or German youth reflecting on or discussing the Hitler period.

These additional texts were in English, French (to accommodate our French-Canadian students), or German, depending on the source, and students could choose one of these languages in which to write a short response to the material. With this particular pedagogical objective, the purpose of these language options was to facilitate the acquisition of knowledge, rather than to increase language proficiency. Each person attached his or her written comments to the articles and then passed them on to fellow students. This established a written discourse that continued during the semester and often provided a basis for discussion. Some students wished to talk outside class about a particular issue that interested or concerned them, and sometimes they asked for more information or additional sources on a specific subject. In each of the four tests, I included questions on the reading material that had been circulated.

The articles revealed to the students the concerns of contemporary Germans and provided a composite picture of today's Germany. Students often expressed surprise that Germany's National Socialist past surfaced frequently and in varying forms in the current debate about the country. It showed them that Germans, after fifty years, still have to deal with that part of their history on an individual as well as an official level. Students became aware of Germany's ongoing process of *Vergangenheitsbewältigung* and the problems this may entail for both Germany's government and its citizens, particularly for the younger generation. The English-language articles from the North American press often contained catchy titles with the word "Nazis" and graphics of large swastikas in order to draw the readers' attention. Students noted that such language and illustrations were absent from the German publications. This led to a revealing class discussion about what expressions and attitudes regarding the Nazi period the law prohibited in Germany.

In addition to this specific material, I invited a guest speaker to introduce a particular subject. Gary Evans, film expert and professor of European history now teaching at the University of Ottawa, presented an excellent lecture including excerpts from the German docudrama *The Wannsee Conference* in January 1997, fifty-five years after the actual event occurred in Berlin on 20 January 1942.[1]

In order to focus further on topics that our textbook and the additional reading material did not adequately cover, I prepared several lectures that deal with political and social developments in Germany that eventually led to the Holocaust. These lectures, which also examine the historical context for antisemitism in culture and literature, are in English for beginners and in German for advanced students. I usually supplement them with handouts, visual material, and transparencies. I treat Nazi propaganda material that contains antisemitic images with caution and thorough explication and sometimes present it only by means of transparencies in order to avoid disseminating it in print.

One handout, in German with English translations, is a timeline containing some of the laws that Nazi Germany passed. Students generally find the Gesetz zum Schutze des deutschen Blutes und der deutschen Ehre (Law for the Protection of German Blood and Honor) both ridiculous and incredible as it deals with the very personal subjects of marriage and sexual relations. After discussion and further explanations, their amusement ceases as they realize the severe impact and consequences these racist laws had on Germany as a whole and on those classified as Jewish.

One of my lectures treats the *Kristallnacht* pogrom of 9 to 10 November 1938 in Germany and Austria from a sociohistorical perspective. Because the days under discussion almost coincide with 11 November, Remembrance Day in Canada, which memorializes fallen Canadian soldiers from all wars, I explain to the students that Germany does not observe 11 November, as to do so would recall its military surrender in 1918 and the subsequent harsh Treaty of Versailles. Students thus become aware of differing perspectives on the same events. The lecture, which uses an interactive teaching method, then covers developments from Hitler's rise to power in 1933 until *Kristallnacht*.

Prior to this lecture, students had learned about another German event that took place on 9 November—the dismantling of the Berlin Wall in 1989. We discussed the issues of German unification, its political and economic meaning, and Germans' joy in celebrating this happy occasion. Because teaching this contemporary development responsibly required tracing the facts that lay behind it, the discussion of unification served as the bridge to the *Kristallnacht* lecture. Thus the students became aware of the importance and irony of these dates in German history.

Conclusion

Since the course taught German composition and conversation, I had to make sure that the content was balanced. By integrating additional material throughout the semester and highlighting certain historical events at the appropriate points, I left much time for the textbook itself. Students could practice conversation and the writing of compositions on aspects of their life, their concerns, and their world. Course evaluations and individual feedback have shown that students liked receiving information that went beyond their textbook. They stated that their new awareness and insights were often useful in their other courses as well as outside the university.

With regard to the Holocaust and the Nazi period, they admitted that they had had a great deal of muddled information before taking the course. This demonstrated the general absence of accurate historical knowledge among today's students. Afterwards, many issues, particularly sociohistorical facts, had become much clearer for them. As mentioned above, besides providing factual information, I alert students to this critical period in recent German history in order to expose them to the dangers of the erosion of democratic processes in general. Early signs of a government's antidemocratic behavior, such as scapegoating a minority group and passing exclusionary laws, may signal to students the need for individuals to take action as responsible citizens in society.[2]

I have been teaching German in this fashion for a few years with good results and positive student feedback. However, in 1997 one of the thirty students in my class took issue with the Holocaust content, which was only a minor component in a six-credit course, because he felt it did not belong in a German class. He launched an official complaint that went from the chair of Modern Languages, to the students' ombudsperson, to the dean, and finally to the president of the university. The student demanded that I be silenced on anything relating to Germany's Nazi past. When his classmates learned of this protest, they disassociated themselves from it and sustained my pedagogical approach.

My professional integrity and academic freedom were defended at each level of university complaint, among other reasons perhaps because the student had manifested an ill-disguised antisemitism in his report. I mention this case only to illustrate that not all of our students may necessarily agree with our well-intentioned endeavors. This incident and the somewhat reactionary attitude that some students bring to German studies also demonstrated to me how German and Germans can be perceived abroad. This particular student, for example, regarded Germans as "pure" and their language as that found in German classical literature. For him, I had destroyed this perfect image.

It is not new that some students harbor the stereotypical view that Germans are successful and hardworking. Others like to focus on the notion of Germany as a powerful world nation with economic success. They believe the country should look to the future, especially after unification, and forget about its ugly past. Although we want our students to feel comfortable in our courses, professors of German should teach their subject in an open and honest manner and with the integrity that it deserves. Sometimes this means dealing with issues that are serious, unpleasant, and often contrary to what students might expect in a German course.

Notes

1. Professor Evans gave a version of this lecture at a pedagogically oriented conference at the University of South Florida in March 1997. He also provided historical source material, references, and guidance, which were an invaluable contribution to my work and course.
2. Montreal poet Sharon H. Nelson used my lecture model, in a 1997 essay, to draw parallels to present-day political developments regarding the desire for independence of the French-Canadian provincial government of Quebec. Unfortunately, she did not emphasize adequately the fact that Quebec within Canada is a democracy.

Concordia University Prof. Karin Doerr

GERM 270A/3, GERMAN COMPOSITION AND CONVERSATION
(ABBREVIATED COURSE OUTLINE)

Books

1) *Weiter! Lesen, Reden und Schreiben* (1994), Textbook and Workbook
2) A German grammar of choice or *Hammer's German Grammar and Usage*
3) Bilingual dictionary and *501 German Verbs*

Other Materials

Handouts, articles

Course Description

This course emphasizes the usage of the essential German grammar and idioms in written and spoken German and includes cultural, geographical, and historical information.

Methodology and Content

- Writing of descriptive and creative compositions
- Directed grammar exercises in the workbook, oral projects
- Conversations, discussions, dialogues, oral presentations
- General class exercises, group and/or team work
- Practice of grammar, vocabulary, pronunciation, and reading
- Listening to audio material in class and viewing videos
- Written and oral testing, final exam
- Reading of and commenting on current affairs newspaper articles in English or French, and German
- Historical, geographical, and cultural information

Sessions Will Cover the Following Topics:

Personal information, family, school and university, hobbies, sports, interests, friends, letter writing, work and professions, city life, food, customs and culture, traveling, geography, history, art and music, German film, authors and poets.

Course Objectives

Students will increase their general knowledge of German; be able to converse in an everyday situation; be able to read and understand information in German; be able to write compositions, letters, and descriptions; do simple translations into English or French; glean sociocultural information on German-speaking countries; be able to express opinions on general issues; be able to give information about themselves; interact in German in various specific situations; know facts of German twentieth-century history.

Evaluation

Final exam	40%
Two tests per semester	20%
Written assignments	
Compositions	10%
Exercises	5%
Oral performance	
Presentations	10%
Class work	5%
Participation/attendance	10%

Special Sessions and Assignments

Semester I: In November, a special lecture on *Kristallnacht* with information on the Nazi era

Semester II: In January, a guest lecture and film excerpts on the Wannsee Conference with information on the Holocaust

One composition topic will be on the Third Reich, and tests will include questions on relevant historical facts of both lectures, as well as on the special handouts and reading material.

Works Cited

Print Sources

Celan, Paul. "Todesfuge." 1952. *Modern Austrian Writing*. Ed. Caroline Markolin. New York: Lang, 1995. 164–65.

Evans, Gary. "The Wannsee Conference: A Turning Point towards the Final Solution." Annual Scholars' Conference on the Holocaust and the Churches. Hearing the Voices: Teaching the Holocaust to Future Generations. University of South Florida, Tampa. 3 March 1997.

Felstiner, Mary Lowenthal. *To Paint Her Life: Charlotte Salomon in the Nazi Era*. New York: Harper Collins, 1994.

Heine, Heinrich. *Lyric Poems and Ballads, English and German*. Trans. Ernst Feise. Pittsburgh: University of Pittsburgh Press, 1961.

Kafka, Franz. "Der Nachbar." *Weiter! Lesen, Reden und Schreiben*. By Isabelle Salaün. New York: Wiley, 1994. 61–63.

Kolmar, Gertrud. *Dark Soliloquy: The Selected Poems of Gertrud Kolmar, English and German*. Trans. Henry A. Smith. New York: Seabury, 1975.

Nelson, Sharon H. "Moving?" *Other Voices* 10.1 (June 1997): 30–45.

Salomon, Charlotte. *Charlotte, Life or Theater? An Autobiographical Play by Charlotte Salomon*. Trans. Leila Vennewitz. New York: Viking, 1981.

"What Did Leni Riefenstahl's Lens See?" *New York Times* 13 March 1994: 15+.

Woltmann, Johanna. *Gertrud Kolmar. Leben und Werk*. Göttingen: Wallstein, 1995.

Films/Videotapes

Anne Frank Remembered. Dir. Jon Blair. Video. Norstar Entertainment, 1995.

The Nasty Girl. Dir. Michael Verhoeven. Video. Sentana, 1989.

Schindler's List. Writ. Thomas Keneally. Dir. Steven Spielberg. Video. MCA Universal Home Video, 1993.

The Wannsee Conference. Dir. Heinz Schirk. 1984. Video. Prism Entertainment, 1988.

Chapter 14

THE HOLOCAUST IN AN INTRODUCTORY GERMAN LITERATURE COURSE
Problematic Responses as a Catalyst for Curricular Change

Miriam Jokiniemi

At the conclusion of his essay "Der Blick auf den Ettersberg. Der Holocaust und die Germanistik," Hans Eichner writes, "Ob wir es wissen oder nicht—wir stehen als Germanisten im Schatten des Ettersbergs ..." (216). My experiences teaching German at York University in Toronto confirm the accuracy of this observation. In the mid to late 1980s especially, the long shadow cast by the Ettersberg, where Buchenwald was located, deepened alarmingly in my classes. These experiences became the catalyst for my reevaluation of how to teach National Socialism and the Holocaust in the undergraduate German curriculum. In this essay I shall describe two of the situations that occasioned my curricular revision and then discuss one of the results: the Holocaust unit that I now teach in German 2200, our introductory literature course.

In winter 1985 I taught Paul Celan's poem "Todesfuge" in that course, as I had many times before without incident, but in this class a group of German-Canadian students claimed that the poem gave an unduly negative portrayal of Germans, encouraging readers to sympathize only with the Jewish victims of the death camps. Later in the day, I found under my office door a letter, which read in part:

Notes for this section can be found on page 207.

Today we discussed "Todesfuge," ... which dealt with the sufferings of Jewish people. "Todesfuge" ... discriminated against the Germans. If we feel sorry for those who suffer, we must not forget all aspects of their nature which come up. I am not saying that what the Nazis did was right, but who ever cuts up the Russians, who treated their prisoners far worse? Hitler did build Germany's economic state before the trouble started. ... War is awful, but why should we dwell on it afterwards, if we can concentrate on building a better society for ourselves?

While I was shocked by such a response, I was not too surprised, for such opinions had a specific context. Between 1985 and 1988, one of Canada's best-known propagators of Holocaust denial theories was on trial in Toronto for "'Verbreitung falscher Nachrichten'" (court decision qtd. in Roche and Webber 335). The situation was the subject of heated debate in the pages of German-Canadian newspapers, and one side of this debate expressed opinions strikingly similar to those of the students in my class.

While teaching the National Socialist period in a third-year literature course after the fall of the Berlin Wall, I found that student reluctance to deal with this topic had increased. When we discussed Richard von Weizsäcker's 1985 speech to the Bundestag, in which he speaks of the crimes of the Hitler regime against the Jews, some German-Canadian students pointed out that their families had also suffered in the war. They expressed *their* feelings of victimization: "We're called Nazis or Krauts," and "We had a big swastika painted on our cottage door" were typical responses. Moreover, when we discussed the 1986 *Historikerstreit,* many students sympathized with the revisionists. Echoing the student response of 1985 and intensified by the prospect of a united Germany, the general feeling in this class was that we should look to the future rather than dwell on the past.

Experiences such as these became the catalyst for my reevaluation of how to teach National Socialism and the Holocaust. I had to find a way of keeping this period an integral part of the German curriculum, while counteracting student resistance to an emotionally charged and disturbing topic. In the early 1990s, the Faculty of Arts of York University encouraged instructors to foreground issues of multiculturalism and diversity in courses wherever possible. Thus, in 1993, I redesigned German 2200 around the twin themes of diversity and universality. Under the theme of diversity, the course explores issues of age, gender, and alterity and Otherness in German literature, including a four-week unit on the Holocaust, focusing on "Europe's ultimate other: the Jew" (Gilman and Katz 1).

The section on alterity and Otherness begins with selections from the anthology *In zwei Sprachen leben. Berichte, Erzählungen, Gedichte von Ausländern.* These texts are written from the perspective of the marginalized or persecuted ethnic Other in contemporary German society, and we concentrate on the problems of this we-they split. Thus, students are already familiar with issues such as discrimination, prejudice, scapegoating, xenophobia and antiforeigner violence before we begin the unit on the Holocaust. In contextualizing the stories and poems from *In zwei Sprachen leben*, we also discuss the political reality of postunification Germany, in which right-wing, neo-Nazi violence has escalated and has included attacks both on minorities perceived as foreign (e.g., the murders in Mölln, 1992; and Solingen, 1993), and on Jewish institutions like synagogues and cemeteries (e.g., Lübeck and Magdeburg, 1994).

Placing a unit on the Holocaust under the theme of alterity and Otherness allows me to emphasize the continuing relevance of the legacy of Nazism and to make connections between past attitudes and present problems. And since most students find Otherness relevant to their own experience,[1] approaching the fate of the Jews in the Third Reich from this point of view motivates students and generates more light than heat on this potentially problematic topic.

The Holocaust unit of German 2200 consists of two stories, a documentary film, a poem, and scenes from a dramatized autobiography, all focusing on the image of the Jew as Other in the Third Reich. The unit emphasizes the interpretation and contextualization of two short stories: Franz Fühmann's "Das Judenauto," which vividly illustrates the nature and corrosive power of antisemitic prejudice in Germany in the 1930s, and Sigrid Wachenfeld's "Meine Geigenstunden," which poignantly exemplifies the fate of one victim of the Nazi assault on the Jews. Since these stories in particular have proven to be a productive learning experience for my students, in this essay I shall concentrate on describing how I approach these two texts in class.

Students quickly notice that, in contrast to the texts we read from *In zwei Sprachen leben*, the Other is not physically present in "Das Judenauto" and does not have a voice. Nonetheless, the story centers on the alleged nefarious influence and destructive power of this absent Other. Thus "Das Judenauto" well illustrates Gilman and Katz's assertion that "anti-Semitism may be able to exist virtually without Jews immediately present within a society in stress ..." (18).

The image of the Jew in "Das Judenauto" has two narrative sources: the grisly tale of an overwrought schoolgirl and the antisemitic propaganda disseminated by adults. Since I use the story to introduce the leitmotif as a literary device, I ask students to focus first on the yellow car of Gudrun's tale from which the story derives its title. Four "schwarze mörderische Juden" (10) carrying long knives allegedly use this car to hunt German girls in order to use their blood to bake bread for Jewish feast days. My students invariably meet this tale of ritual murder and blood sacrifice with disbelief, seeing it as merely the hysterical fabrication of an attention-seeking class gossip. However, when I ask why the young boy who is the narrator and central character in "Das Judenauto" accepts this bloodthirsty tale without question, they realize that it is not only because he is young and impressionable, but because Gudrun's tale corroborates his social conditioning. We discuss the significance of the historical context of the story: the year is 1931, a worldwide depression has brought extreme economic hardship to Germany, and the narrator's father is among the small businessmen threatened with ruin. Working in small groups, students list all the information about the Jews that the young narrator, who admits to never having seen a Jew himself, has gleaned from adults. A summary of their findings reads like a compendium of the antisemitic propaganda of the times: Jews are the archenemies of the Germans, whom they are plotting to destroy. As dark and crooked in appearance as the deeds they perpetrate, they swindle people out of their savings and destroy crops and cattle, so as to starve the Germans to death. Jews are also to blame for the Great Depression, the ruin of German businesses, and virtually every other ill afflicting Germany. "[Sie] waren schuld an allem Schlechten in der Welt,"[2] states the narrator (11).

In this social climate, where the Jew is the scapegoated, demonized, and feared Other, the young narrator becomes the victim of his own overactive imagination about the four murderous Jews of Gudrun's tale. Exposed to public humiliation and ridicule, he then acts in the spirit of his social conditioning and blames not himself but the (nonexistent) Jews for his predicament, seeing it as one more example of their devious machinations. The story ends with his screaming tirade of antisemitic hatred.

In my experience, "Das Judenauto" is very well received by students. However, initially, many were quite skeptical about most of the charges against the Jews in the story. "No sane person of the twentieth century could believe such things" was a typical response. Thus, in recent years, I have incorporated "From the Cross to the Swastika," Part One of the documentary film *The Longest Hatred: The History of Anti-Semitism*, into our examination of the Jew as Other. "From the Cross to the Swastika" illuminates the origins of Nazi hostility to the Jews in both Christian anti-Judaism and nineteenth-century racial antisemitism. It explains the myth of the murder of Christian children by Jews and features in one segment an Austrian church, where the remains of a child allegedly killed by Jews are still venerated. This documentary also makes the long history of many of the negative stereotypes of Jews clear, for instance, the images of the

Jew as demon or devil, as financier and usurer, as parasitic exploiter, and as anti-German conspirator, plotting worldwide Jewish domination. Student response to "From the Cross to the Swastika" has been consistently positive. After one screening, a student spontaneously exclaimed: "The propaganda in 'Das Judenauto' was the opposite of the truth: Jews were not the hunters, but the hunted!"

The written assignment on this documentary consists of two parts. During the film screening, students fill in a handout and briefly explain the significance of some key figures and events in the history of antisemitism (e.g., Pope Innocent III, the Spanish Inquisition, Martin Luther, and Wilhelm Marr). As a homework assignment, they answer two prompts: (1) In what way did this documentary help you to understand "Das Judenauto" better? and (2) Name and explain at least three aspects of antisemitism found in both the story and the film.

After a brief discussion of Brecht's satirical poem "Der Jude, ein Unglück für das Volk," which brilliantly exposes the scapegoating of Jews in Hitler's regime to ridicule and unmasks the true cause of the socioeconomic ills of the time—the regime itself—we move on to Sigrid Wachenfeld's short story "Meine Geigenstunden." This story shares the narrative point of view of "Das Judenauto"—that of a nine-year-old child. The fate of the narrator's Jewish violin teacher, Herr Pedczi, is central to the story. Students discuss the relationship between the narrator and her teacher, concentrating on the portrayal of the latter. They discover that although Herr Pedczi is doubly Other, both Jewish and Hungarian, in this story he is not stigmatized in any way. The young narrator's ignorance of antisemitic prejudice allows her to see Herr Pedczi as a kindly, cultured father figure, even after he has become *persona non grata*. Students also experience how the child's naive perspective heightens the senselessness and inhumanity of Herr Pedczi's fate. When he is dismissed as concertmaster of the Düsseldorf Symphony, for example, his student reflects: "Herr Pedczi, der erste Geiger, war entlassen worden.—Er war Jude. Jude. Was war das? Jemand, der sich am Morgen nicht die Zähne putzte? Jemand, der etwa gelogen hatte? Oder gar ein Dieb?" (136).[3]

However, although the narrator and her parents focus on Herr Pedczi's essential humanity rather than his roots, in the Nazi state these values are reversed. As the despised Other, Herr Pedczi becomes the victim of an unprovoked brutal street beating. While my students have usually heard of the persecution of the Jews under Hitler and of the "Final Solution," they have little conception of the extent and gradual escalation of Hitler's anti-Jewish legislation. Thus I use Herr Pedczi's fate to show that in Hitler's Germany the persecution of the Jews was far more than just a problem of individual behavior. Students come to realize that the assault on the Jews was state policy, embodied in government laws and decrees, which systematically stripped Jews of their human dignity, their civil rights, their property, and, ultimately, their lives. I distribute a handout with the dates of laws and key events from January 1933 to May 1945, based on the timelines compiled by Rado Pribic (xiv–xvii) and Hans Peter Richter (121–23). With the help of this handout, students follow the fate of Herr Pedczi: after he is dismissed from his post with the symphony and forbidden to give private lessons to Aryan students, his apartment is ransacked, his property confiscated, and he is finally deported. A notice at the door of his former home then proclaims: "Unser Haus ist judenfrei" (137).[4]

Compared to the fate of the Other in texts from *In zwei Sprachen leben*, Herr Pedczi's fate stands out in sharp relief. "Meine Geigenstunden" shows that in Nazi Germany the persecution of the Jew as Other went far beyond marginalization, victimization, and verbal and physical abuse. Antisemitism was legitimate government policy. Indeed, as I remind my students, Hitler's goal was the annihilation of the Jewish people. Elie Wiesel emphasizes the significance of this in a 1984 interview with Stephen Lewis: "Only the Jewish people were designated for total murder. Only the Jew was guilty simply because he was a Jew. ... [F]or the first time in history, 'being' became a crime. And that was true only for the Jew and the Jewish victim, and nobody else" ("Elie Wiesel" 156–57).

The homework assignment on "Meine Geigenstunden" focuses on the narrator's last lesson with Herr Pedczi. He plays the Air in G from Bach's Orchestral Suite in D Major and concludes with the words "Hör gut zu, das hier—diese Klänge, das ist Deutschland" (136).[5] I play a tape of Bach's famous Air in class and have students write an interpretation of the significance of Herr Pedczi's words. The consensus is that it is both poignant and ironic that a victim of Nazi barbarism is the story's main exponent of Germany's humanistic legacy, as exemplified in the music of Bach. Since many students interpret Herr Pedczi's last words as an indication of his faith in the ultimate triumph of the "other" or "good" Germany, we then consider Anna Seghers's question posed at a *Schriftstellertreffen* in Weimar in 1965: "'Wie war dieser Riß möglich geworden, den Sie vor sich hier sehen: Weimar und Buchenwald?'" (qtd. in Cohen 192).[6]

I seek to emphasize analogies between the two stories in the Holocaust unit of German 2200 and the texts we read earlier in the section on alterity and Otherness. For example, the word "judenfrei," with which the story "Meine Geigenstunden" ends, reminds students of the word "[a]usländerfrei." In 1991, the latter won the "Un-Word" of the year award because it most strikingly demonstrated "inhumane language usage" ("'Un-Word' of 1991: 'Foreigner-free'" 7). The parallelism of the terms "judenfrei" and "[a]usländerfrei," separated by some sixty years of German history, heightens student awareness of the way in which the past continues to cast its shadow on the present. Such connections also help students to understand why the alarming rise in right-wing, neo-Nazi activities all over the world is especially disturbing in the German context, despite candlelight parades and other public demonstrations of solidarity with the victims.

The Holocaust unit of German 2200 concludes with excerpts from *Ab heute heißt du Sara. 33 Bilder aus dem Leben einer Berlinerin*. This is the GRIPS Theater Berlin's dramatization of *Ich trug den gelben Stern*, Inge Deutschkron's autobiographical account of how she survived the years 1933 to 1945 in the German capital. Furthermore, the audiocassette with the songs from *Ab heute heißt du Sara* is a very useful teaching aid. I have found that songs such as Scene 14's "Seht her, seht ruhig her," which expresses Inge's fear and humiliation on 2 September 1941, when she wears the obligatory yellow Star of David in public for the first time, lend themselves most effectively to classroom use.

Concerning the relevance of the Holocaust in contemporary Germany, Frank Stern has written: "[T]his past ... is not simply an inconvenient shadow Germans can shake off and leave behind. [It] is an ideological and social reality. ... Every struggle for the opening of a new museum dealing with national German history or the history of the Jews, every debate and dispute over the reconstruction of a former synagogue confronts the public anew with this disturbing reality" (84). Once they have been sensitized to issues raised by National Socialism and the Holocaust, students readily find parallels in the Canadian context. The news story about the problems associated with the property chosen for Canada's new embassy in Berlin is but one example. Leipziger Platz 17, where the new Canadian embassy is to be built, once housed the wartime office of Nazi Germany's propaganda minister, Joseph Goebbels. "[B]efore that, it belonged to the prominent Jewish-owned Wertheim department-store chain. ... [T]he Wertheim business was 'Aryanized' and the Nazi Party got its hands on the property. ... That story has only now been uncovered by a Berlin historian and promises to be the subject of investigation and controversy for years" (Freeman A1).

The Ettersberg, capped today by the Buchenwald memorial site honoring the victims of National Socialism, will continue to cast its shadow on our work as Germanists and to challenge us in our classrooms. The next time I teach German 2200, I plan to incorporate *Gegen das Vergessen*, a new CD-ROM with over five hundred archival photographs and a wealth of film, audio, and text documentation on the Holocaust. In its current form, the Holocaust unit of German 2200 is an attempt to illuminate some of the issues central to that darkest period of German history of which Buchenwald is emblematic. Focusing on the image of the Jew as Other in the Third Reich, it emphasizes the enormity and uniqueness of the Nazi assault on the Jews, as well as the continuing relevance of that past to the present.

Notes

1. Toronto is the most ethnically diverse city in the world; more than one hundred languages are spoken here. The city's immigrant communities make up forty-eight percent of its population, and this figure is expected to rise in the near future (Carey A1). The student body at York University reflects Toronto's ethnocultural diversity.
2. "[They] were to blame for everything bad in the world" (Fühmann, in Hörnigk and Stephan 219).
3. "Herr Pedczi, the first violinist, had been dismissed. He was a Jew. A Jew. What was that? Someone who didn't brush his teeth in the morning? Someone who had perhaps told a lie? Or was perhaps even a thief?" [Unless otherwise indicated, all translations in these notes are by Miriam Jokiniemi.]
4. "Our house is free of Jews."
5. "Listen carefully; these sounds are Germany."
6. "'How was this caesura which you see here before you possible: Weimar and Buchenwald?'"

York University   **Prof. Miriam Jokiniemi**

GERMAN 2200.06, READING GERMAN LITERATURE: AN INTRODUCTION

This is a required course for German majors and minors, as well as for German Studies majors. There are two seventy-five-minute meetings per week, and the format combines lectures and discussions.

Grading for the entire course:

Three papers	35%
Class participation	15%
Short tests	25%
Final examination	25%

    Holocaust Unit: The Jew as Other (Abbreviated Syllabus)

Week 1

Franz Fühmann: "Das Judenauto"

Week 2

The Longest Hatred, Part One: "From the Cross to the Swastika" (Video)
Bertolt Brecht: "Der Jude, ein Unglück für das Volk"

Week 3

Sigrid Wachenfeld: "Meine Geigenstunden"

Week 4

Ab heute heißt du Sara (Textbook and audiocassette: excerpts)
Summary

Works Cited

Print Sources

Ackermann, Irmgard, ed. *In zwei Sprachen leben. Berichte, Erzählungen, Gedichte von Ausländern.* 1983. 3rd. ed. Munich: dtv, 1992.

Brecht, Bertolt. "Der Jude, ein Unglück für das Volk." 1939. *Gesammelte Werke.* Vol. 9. Ed. Elisabeth Hauptmann with Rosemarie Hill. Frankfurt am Main: Suhrkamp, 1967. 713–14.

Carey, Elaine. "Minorities set to be majority." *Sunday Star* [Toronto] 7 June 1998, metro ed.: A1+.

Celan, Paul. "Todesfuge." 1952. *Ausgewählte Gedichte.* Frankfurt am Main: Suhrkamp, 1970. 22–24.

Cohen, Robert. "Die befohlene Aufgabe machen: Anna Seghers' Erzählung 'Der Ausflug der toten Mädchen.'" *Monatshefte* 79 (1987): 186–98.

Deutschkron, Inge. *Ich trug den gelben Stern.* 1978. Munich: dtv, 1990.

Eichner, Hans. "Der Blick auf den Ettersberg. Der Holocaust und die Germanistik." *Modernisierung oder Überfremdung? Zur Wirkung deutscher Exilanten in der Germanistik der Aufnahmeländer.* Ed. Walter Schmitz. Stuttgart: Metzler, 1994. 199–216.

"Elie Wiesel." *Art out of Agony: The Holocaust Theme in Literature, Sculpture and Film.* Stephen Lewis in conversation. Based on programs from the CBC radio series Stereo Morning, 30 May–3 June 1983. Toronto: CBC Enterprises, 1984. 151–69.

Freeman, Alan. "Past haunts Canada's embassy site in Berlin." *Globe and Mail* [Toronto] 26 December 1997: A1+.

Fühmann, Franz. "The Jew Car." Trans. Jan van Heurck. *The New Sufferings of Young W. and Other Stories from the German Democratic Republic.* Ed. Therese Hörnigk and Alexander Stephan. The German Library 87. Gen. ed. Volkmar Sander. New York: Continuum, 1997. 216–24.

———. "Das Judenauto." 1962. *Das Judenauto. Vierzehn Tage aus zwei Jahrzehnten.* Zurich: Diogenes, 1968. 7–18.

Gilman, Sander L., and Steven T. Katz, eds. Introduction. *Anti-Semitism in Times of Crisis.* New York: New York University Press, 1991. 1–19.

Ludwig, Volker, and Detlef Michel. *Ab heute heißt du Sara. 33 Bilder aus dem Leben einer Berlinerin.* Textbook. Berlin: GRIPS Theater, 1989.

Pribic, Rado. "Fifty-Five Years after 'Reichskristallnacht.'" *The German Public and the Persecution of the Jews, 1933–1945: "No One Participated, No One Knew."* Ed. Jörg Wallenberg. English edition translated and edited by Rado Pribic. Atlantic Highlands, NJ: Humanities Press International, 1996. xi–xviii.

Richter, Hans Peter. "Zeittafel." *Damals war es Friedrich*. Munich: dtv, 1980. 121–23.

Roche, Jörg Matthias, and Mark Joel Webber. "Themenbereich V. Zur Aktualität der Vergangenheit." *Für- und Wider-Sprüche. Ein integriertes Text-Buch für Colleges und Universitäten*. New Haven: Yale University Press, 1995. 288–360.

Stern, Frank. "German-Jewish Relations in the Postwar Period: The Ambiguities of Antisemitic and Philosemitic Discourse." *Jews, Germans, Memory: Reconstructions of Jewish Life in Germany*. Ed. Y. Michal Bodemann. Ann Arbor: University of Michigan Press, 1996. 77–98.

"'Un-Word' of 1991: 'Foreigner-free.'" *The Week in Germany* [German Information Center, New York] 14 February 1992: 7.

Wachenfeld, Sigrid. "Meine Geigenstunden." 1982. *Tee und Butterkekse. Prosa von Frauen*. Ed. Ingeborg and Rodja Weigand. Munich: Schwiftinger, 1982. 133–37.

Audio/Visual Sources

Ab heute heißt du Sara. Audiocassette. GRIPS Theater Berlin, 1989.

Gegen das Vergessen. [Eine Dokumentation des Holocaust]. Scholarly advisor: Erika Weinzierl, Institut für Zeitgeschichte der Universität Wien. CD-ROM. Navigo Multimedia, 1997.

The Longest Hatred: The History of Anti-Semitism. Dir. Rex Bloomstein. Nucleus for Thames TV and WGBH. 1991. PBS. 21 April 1993. Video. WGBH-Boston Video, 1993.

Chapter 15

BEYOND CULTURAL LITERACY
"Interactive Autobiography" as Holocaust Pedagogy

William Collins Donahue

In order to clarify the need for Holocaust pedagogy, we often point to widespread ignorance of the subject. And while this ignorance is undeniable, as Tom W. Smith's study clearly shows,[1] there may be other factors, particularly in the undergraduate German program, that merit our attention. First, the focus on knowledge gaps may lead us, however inadvertently, to conceive of our students statically, as mere empty vessels to be filled with various doses of historical data, without considering those factors that determine how—and whether—these students will digest this information. Second, the knowledge deficit model can easily become a "dodge": pedagogues can forever debate, for example, whether *their* students belong to that minority capable of supplying what Smith terms "fully correct answers" about the Holocaust (3).[2] In this essay, I suggest that we take a more dynamic approach by conceiving of our students not merely as people who lack knowledge, but as learners whose attitudes, emotions, prejudices, and intellectual curiosity will play crucial roles in learning outcomes. There can be little doubt that, when it comes to teaching the Holocaust within the collegiate German program, the notorious "affective filter" can become the decisive factor in the success or failure of the effort. Therefore, paying close attention to what students know, think they know, want to know, and even to what they don't want to know will be an essential ingredient in any successful Holocaust pedagogy. The unit I describe below,

---

Notes for this section begin on page 219.

while providing basic structure and content, is fundamentally student-propelled. The flexibility I claim for this strategy addresses not only the variety of needs within any one classroom, but also the wide array of postsecondary institutions included under the rubric "college level." Given this diversity, would it not seem presumptuous to espouse a rigidly content-based curriculum designed to meet the needs of *all* these institutions?

In constructing this unit, I have been guided by the following principles:

(1) While there remains a need for specialty courses on the Holocaust, it is also desirable to integrate the teaching of the Holocaust into larger courses on twentieth-century German literature and culture. In doing so, I feel I am responding to a long-standing desire of scholars in this field to reverse the "ghettoization" of Holocaust Studies.

(2) There is a distinct advantage to conducting the unit (and course) in German, if the course is offered within the context of the German Department or program. Though some ancillary readings are in English, primary texts and discussion are in German. There is an undeniable trade-off implied in this decision: one simply cannot cover the same amount of ground in German. Yet the benefit is that students learn that the Holocaust is deeply related to everything else they have been studying about German culture. Though this position stands in diametric opposition to the view of some colleagues, who hold that the Holocaust is so complex that it cannot possibly be treated in the foreign language classroom at the undergraduate level, my experience proves otherwise.

(3) It is advisable to provide basic historical information as a matter of course to all students, but unnecessary to replicate the efforts of history and political science courses. Rather than worry about what students do or do not know, I simply provide background material that can be varied to accommodate students' needs and interests. In addition, I direct students to other relevant courses in the university and to books they might want to read outside of class. The particular course I will refer to below focuses on autobiography in the context of wider culture; thus while we are primarily concerned with the individual's experience, the broader context is also of importance. Indeed, it is crucial that the instructor be in a position to place the individual survivor's (or refugee's) experience within the larger context of Holocaust scholarship.

(4) It is necessary to impart an appreciation of the ongoing significance of the Holocaust within the German polity. I strive to illustrate how the Holocaust lives on in the memories and imagination of survivors (and their progeny), and continues to inform political and cultural events from the Bitburg debacle to the controversial Haus der Geschichte der Bundesrepublik Deutschland in Bonn, to name just a few recent examples. In brief, I share Eric Santner's view, articulated in *Stranded Objects: Mourning, Memory, and Film in Postwar Germany,* that "post-Holocaust Germany" is still deeply and complexly involved in coming to terms with its Nazi past.

(5) Given the fact that our students often identify in some way with Germany due to heritage or other bonds, it is particularly advisable to afford these students the opportunity to engage personally with the material, to relate it as much as possible to their own lives, and to reverse the traditional, unilateral didactic model (teacher as supplier, student as recipient) by having students develop their own active, investigative skills.

* * * * *

Ruth Gutmann witnessed the so-called *Reichskristallnacht* as a young girl. She and her twin sister Eva were safe in Holland when their father, believing he would receive visas that would allow the entire family to emigrate to safety, recalled them to Germany. Not long thereafter, the family was sent to Theresienstadt, and, finally, to Auschwitz. I invited Ruth to speak in the context of a course entitled Autobiography and Culture, a junior-level culture course in German.[3]

Just prior to Ruth's visit we read an excerpt of a memoir by Lucie Begov who had also been incarcerated at Auschwitz, as well as some very moving diary entries by a young boy who had been sent along with his younger sister to England on a *Kindertransport* ("Für Susie"). In preparation for the presentation, students received a timeline (in English) outlining Ruth's life, an autobiographical account (in German) of Ruth's experience of *Kristallnacht*,[4] and a brief article (in English) by Omer Bartov that outlines the main historiographic approaches to the Holocaust.[5] During the session preceding Ruth's arrival, students broke up into small groups to discuss the German text and to help each other compose questions and comments; each student was to have a list of ten questions to pose during the discussion period. In order to give the students a chance to accustom themselves to Ruth's speaking voice (and to reassure them that she is an approachable and candid person), I played a ten-minute segment from a videotaped interview that I had conducted with Ruth in German several years prior to this classroom visit.

On the morning of the presentation, each student contributed one item (pastries, coffee, juice, etc.), which collectively helped to transform our dusty seminar room into an aromatic café. After introducing Ruth, I asked the students to introduce themselves and say something about their studies. I assumed that this would proceed rather uneventfully, and that Ruth would soon begin expatiating on her traumatic experience of *Kristallnacht*. But instead she began to engage students and ask questions about *their* lives. Before long they seemed to feel part of a conversation, rather than the target of a talk. Time flew by. I limited myself largely to the role of language facilitator, writing unfamiliar vocabulary on the board, and asking Ruth to rephrase or repeat things whenever I noticed that students were not following her German.

When just twenty minutes of the eighty-minute period remained, I interrupted to remind Ruth that the students had some prepared questions. A number of students wanted to know how her experience in the camps had affected her religious beliefs; had she, specifically, come to doubt the existence of God? Ruth responded that since the destruction of her synagogue on *Kristallnacht*, she has never entered another synagogue for the purposes of worship; that while she is not opposed to religious belief, she is not herself a religiously observant Jew; and that the Holocaust affected others in the exact opposite manner. Her older sister, for example, has since become very pious. A number of questions focused on her personal life: How had she raised her children? Did she discuss the Holocaust with them? How did she meet her husband? Ruth replied that she and her husband had discussed the Holocaust with their children once they were old enough; she feels this is too great a burden for young children. Another group of questions clustered around Ruth's relationship to postwar Germany: Has she gone back? What does she think of Germans now? When does she speak German? Ruth responded that she has visited Germany, that she has German friends, that she and her husband read German regularly, and that she corresponds occasionally in German. Still, the relationship is not unproblematic. Her German friends tend to be of the "second generation"; she generally prefers to speak English, which now comes more naturally to her; and though she feels strongly that young Germans should not be overburdened with the Nazi past, she recounted some questionable expressions of "Vergangenheitsbewältigung" by members of that very second generation.

Though it is not my purpose to recapitulate the conversation in detail, the above will provide some sense of the discussion. As the end of the period drew closer, I reminded the students that Ruth had spent a considerable amount of time in Auschwitz; did anyone wish to ask about this? Students did want to know, as I later learned when I read their lists of questions, but no one posed this one. As the hour came to an end, I felt satisfied about the way things had gone, but also a little unsettled that no one had asked "the question." Subsequently, I discovered one reason: two students confided that they were worried that such a question might cause Ruth (and themselves) to cry, and this kind of emotional outburst they wanted to avoid at all costs.

How could we extend the discussion? I asked each student to write a one-page letter to Ruth, in which one might thank her, pose further questions, and make any remarks on the presentation. My intent was to give students an opportunity to compensate for a lack of time, shyness, or the limitations imposed by speaking a foreign language more or less spontaneously. They wrote their letters in German, but had more time, and some emotional distance, to formulate their thoughts. A few letters were routine thank-you notes that merely reiterated thoughts already expressed in class. But most were substantive, and actually broke new ground, asking about more delicate matters that may have been too difficult for them to raise face to face.

A number of students confessed explicitly that they had felt too uncomfortable to pose certain questions in class, but wished to make up for that missed opportunity in their letters. Ruth urged them to be bold:

> Ich scheine Ihnen allen ja allerlei Furcht eingejagt zu haben. Einige von Ihren Mitschülerinnen haben mir geschrieben, daß sie Angst hatten, dieses und jenes zu fragen. Ich kann Ihnen nur versichern—obwohl es leider für dieses Mal zu spät ist—It's a free country! (So kann man das nur auf Englisch sagen.) Wenn man nicht antworten will, wird der oder die Befragte sich nicht genieren es Ihnen zu sagen.[6]

Obviously, students' anxieties cannot be dismissed or answered with a mere exhortation to "get over it," yet just knowing that others share these very same inhibitions may offer some consolation and reassurance.

The variety of questions was notable. One student remarked that her German heritage had played a significant role in her life, and that she had learned a lot about Germany by corresponding with her German relatives: "Es interessiert mich sehr, aber ich höre sehr wenig über den Holocaust."[7] Ruth noted in response that this was not at all surprising, and suggested that talking about the Holocaust remains "ein sehr heikeles Thema" for Germans in the second and third generation. Many students, in my experience, insist on a clean slate for the Federal Republic; these students are not willing to consider what Benjamin Korn has termed the Holocaust's "aftershock"—the ways in which it has shaped and distorted postwar German politics and culture. Whereas it would be foolish to speak of the second (and each successive) generation's guilt with regard to Nazi crimes, it would be equally foolhardy to overlook the evidence of anguish and antagonism between the generations that is directly attributable to the Nazi genocide. Ruth puts it rather succinctly: "Denn wenn man darüber nachdenkt, muß man ja auf den Gedanken kommen, daß die ältere Generation viel mehr darüber weiß als sie wahrhaben möchte. Und das ist auch sehr unangenehm für die jüngeren Menschen. ... 'Vater (oder Großvater), weißt Du irgendetwas über den Holocaust?' Ich glaube nicht, daß man das leicht fragen oder schreiben kann."[8]

Some students expressed their respect for Ruth for all she had gone through. Others mused that she is perhaps a better person for having survived the horrors of Auschwitz. Both comments assume a fundamentally salvific, and thus usually religious, conception of suffering, the appropriateness of which Lawrence Langer has thoughtfully challenged (25–30). Ruth made a similar point in language easily accessible to my students: "Ich denke nicht, daß ich Respekt verdiene, weil ich in einem Konzentrationslager war. Ich habe mich ja nicht freiwillig gemeldet und mein Überleben war mehr Chance als Verdienst."[9] Although Ruth is fundamentally optimistic about the future and very sensitive about burdening young people with the atrocities she witnessed, she nevertheless rejects the notion of a "silver lining in every cloud" when applied to the Holocaust: "Ich glaube nicht, daß im Grausamen etwas Positives gefunden werden muß. Es ist besser sich zuzugestehen, daß man Erfahrungen gemacht hat, die sehr schwer zu ertragen waren. Ehrlichkeit verbietet das Beschönigen. Es ist besser zu sagen: 'So war es' und dann das Leben trotzdem fortzusetzen. Ich weiß nicht, ob Sie auch so darüber denken und, ob Sie mich verstehen."[10] With this, Ruth effectively challenged the students' overly sanguine assumptions about the Holocaust. And in doing so, she has given my students a vantage point from which to assess those larger cultural forces at work in what Alvin Rosenfeld has termed "The Americanization of the Holocaust."

Several students had asked about Ruth's relationship to postwar Germany during the discussion period, and a few pursued this line of inquiry in their letters. They wanted to know how Ruth and her husband identify themselves today: "Wie nennen Sie sich," one person queried, "deutsche Juden, jüdische Amerikaner, oder vielleicht nur Amerikaner? Bitte, antworten Sie nur, wenn Sie wollen."[11] The potentially sensitive issue here, I think, is the question of "Germanness." A number of my students feel quite closely tied to Germany, either because of close German relatives (in one case, the parents themselves are German), or due to other kinds of bonds such as high school *Gastfamilien*, college study abroad programs, and the like. Yet neither Ruth nor Al, both born in Germany, and both native speakers of German, identify themselves as "German" any longer. Ruth answers the question in this way: "Heute früh fragte ich Alfred: 'Also, wie nennst Du Dich?' Ohne auch nur einen Augenblick zu zögern, antwortete er: 'Ich bin Amerikaner, weil ich das wählte, und Jude weil ich so geboren bin.' Ich nenne mich meistens nicht so genau, aber wenn ich es muß, nenne ich mich erstens 'einen Menschen,' dann 'eine Frau,' und erst danach eine jüdische Amerikanerin."[12] What I hope students will glean from this response, which I have only given in part, is the sense of complex ambivalence which characterizes Ruth's relationship to Germany and Germans. This survivor of the Holocaust neither wholeheartedly embraces Germany and the Germans, nor does she indiscriminately deplore it and them. Is it too optimistic to hope that the students themselves may come to see that there are not just two simplistic options when it comes to judging a complex and multifaceted culture?

In fact, if there is a unifying theme to these disparate letters, it is Ruth's repeated admonition not to be satisfied with simple, monolithic answers. Especially when it comes to her experiences at Auschwitz, a topic frequently broached by students in their letters, Ruth repeatedly draws students' attention to the diversity of such experience. Echoing the concerns some historians have voiced regarding an overreliance on autobiographical accounts (they are worried that readers may draw unwarranted conclusions from what are perhaps atypical stories), Ruth writes:

> Über Auschwitz zu sprechen ist aus verschiedenen Gründen nicht leicht: erstens hat jeder nur das seinige erlebt und für jeden Überlebenden war es etwas anders, und zweitens fühlt jeder seine Erlebnisse auf seine eigene Art. Das beste Beispiel, welches ich Ihnen dafür geben kann, waren meine Zwillingsschwester und ich: es kam sehr oft vor, daß wir uns zankten, wenn wir uns in späteren Jahren über diese schlimmen Zeiten unterhielten. ...[13]

In order to give students a feel for the diverse experience of the camps, Ruth recommends first that they turn to Primo Levi's widely acclaimed (and very accessible) *Survival in Auschwitz*, and offers to make further suggestions for those wishing to pursue the topic more seriously.

Yet talking about Auschwitz is made difficult not only because of the variety of the inmates' experiences; nor does my students' noted hesitation about asking the tough questions fully account for the problem. Ruth herself finds it hard. A number of her letters provide glimpses of her experience of Auschwitz, but one, written at the request of a particularly inquisitive student, contains a much fuller account of this time. At the outset Ruth tellingly remarks: "Sie haben anscheinend gemerkt welche Geschichten und Erlebnisse ich beiseite gelassen habe—meiner UND Ihrer halber!"[14] After relating some of the "Erlebnisse" she and her twin sister experienced together yet so differently, including tragedies that ensued decades after the war was already over, Ruth asserts: "So, jetzt werden Sie verstehen, warum ich manche Themen umgangen bin. Ich beunruhige junge Leute auch furchtbar ungern. Hoffnung und Jugend dürfen nicht auseinander gerissen werden, und, wenn das passiert, ist es schwer zu heilen. Zu solch einem Riß möchte ich gar nicht beitragen. Ganz im Gegenteil."[15] In expressing what she hopes to spare her listeners, Ruth is indirectly stating what happened to her in the Holocaust when hope and youth were indeed rent asunder. The story itself, which I have omitted, provides a very personal, concrete, and readable account that will not allow students the comforting illusion that the ill effects of the Holocaust ceased with the liberation of the camps in 1945.

Ruth's own admission regarding certain themes she initially avoided may have some transfer application to other pedagogical settings, for her concern about her audience is part of a larger phenomenon well documented by oral historians. The letter stage of the Holocaust unit can provide a kind of reprieve, then, not only for timid students, but also for solicitous speakers such as Ruth. The distance implied in writing sometimes allows us to say things we would otherwise have carefully avoided.

The letters included many other topics: one student pursued the question of religious belief in the wake of the Holocaust; another thoughtfully compared racism in America to that in Nazi Germany; one raised the thorny issue of "historical lessons," mentioning Bosnia specifically; another sought advice on literary reflections on the Holocaust. Ruth took up each of these in turn. Eschewing generalizations, she challenged students' assumptions, even while she found some common ground. The final phase of the unit involved copying all of Ruth's letters and distributing them to the entire class. There were no texts that students read with greater enthusiasm in the entire course, according to their course evaluations.

Autobiography's accessibility to students has been well documented by Andreas Lixl-Purcell ("Mehr Memoiren!"). The question to be asked now, I think, is not whether, but *how*, to employ this genre. With the advent of videotaped testimony, the temptation may be greater than ever to assume that these autobiographical accounts simply "speak for themselves." Of course they do "speak," but are they heard? The historian Reinhard Rürup tells the story of German visitors to the *Topographie des Terrors* exhibition in Berlin who remark repeatedly in a visitors' log that they are seeing these things for the first time. Rürup notes that this cannot possibly be true, given the attention afforded the Holocaust and Nazism on German television and in the German school curricula. He concludes that mere *exposure* apparently has little effect; learners must be respected and allowed to pursue their own interests and questions if this information is to be integrated at any meaningful level.[16] This insight has informed my own teaching of the Holocaust, and it is the reason I seek to have students take on an active and creative role in this unit.

The greatest advantage of this interactive arrangement is that it takes into account students' linguistic and emotional inhibitions, permitting them greater freedom to formulate personally relevant questions in a relatively low-pressure kind of exercise (i.e., letter writing). Above all, it has been my aim to put students "in the driver's seat," fully realizing that without some background and direction, they may not even know where to begin their inquiry. At the same time, I fervently hope that they will not end this journey prematurely, satisfied with clichéd commonplaces about evil, suffering, and the "inevitability" of history. Of one thing we can be sure: a pedagogical approach that combines student autonomy with a respect for emotional inhibitions and individual curiosity will still be necessary even when survivors such as Ruth Gutmann can no longer relate their stories personally.

Notes

1. In his *Holocaust Denial: What the Survey Data Reveal*, Smith reports that in general "knowledge of the Holocaust is shallow, incomplete, and imperfect"; indeed, "only 25–35 percent gave what were considered fully correct answers—those that mentioned three key elements: (1) the persecution, extermination, etc. of the (2) Jews by the (3) Germans, Nazis, etc." (3).
2. Generalizations about students' background knowledge are notoriously impressionistic and, in fact, contradictory. Since evidence gathered by Germanists on the status of North American college students' knowledge of the Holocaust is strictly anecdotal, it is not surprising to find that the assessments of two instructors, both of whom strongly advocate Holocaust pedagogy in the undergraduate German program, are diametrically opposed: see Roche 28 and Wuerth 201.
3. I gratefully acknowledge permission to quote and paraphrase Ruth Gutmann's remarks from this visit and from her letters to my students.
4. The essay is entitled "Die Erfahrungen meiner Familie 1938 während Kristallnacht." I hope to make it and her letters available to other instructors in the near future.

5. The article in question is "Ordinary Monsters," Bartov's review of Daniel J. Goldhagen's much discussed *Hitler's Willing Executioners: Ordinary Germans and the Holocaust*. The review begins with a brief but magisterial overview of Holocaust historiography; it is this very accessible account that is most relevant to students' need for background information. A very useful orientation (for instructors and students) can be found in Robert Bernheim's "Chronology of Significant Events in the History of the Third Reich 1933–1945."
6. "I seem to have frightened you all in all sorts of ways. Some of your classmates wrote me that they were afraid to ask this or that. I can only assure you—although it's unfortunately too late for this time—It's a free country! (You can only say it that way in English.) If one doesn't want to answer, the person being asked won't be embarrassed to tell you." [This and all translations in these notes are by William Collins Donahue.]
7. "It interests me a lot, but I hear very little about the Holocaust."
8. "Because if you think it over, you have to come to the conclusion that the older generation knows much more about it than it would like to admit. And that is also very unpleasant for the younger people. … 'Father (or Grandfather), do you know anything about the Holocaust?' I don't think that you can easily ask or write that."
9. "I don't think that I deserve respect because I was in a concentration camp. I didn't volunteer after all and my survival was more [a matter of] chance than merit."
10. "I don't think that something positive must be found in what is horrible. It is better to admit to yourself that you've had experiences that were very difficult to bear. Honesty forbids one to glorify them. It's better to say: 'That's how it was' and then to go on with life despite it. I don't know if you think that way about it too and whether you understand me."
11. "What do you call yourselves, German Jews, Jewish Americans, or maybe just Americans? Please answer only if you want to."
12. "This morning I asked Alfred: 'So, what do you call yourself?' Without hesitating even a moment, he answered: 'I am an American, because I chose to be, and a Jew because I was born one.' I usually don't identify myself so explicitly, but when I have to, I call myself 'a human being' first, then 'a woman,' and only after that a Jewish American."
13. "It isn't easy to talk about Auschwitz for various reasons: first of all, each person only had his or her own experiences and it was somewhat different for each survivor, and secondly, everyone feels his or her experiences in his or her own way. The best example I can give you for this was my twin sister and I: it happened very often that we quarreled when we talked with each other about these bad times in later years. …"
14. "You apparently noticed what stories and experiences I left out—for my sake AND yours!"
15. "So, now you'll understand why I avoided some topics. I really hate to upset young people too. Hope and youth mustn't be torn apart, and if that happens, it's difficult to mend. I wouldn't want to contribute to such a rift at all. Quite the opposite."
16. On this comment by Rürup and related aspects of Holocaust pedagogy in Germany, see William Collins Donahue and Robert L. Cohn, "Cultural Reparations? Jews and Jewish Studies in Germany Today."

Rutgers University   **Prof. William Collins Donahue**

GERMAN 391, AUTOBIOGRAPHY AND CULTURE

Texts:

1. Andreas Lixl-Purcell, *Stimmen eines Jahrhunderts 1888-1990: Deutsche Autobiographien, Tagebücher, Bilder und Briefe.* Fort Worth: Holt, Rinehart and Winston, 1990. Abbreviation: SeJ.
2. Henry R. Stern and Richey Novak, *A Handbook of English-German Idioms and Useful Expressions.* New York: Harcourt Brace Jovanovich, 1973.
3. Photocopied texts (from instructor).

Abbreviated Syllabus:

Woche 1

Nazismus und der Holocaust. Arbeit 2: "Meine Jugend" (zwei bis drei Seiten). Ernst Toller (Kap. 17 *SeJ* 143–49).
E. Toller, "Offener Brief an Herrn Goebbels" (Photokopie); L. Begov, "Auschwitz-Birkenau" (Kap. 21 *SeJ* 179–90).

Woche 2

"Für Susie" (Photokopie).
R. Gutmann: Timeline & Kristallnachtbericht.

Woche 3

Besuch von Ruth und Al Gutmann (Vortrag & Gespräch).
Ruth & Sam Dreifus, "Da war keine Zukunft mehr für uns" (Photokopie).

Woche 4

Quiz 3.

Woche 5

Vergangenheitsbewältigung & Nachkriegszeit. Film: *Das schreckliche Mädchen.*
Filmdiskussion; Bertolt Brecht (Kap. 9 *SeJ* 161–68).

Woche 6

Drei Texte: "Vom Nullpunkt anfangen" (Kap. 24 *SeJ* 205–10); "Gedanken zur Atombombe" (Kap. 26 *SeJ* 223–27); "Das Ende der Autobiographie" (B. Neumann, Photokopie).

Assignments:

1. **Daily "Zusammenfassung"**: Summarize in German the main points of the day's reading in approximately eight sentences. Mark passages that are difficult and note any questions you may have.
2. **Short paper**: This will take the form of a letter to Ruth Gutmann (your comments and questions based on her class visit); typed, one to two pages.
3. **Quiz**: Short answers, thirty minutes, based on reading.
4. **Short oral presentation**: Three to five minutes, accompanied by one-page handout providing essential vocabulary on a topic or person relevant to the course. To be scheduled individually.
5. **Final exam**: A list of ten essay questions will be distributed in advance; three questions will be drawn from this list for the actual exam.

Grading (for entire course):

The "floor": In order to qualify for a grade other than INC (incomplete), each student must attend on a regular basis (missing no more than three sessions per semester), submit the daily *Zusammenfassung* punctually and regularly (again, missing no more than three per semester), and participate in class discussions by offering to answer questions (or posing questions) at least once per class meeting. If and only if these conditions have been met, then the following formula will be used to calculate your grade:

1. *Zusammenfassungen*	15%
2. Two Papers	20%
3. Quizzes	15%
4. Kurzreferate	15%
5. Oral Participation (beyond mere attendance)	10%
6. Final Exam	25%

Works Cited

Print Sources

Bartov, Omer. "Ordinary Monsters." *The New Republic* (29 April 1996): 32–38.
Bernheim, Robert. "Chronology of Significant Events in the History of the Third Reich 1933–1945." *The Holocaust: Introductory Essays.* Ed. David Scrase and Wolfgang Mieder. Burlington, VT: The Center for Holocaust Studies at the University of Vermont, 1996.
Donahue, William Collins. "'We shall not speak of it': Nazism and the Holocaust in the Elementary College German Course." *Die Unterrichtspraxis* 27.1 (1994): 88–104.
Donahue, William Collins, and Robert L. Cohn. "Cultural Reparations? Jews and Jewish Studies in Germany Today." *German Politics and Society* 15.1 (Spring 1997): 94–116.
Dreifus, Ruth, and Sam Dreifus. "Da war keine Zukunft mehr für uns." Interview. Donahue Appendix B 100–103.
"Für Susie." *Newsletter.* London: Association of Jewish Refugees in Great Britain, June 1996. N. pag.
Gutmann, Ruth. "Die Erfahrungen meiner Familie 1938 während Kristallnacht." Unpublished essay. Fall 1996.
———. Unpublished Letters to Students in German 391. Fall 1996.
Korn, Benjamin. "Shock and Aftershock." 1988. *Jewish Voices, German Words: Growing Up Jewish in Postwar Germany and Austria.* Ed. Elena Lappin. Trans. Krishna Winston. North Haven, CT: Catbird Press, 1994. 19–37.
Langer, Lawrence. *Admitting the Holocaust: Collected Essays.* New York: Oxford University Press, 1995.
Levi, Primo. *Survival in Auschwitz: The Nazi Assault on Humanity.* New York: Simon and Schuster, 1996.
Lixl-Purcell, Andreas. "Mehr Memoiren!: Exil, Faschismus und Holocaust im Deutschunterricht." *Die Unterrichtspraxis* 25.2 (1992): 134–43.
———. *Stimmen eines Jahrhunderts 1888–1990: Deutsche Autobiographien, Tagebücher, Bilder und Briefe.* Fort Worth: Holt, Rinehart and Winston, 1990.
Neumann, Bernd. "Das Ende der Autobiographie." *Autobiographische Texte: Arbeitstexte für den Unterricht.* Ed. Klaus G. Imgenberg and Heribert Seifert. Stuttgart: Reclam, 1985. 180–81.
Roche, Jörg. "Das Thema Nationalsozialismus in nordamerikanischen DaF-Lehrwerken: Widerstände und Möglichkeiten." Warmbold, Koeppel, and Simon-Pelanda 22–39.

Rosenfeld, Alvin H. *The Americanization of the Holocaust*. David W. Belin Lecture in American Jewish Affairs 5. Ann Arbor: Frankel Center for Judaic Studies, 1995.

Santner, Eric L. *Stranded Objects: Mourning, Memory, and Film in Postwar Germany*. Ithaca: Cornell University Press, 1990.

Smith, Tom W. *Holocaust Denial: What the Survey Data Reveal*. Working Papers on Contemporary Antisemitism. New York: The American Jewish Committee, 1995.

Toller, Ernst. "Offener Brief an Herrn Goebbels." Donahue Appendix D 104.

Warmbold, Joachim, E.-Anette Koeppel, and Hans Simon-Pelanda, eds. *Zum Thema Nationalsozialismus im DaF-Lehrwerk und -Unterricht*. Munich: iudicium, 1994.

Wuerth, Hans Martin. "Erinnerungen an die Opfer: Reaktionen amerikanischer College-Studenten auf die nationalsozialistische Vergangenheit." Warmbold, Koeppel, and Simon-Pelanda 198–204.

Film/Videotape

Das schreckliche Mädchen (The Nasty Girl). Dir. Michael Verhoeven. 1989. Video. Miramax, 1990.

Chapter 16

THE TEACHING (AND NOT TEACHING) OF "THE DISASTER"

Leslie Morris

Sarah Kofman, in her memoir *Paroles Suffoquées*, makes the following comment about her father's death in Auschwitz: "[C]omment ne pas le dire? Et comment le dire?" (15–16). The questions "[H]ow can one not say it? And how can it be said?" shape, I will argue, the acts of thinking, writing, and teaching about the Holocaust. The title of my essay draws on Maurice Blanchot's exploration of the fundamentally unspeakable nature of the Holocaust in his book *The Writing of the Disaster*, in which he replaces the terms "Shoah" or "Holocaust" with the more evocative word "Disaster." The injunction to narrate or explain "the Disaster" and the uncertainty of how "it" might be told form the paradox that accompanies any attempt to teach the Holocaust. As Jean-François Lyotard reminds us, Holocaust art "does not say the unsayable, but says that it cannot say it" (47). With Kofman and Lyotard and others in mind, I will explore how this paradox of the fundamental unrepresentability of the Holocaust, which is, at the same time, the subject of nearly constant discussion and writing, affects the possibilities offered by teaching (and not teaching) "the Disaster."

This paradox lies at the center of my attempts to "teach the Holocaust"—an attempt that challenges, always, the idea that the Holocaust can ever be taught. One course I designed, entitled History, Memory, Narrative: Postwar German Literature in Translation, examines a variety of texts that underscore the failures of memory and of language to recapture

---

Notes for this section can be found on page 232.

experience. Through a selection of literary, film, and theoretical texts, we explored the viability of writing in German, about German history, after the Shoah. Although this was a German Studies and not a Jewish Studies course, the question that was in the back of my mind as I designed the course was what it might mean to "teach the Holocaust" and whether I was in fact doing so. If to "teach the Holocaust" means to investigate in the classroom the questions of silence, of the unspeakable, of the representation of historical reality, then I did indeed "teach the Holocaust" as I taught this class. Yet how are these questions different when teaching and writing about postwar German culture?

The first answer to this question lies not only with the speakable and the unspeakable, but with the absence of Jews in Germany.[1] In a rather brutal assessment of his generation of male Jews after what he calls "the Catastrophe," the French writer Alain Finkielkraut speaks of "imaginary Jews," whom he characterizes as living "in borrowed identities. They have taken up residence in fiction. The Judaism they invoke enraptures and transports them magically to a setting in which they are exalted and sanctified" (15). Finkielkraut's description of Jewishness as having migrated inward to the realm of the imaginary is, I believe, a useful insight when contemplating the absence and erasure of Jewish life in Germany, a critical issue in German culture today. It is the Jewish absence that defines any possible German relationship to Holocaust literature, and it is the Jewish absence in post-Shoah Germany that I believe must be placed at the center of any postwar German literature course.

How, then, to structure a "real live" course to real students around this elusive notion of absence? I chose a variety of literary texts that shared a common distrust or skepticism about the possibility of narrative or representation after Auschwitz, texts that fulfill Lyotard's dictum that Holocaust art "does not say the unsayable, but says that it cannot say it." My starting point with the course is to explore the ways in which the question of the Shoah, as phrased by Kofman, Lyotard, and Blanchot—how, or whether, to speak about "it" at all, while at the same time insisting on speaking about it, at times almost compulsively—might be brought into the syllabus for an upper-level literature class taught in English. As such, the absence of Jewishness, or rather the specter of the imaginary Jew (or an imaginary Jewish culture), to use Finkielkraut's term, in these texts by non-Jewish Germans, is what defines "the Holocaust" in this course: again, an example of teaching, and at the same time *not* teaching, the Holocaust.

This course was taught in English and cross-listed as part of the "literature" offering, thus setting it apart from the courses in German literature taught in German. This is significant, I think, for a number of reasons.

First, that such a course would fall under the broader domain of "literature" and not be "ghettoized" in a language department somehow implies that the act of teaching about the Holocaust in German would entail different questions than it does in English. Teaching texts in translation automatically raises the question of the origin and the authenticity of a literary work. Whereas any text read in a class frequently runs the risk of becoming a holy or devotional object, not always subject to the sort of scrutiny that it deserves, the translated text in particular forbids any easy notions of literary production and urges students, by its very status as nonoriginal, to question the relationships raised among narrative, history, and memory. The translated text, by virtue of its not being the original, forces an inquiry into the meaning and significance of the act of reading as well.

Although the reading was comprised entirely of translated texts, they were not exclusively "Jewish" texts. I attempted to bring together an array of texts that foreground the difficulties of historiography and of narrative and that challenge the supposed seamlessness, objectivity, and "truth telling" of documentary or "historical" accounts. These are all texts that question the privileging of "experience" as an epistemological category, focusing instead—indeed, insisting—on the way it is always mediated through language, narrative, text. In addition to some works from the canon of postwar German literary texts, such as Christa Wolf's *Patterns of Childhood* and Wolfgang Koeppen's *Pigeons on the Grass*, the class read some of the classic "Jewish" texts that explore the relationship between memory and experience, such as Primo Levi's *Survival in Auschwitz*, Sara Nomberg-Przytyk's *Auschwitz: True Tales from a Grotesque Land*, and Cynthia Ozick's *The Shawl*. In order to set these questions in a contemporary German context, I placed on reserve in the library the entire corpus of articles and books pertaining to the *Historikerstreit*. Since the course was offered in 1991, it was quite contemporaneous with the debate that was still being generated.

Although the focus of the course was on literature, we explored the relationships among history, memory, and narrative in a number of films, essays, and historical texts. The first piece that the class read was Anna Seghers's "The Excursion of the Dead Girls," a short story that manages in its brevity to raise significant questions not only about how history and memory can be represented in a literary text, but also about how various subject positions (victim, collaborator, child) affect the telling of the tale. In that first week, the students began their reading of the *Historikerstreit*, which continued for the next three weeks, and discussion focused on the role that texts play in the public shaping of history and memory.

The novels that we read shared a common concern with the relationship between writing and memory. Since part of the aim of the course was to introduce literature students, and not necessarily German majors, to the important works of German and Austrian literature written in the postwar period, I selected Wolfgang Koeppen's *Pigeons on the Grass*, Alexander Kluge's *Case Histories*, Heinrich Böll's *Billiards at Half-Past Nine*, Christa Wolf's *Patterns of Childhood*, Ingeborg Bachmann's *Malina*, Peter Handke's *A Sorrow beyond Dreams*, and Elfriede Jelinek's *Wonderful, Wonderful Times*. All of these novels negotiate the difficult shoals of memory and history and point, at the same time, to the necessity and difficulties of saying "the unsayable." For American students who had had no previous exposure to German literature of any period, these novels were illuminating for a number of reasons.

The two novels that sparked the most intense discussion and debate were Koeppen's *Pigeons on the Grass* and Bachmann's *Malina*.[2] The open narrative structure of both novels enabled students to enter the text, giving them a sense of freedom of interpretation and authorizing them to produce their own readings of the works. Similarly, students responded quite strongly to Christa Wolf's *Patterns of Childhood*. In order to help students gain access to the Wolf novel, I began with an in-class writing exercise in which they had to narrate an event from their childhood. After they had written for about fifteen minutes, I had them rewrite what they had just narrated, but this time using the third person. The students then broke into groups and read and discussed what they had written. I used this exercise to generate a discussion of the technique that Wolf uses in her novel and to help the students to focus on the question of the elusiveness of memory and the way in which writing and language shape how memory is captured and conveyed. From this exercise we were able to move into a lively and productive discussion of the novel. I believe that this writing exercise also helped to offset the perception of the "foreignness" of these texts. By enabling students to explore the meaning of memory and narrative in their own lives and then to bring this back to their reading of the novel, I feel I gave them access to another layer of the Wolf novel. The films that I showed as part of the course also, I believe, helped allay students' initial anxiety about the utter "foreignness" of German culture.

The very fact of reading texts in translation highlighted the question of "foreignness" in the course. Reading a translated text forces students to look at a work of literature in a different light and can make them aware, sometimes for the first time, of a literary text as something that is produced, and in the case of a translation, changed from the original to the translation. This is a key concept in a course that explores the interplay between memory and narrative, for it also forces the student to see all texts as being generated by a series of factors—cultural, linguistic, political. Reading in translation makes it much more difficult for students to approach a literary work as inviolable truth; rather, it leads them to examine the various factors that might shape the novel and, ultimately, foregrounds the very "foreignness" that might at first have caused the students to balk at taking the course. I see this as a great benefit of teaching in translation, and for this reason I always highlight the act of translation in a course. The Jelinek novel, for instance, (the translation of *Die Ausgesperrten*) is a "bad" translation, the English cumbersome, awkward, and often obscuring the meaning that might be found in the original. The very awkwardness of the prose, however, enabled me to steer students to a reading of the text that highlighted it *as* text, as part of a mediated discourse, rather than as a seamless re-presentation of historical reality. Hyperliterary conventions in Koeppen's novel—for instance, the extensive use of a stream-of-consciousness narrative voice—also helped raise questions about the interplay among history, memory, and narrative.

Perhaps the text that most successfully contributed to a reexamination of the role of history and memory in the production of narrative was an ancillary text that I had placed on the reserve reading list: Sara Nomberg-Przytyk's fictionalized memoir *Auschwitz: True Tales from a Grotesque Land*, a text that by its nature raises questions about the role of legend in Holocaust memoirs, of the author, and of publication and translation in the dissemination and production of information about the Holocaust. The ironically entitled "True Tales" never aspire to this impossible condition of "truth"; rather, Nomberg-Przytyk weaves together a series of vignettes about life in Auschwitz, vignettes that are as dependent on legend as they are on the process of witnessing and testimony, both of which, given the legal origins of the terms, set up an assumption of a truth that can be attained. This is in many ways an exemplary Holocaust text in that it raises questions about the authenticity of experience, authorial voice, and the role of "Holocaust" literature.

The postwar German text that most strikingly raises these issues of authenticity of voice and truth telling is Wolfgang Koeppen's *Jakob Littners Aufzeichnungen aus einem Erdloch*.[3] The book was originally written and published in 1948 by the Kluger Verlag (Munich) as the "real" diaries of a survivor named Jakob Littner. The recent edition, published in 1992 by the Jüdischer Verlag, reveals that in fact Wolfgang Koeppen had been the ghostwriter of the original diary, and that Jakob Littner was a survivor who had told his story to a Munich publisher shortly after the war. The complex publication history of the book and Koeppen's later acknowledgment of his role in its publication in the foreword to the 1992 edition point to the complexities of representation of the Holocaust in a German context. As Koeppen states at the end of the foreword about the act of writing Littner's experience as if it were his own: "Ich aß amerikanische Konserven und schrieb die Leidensgeschichte eines deutschen Juden. Da wurde es meine Geschichte" (6).[4] This unabashed willingness to identify with a victim of National Socialism and, in so doing, to cross the line from interpretation to representation, raises complex legal, ethical, and political questions. Ultimately, however, it points to what I have been identifying as the central question of Holocaust literature and the central question of my course: can there ever be an "authentic" representation of the Holocaust? Like Nomberg-Przytyk's "memoir," *Jakob Littners Aufzeichnungen aus einem Erdloch* relies as much on legend and narrative as on "historical truth" to convey some of "what happened."

In 1995, I offered an entirely different course that nonetheless raises similar questions. I had been thinking for a long time about teaching a course that would bring the poetics of writing after Auschwitz into as broad and comparative a context as possible. I designed a comparative literature course entitled Poetry of Place/Poetry of Exile, in which we read poetic texts from diverse literary traditions that deal with questions of Diaspora, place, and exile in modernist and postmodern poetry and theory. In order to highlight the idea of "place" as a constantly shifting semiotic sign, I began the course with Italo Calvino's *Invisible Cities* and continued with an exploration of diasporic identity in poetic texts by writers such as Paul Celan, Edmond Jabes, Mahmoud Darwish, Aimé Cesaire and Yehuda Amichai. This sort of course encourages an exploration of the larger questions that link German Studies and Jewish Studies beyond the more obvious rubric of German-Jewish literature or Holocaust literature, and enables students to explore, through literary and nonliterary texts, questions about the meaning of national, linguistic, and literary borders. I designed this course to investigate modernist and postmodern conceptions of place and displacement, looking at the consonance and dissonance between the postmodern concern with Diaspora and displacement (as seen in writers such as Edmond Jabes and Jean Baudrillard) and the modernist exploration of exile. The course draws on diverse literary traditions, including texts by Italian, German, French, Palestinian, Hebrew, English, and American authors as a way to encourage students to explore what it means to dwell in the polyphony "between" languages. I would, if pressed, choose to describe this as a course that cannot be separated from thinking about the Holocaust, since it is the thinking and writing about the Shoah by writers from diverse literary traditions that lie at the center of the reflections about art, poetics, and language that form the basis of this course.

I confess that I really cannot imagine a course that could even "teach" the Holocaust, and especially teach it from a German perspective. What would be covered in such a course? Survivor narratives, texts by Jewish authors, texts that use the Holocaust as a "theme" or backdrop, texts whose writers were affected in some way by the Holocaust? Such a course would have to first examine the ethical and philosophical issues that are raised by any attempt at representation of the Shoah. One must walk the fine line between saying "the unsayable" and recognizing the fundamental impossibility of articulating what Blanchot calls "the Disaster," what Finkielkraut describes as "the Catastrophe," what others refer to as "the Shoah" or simply as "Auschwitz." As Blanchot commands us: "[K]now what has taken place, do not forget, and at the same time never will you know" (82). This is the dilemma that we face when undertaking to "teach the Holocaust," and it is this dilemma that accompanies me in all of my teaching. Rather than "teaching the Holocaust," as a Germanist who writes and teaches on the borders of Jewish Studies and German Studies, I feel that my task is to problematize the enterprise of talking about, or representing, the Shoah. This involves an exploration of the interplay between memory and narrative, and an interrogation of the elusive nature of memory and forgetting.

I might not be teaching "the" Holocaust, but I feel that courses such as these lead students to contemplate the void that the Holocaust has left us, to crawl into the space that separates the German from the Jew, to ponder what Finkielkraut calls the "imaginary Jew." The various writers—Paul Celan, Anna Seghers, Edmond Jabes, Ingeborg Bachmann, Christa Wolf—whom we read in these courses all point to the difficulty of writing in German after the Shoah. While their own subject positions—as Jew, as German, as woman—are significant, equally significant are their various navigations through the landscape of postwar German identity and culture.

Perhaps a way out of the paradox of speaking the unspeakable and teaching the unteachable lies in a more poetic formulation. To offer a different way of thinking about teaching about or around the Holocaust, I turn to Paul Celan's idea, articulated in his Bremen prize speech, of the poem as being "unterwegs." I would like to propose that the act of teaching depends on a similar indeterminacy and rootlessness as Celan's conception of the poem. Like the poem that Celan describes as never fixed or static, but instead always "en route" to the "inhabitable" (35), lingering in the liminal state he identifies as "unterwegs," teaching the Holocaust, in particular, also demands that we constantly reformulate and recast the parameters of history, memory, and narrative, keeping ourselves and our students "en route" to an understanding of the gulf between the speakable and the unspeakable. To craft a syllabus that urges a group of students to contemplate how language and memory shape experience and how experience, in turn, is shaped by language, is part of this process of being "unterwegs." The texts in the Poetry of Place/Poetry of Exile course are not texts that can be "taught" in any traditional sense of the word, but rather texts that evoke, provoke, and begin an inquiry that does perhaps lead to one of the central questions posed by the Holocaust: What is the relationship among art, language, music, poetry in a world still shaped by "the Disaster"? I like to think of teaching the Holocaust as a state of moving *toward*, of being "unterwegs," and of not being willing or able to reduce experience, lived or historical or literary or artistic, to any single cause or reason. To teach the Holocaust, with Celan's idea of the poem as a movement *toward*, is to keep open the impossibilities and the failures, as well as to live the paradoxical injunction to keep teaching what cannot be taught.

Notes

1. Despite the resurgence of Jewish life in Germany since the *Wende*—what many refer to as a renaissance of Jewish culture—I maintain the distinction between this partly artificial, self-conscious recreation of Jewish life and the vital Jewish presence in Germany that existed before the Holocaust. Jewish culture in Germany today is chic, marketable, and, I would argue, fetishized precisely because of the absence that has defined it for the past fifty years. For more discussion of this topic, see Sander L. Gilman and Karen Remmler, eds., *Reemerging Jewish Culture in Germany*.
2. Jelinek's *Wonderful, Wonderful Times* caused a bit of a sensation due to the graphic sexuality and violence depicted in the novel, but the translation is unfortunately so weak that it impaired effective discussion of the work in class. The other translations were all of high quality.
3. Unfortunately, this book by Koeppen has not been translated into English. It was published by the Jüdischer Verlag in 1992, the year after I taught History, Memory, Narrative. However, I can imagine that an upper-level German student could discuss the novel for an in-class presentation. I would certainly try to do this the next time I teach the course.
4. "I ate American preserves and wrote the story of a German Jew's suffering. Then it became my story" [translation by Leslie Morris].

Bard College   **Prof. Leslie Morris**

GERMAN/ENGLISH 334
HISTORY, MEMORY, NARRATIVE:
POSTWAR GERMAN LITERATURE IN TRANSLATION

Week 1
Introduction

Week 2
Anna Seghers, "The Excursion of the Dead Girls"
Luise Rinser, "Nina's Story"

On reserve:
Jürgen Habermas, "Concerning the Public Use of History"
Theodor Adorno, "What Does Coming to Terms with the Past Mean?"
Primo Levi, *Survival in Auschwitz*
Cynthia Ozick, *The Shawl*

Week 3
Christa Wolf, "Change of Perspective"

On reserve:
Broszat/Friedländer, "A Controversy about the Historicization of National Socialism"
James Young, Introduction to *Writing and Rewriting the Holocaust*
Sara Nomberg-Przytyk, *Auschwitz: True Tales from a Grotesque Land*

Week 4
Wolfgang Borchert, *The Man Outside*

Week 5
Wolfgang Koeppen, *Pigeons on the Grass*

Week 6
Heinrich Böll, *Billiards at Half-Past Nine*

Week 7
Film Screening: Helma Sanders-Brahms, *Deutschland bleiche Mutter*

Week 8
Discussion of *Deutschland bleiche Mutter*
FIRST PAPER DUE

Week 9
Alexander Kluge, *Case Histories*
Walter Benjamin, "Theses on the Philosophy of History"

Week 10
Film Screening: Alexander Kluge, *Abschied von gestern*

Week 11
Discussion of Kluge, *Abschied von gestern*
On reserve:
Eric Rentschler, "Remembering Not to Forget: A Retrospective Reading of Kluge's *Brutality in Stone*."
Anton Kaes, *From Hitler to Heimat: The Return of German History as Film*

Week 12
Ingeborg Bachmann, from *The Thirtieth Year*: "Everything," "Youth in an Austrian Town," "Undine Goes," "A Step towards Gomorrah"

Week 13
Bachmann, *Malina*

Week 14
Christa Wolf, *Patterns of Childhood*

Week 15
Peter Handke, *A Sorrow beyond Dreams*

Week 16
Elfriede Jelinek, *Wonderful, Wonderful Times*

Books Available in Bookstore:
Ingeborg Bachmann, *Malina*
Heinrich Böll, *Billiards at Half-Past Nine*
Wolfgang Borchert, *The Man Outside*
Elfriede Jelinek, *Wonderful, Wonderful Times*
Alexander Kluge, *Case Histories*
Wolfgang Koeppen, *Pigeons on the Grass*
Christa Wolf, *Patterns of Childhood*

Course Requirements:
One short paper (five pages)
One longer paper (twelve to fifteen pages, due last week of class)
Six short (two pages) response papers
In-class presentation

Works Cited

Print Sources

Adorno, Theodor. "What Does Coming to Terms with the Past Mean?" Trans. Timothy Bahti and Geoffrey Hartman. *Bitburg in Moral and Political Perspective*. Ed. Geoffrey Hartman. Bloomington: Indiana University Press, 1986. 114–29.

Bachmann, Ingeborg. *Malina*. Trans. Philip Boehm. New York: Holmes and Meier, 1990.

———. *The Thirtieth Year*. Trans. Michael Bullock. New York: Holmes and Meier, 1987.

Benjamin, Walter. "Theses on the Philosophy of History." *Illuminations*. Trans. Harry Zohn. Ed. Hannah Arendt. New York: Schocken, 1969. 253–64.

Blanchot, Maurice. *The Writing of the Disaster*. Trans. Ann Smock. 1986. Lincoln, NE: University of Nebraska Press, 1995.

Böll, Heinrich. *Billiards at Half-Past Nine*. New York: McGraw Hill, 1962.

Borchert, Wolfgang. *The Man Outside*. Trans. David Porter. 1952. New York: New Directions, 1971.

Broszat, Martin, and Saul Friedländer. "A Controversy about the Historicization of National Socialism." *New German Critique* 44 (Spring/Summer 1988): 85–126.

Calvino, Italo. *Invisible Cities*. Trans. William Weaver. New York: Harcourt Brace, 1974.

Celan, Paul. "Speech on the Occasion of Receiving the Literature Prize of the Free Hanseatic City of Bremen." *Collected Prose*. Trans. Rosemary Waldrop. Manchester: Carcanet Press Ltd., 1986. 33–35.

Finkielkraut, Alain. *The Imaginary Jew*. Trans. Kevin O'Neill and David Suchoff. Lincoln, NE: University of Nebraska Press, 1994.

Gilman, Sander L., and Karen Remmler, eds. *Reemerging Jewish Culture in Germany: Life and Literature since 1989*. New York: New York University Press, 1994.

Habermas, Jürgen. "Concerning the Public Use of History." *New German Critique* 44 (Spring/Summer 1988): 40–50.

Handke, Peter. *A Sorrow beyond Dreams*. Trans. Ralph Manheim. New York: Farrar, Straus & Giroux, 1975.

Herrmann, Elisabeth Rütschi, and Edna Huttenmaier Spitz, eds. *German Women Writers of the Twentieth Century*. Oxford: Pergamon Press, 1978.

Jelinek, Elfriede. *Wonderful, Wonderful Times*. Trans. Michael Hulse. London: Serpent's Tail Press, 1990.

Kaes, Anton. *From Hitler to Heimat: The Return of History as Film.* Cambridge, MA: Harvard University Press, 1989.

Kluge, Alexander. *Case Histories: Stories.* Trans. Leila Vennewitz. New York: Holmes and Meier, 1988.

Koeppen, Wolfgang. *Jakob Littners Aufzeichnungen aus einem Erdloch.* 1948. Foreword by Wolfgang Koeppen. Frankfurt am Main: Jüdischer Verlag, 1992.

———. *Pigeons on the Grass.* Trans. David Ward. New York: Holmes and Meier, 1990.

Kofman, Sarah. *Paroles Suffoquées.* Paris: Editions Galilee, 1987.

Levi, Primo. *Survival in Auschwitz and the Reawakening.* Trans. Stuart Woolf. New York: Summit Books, 1986.

Lyotard, Jean-François. *Heidegger and "the jews."* Trans. Andreas Michel and Mark Roberts. Minneapolis: University of Minnesota Press, 1990.

Nomberg-Przytyk, Sara. *Auschwitz: True Tales from a Grotesque Land.* Trans. Roslyn Hirsch. Chapel Hill, NC: University of North Carolina Press, 1985.

Ozick, Cynthia. *The Shawl.* New York: Knopf, 1989.

Rentschler, Eric. "Remembering Not to Forget: A Retrospective Reading of Kluge's *Brutality in Stone*." *New German Critique* 49 (Winter 1990): 23–41.

Rinser, Luise. "Nina's Story." Trans. Richard and Clara Winston. Herrmann and Spitz 60–66.

Seghers, Anna. "The Excursion of the Dead Girls." Trans. Elizabeth Rütschi Herrmann and Edna Huttenmaier Spitz. Herrmann and Spitz 39–52.

Wolf, Christa. "Change of Perspective." Trans. A. Leslie Willson. Herrmann and Spitz 94–100.

———. *Patterns of Childhood.* Trans. Ursule Molinaro and Hedwig Rappolt. New York: Farrar, Straus & Giroux, 1984.

Young, James. *Writing and Rewriting the Holocaust: Narrative and the Consequences of Interpretation.* Bloomington: Indiana University Press, 1988.

Film Sources

Abschied von gestern (Yesterday Girl). Dir. Alexander Kluge. West Glen Communications, 1966.

Deutschland bleiche Mutter (Germany Pale Mother). Dir. Helma Sanders-Brahms. New Yorker Films, 1980.

IMPORTANT HISTORICAL READINGS ON THE HOLOCAUST AND THE NAZI ERA

Compiled by Ronald Webster

I. Reference Works

Fischel, Jack. *Historical Dictionary of the Holocaust*. Lanham, MD: Scarecrow Press, 1999.

Kershaw, Ian. *The Nazi Dictatorship: Problems and Perspectives of Interpretation*. 1985. 3rd ed. London: Edward Arnold, 1993.

Zentner, Christian, and Friedemann Bedürftig, eds. *The Encyclopedia of the Third Reich*. New York: Da Capo Press, 1997.

II. Monographs

Bankier, David. *The Germans and the Final Solution: Public Opinion under Nazism*. Cambridge, MA: Basil Blackwell, 1992.

Bauer, Yehuda. *A History of the Holocaust*. New York: F. Watts, 1982.

Berenbaum, Michael, and Abraham Peck, eds. *The Holocaust and History: The Known, the Unknown, the Disputed and the Reexamined*. Bloomington, IN: Indiana University Press, 1998.

Breitman, Richard. *The Architect of Genocide: Himmler and the Final Solution*. London: Bodley Head, 1991.

Browning, Christopher R. *Fateful Months: Essays on the Emergence of the Final Solution*. New York: Holmes & Meier, 1985.

_____. *Ordinary Men: Reserve Police Battalion 101 and the Final Solution in Poland*. New York: Aaron Asher Books-HarperCollins, 1992.

Burleigh, Michael, and Wolfgang Wippermann. *The Racial State: Germany, 1933–1945*. Cambridge: Cambridge University Press, 1991.
Dawidowicz, Lucy S. *The War Against the Jews 1933–1945*. 1975. Rev. ed. New York: Bantam Books, 1986.
Fleming, Gerald. *Hitler and the Final Solution*. Introduction by Saul Friedländer. Berkeley: University of California Press, 1984.
Friedländer, Henry. *The Origins of Nazi Genocide: From Euthanasia to the Final Solution*. Chapel Hill, NC: University of North Carolina Press, 1995.
Friedländer, Saul. *Nazi Germany and the Jews*. Vol. I: *The Years of Persecution, 1933–1939*. New York: HarperCollins, 1997.
Gilbert, Martin. *The Holocaust: The Jewish Tragedy*. 1985. London: Collins, 1986.
Goldhagen, Daniel Jonah. *Hitler's Willing Executioners: Ordinary Germans and the Holocaust*. New York: Knopf, 1996.
Gordon, Sarah. *Hitler, Germans and the "Jewish Question."* Princeton, NJ: Princeton University Press, 1984.
Hilberg, Raul. *The Destruction of the European Jews*. New York: Holmes and Meier, 1985.
Kaplan, Marion. *Between Dignity and Despair: Jewish Life in Nazi Germany*. New York: Oxford University Press, 1998.
Kershaw, Ian. *Popular Opinion and Political Dissent in the Third Reich, Bavaria 1933–1945*. Oxford: Oxford University Press, 1983.
Kren, George M., and Leon Rappoport. *The Holocaust and the Crisis of Human Behavior*. New York: Holmes and Meier, 1980.
Lipstadt, Deborah E. *Beyond Belief: The American Press and the Coming of the Holocaust, 1933–1945*. New York: Free Press, 1993.
Marrus, Michael R. *The Holocaust in History*. London: Penguin Books, 1988.
Marrus, Michael R., ed. *The Nazi Holocaust: Historical Articles on the Destruction of European Jews*. 9 nos. in 15 vols. Westport, CT: Meckler, 1989.

    No. 1. *Perspectives on the Holocaust.*
    No. 2. *The Origins of the Holocaust.*
    No. 3. *The "Final Solution": The Implementation of Mass Murder.*
    No. 4. *The "Final Solution" outside of Germany.*
    No. 5. *Public Opinion and Relations to the Jews in Nazi Europe.*
    No. 6. *The Victims of the Holocaust.*
    No. 7. *Jewish Resistance to the Holocaust.*
    No. 8. *Bystanders to the Holocaust.*
    No. 9. *The End of the Holocaust.*

Mayer, Arno J. *Why Did the Heavens Not Darken? The "Final Solution" in History.* New York: Pantheon Books, 1988.

Niewyk, Donald, ed. *The Holocaust: Problems and Perspectives of Interpretation.* Lexington, MA: D. C. Heath, 1992.

Poliakov, Leon. *A History of Anti-Semitism.* 4 vols. New York: Vanguard Press, 1965–85.
- Vol. 1. *From the Time of Christ to the Court Jews.* 1965.
- Vol. 2. *From Mohammed to [the] Marranos.* Trans. Natalie Gerardi. 1973.
- Vol. 3. *From Voltaire to Wagner.* Trans. Miriam Kochan. 1975.
- Vol. 4. *Suicidal Europe, 1870–1933.* 1985.

Reitlinger, Gerald. *The Final Solution: The Attempt to Exterminate the Jews of Europe, 1939–1945.* 1953. 2nd rev. and aug. ed. London: Vallentine & Mitchell, 1968.

Schleunes, Karl A. *The Twisted Road to Auschwitz: Nazi Policy toward German Jews, 1933–1939.* Urbana, IL: University of Illinois Press, 1970.

Schmidt, Gilya Gerda, ed. and trans. *National Socialism and Gypsies in Austria.* By Erika Thurner. Foreword by Michael Berenbaum. Tuscaloosa, AL: University of Alabama Press, 1998.

Shandley, Robert R., ed. *Unwilling Germans? The Goldhagen Debate.* Minneapolis: University of Minnesota Press, 1998.

Ziegler, Jean. *The Swiss, the Gold and the Dead.* New York: Harcourt Brace, 1998.

III. Periodical Literature, Contributions to Anthologies

Browning, Christopher R. "Nazi Resettlement Policy and the Search for a Solution to the Jewish Question 1939–41." *German Studies Review* 9.3 (1986): 497–519.

Conway, J. S. "The Silence of Pope Pius XII." *The Papacy and Totalitarianism between the Two World Wars.* Ed. Charles F. Delzell. New York: Wiley, 1974. 79–108.

Friedländer, Henry. "Publications on the Holocaust." *The German Church Struggle and the Holocaust.* Ed. Franklin Hamlin Littell and Hubert G. Locke. Detroit: Wayne State University Press, 1974. 69–94.

Friedländer, Saul. "From Anti-Semitism to Extermination: A Historiographical Study of Nazi Policies toward the Jews and an Essay in Interpretation." *Yad Vashem Studies* 16 (1984): 1–50.

Graubart, J. "The Vatican and the Jews: Cynicism and Indifference." *Judaism* 24 (Spring 1975): 168–80.

Hillgruber, Andreas. "War in the East and the Extermination of the Jews." *Yad Vashem Studies* 18 (1987): 103–32.

Jäckel, E. "Hitler Orders the Holocaust." *Holocaust and Genocide Studies* 1.1 (1987): 61–80.

Kater, Michael H. "Everyday Anti-Semitism in Prewar Nazi Germany: The Popular Bases." *Yad Vashem Studies* 16 (1984): 129–59.

Kershaw, Ian. "The Persecution of the Jews and German Popular Opinion in the Third Reich." *Leo Baeck Institute Year Book* 26 (1981): 261–89.

Kolinsky, Eva. "Remembering Auschwitz: A Survey of Recent Textbooks for the Teaching of History in German Schools." *Yad Vashem Studies* 22 (1992): 287–307.

Kulka, O. "'Public Opinion' in Nazi Germany and the 'Jewish Question.'" *Jerusalem Quarterly* 25 (1982): 121–44.

Lifton, Robert J. "Reflections on Genocide." *Psychohistory Review* 14 (1986): 39–54.

Mark, B. "The Study of the Jewish Resistance Movement." *Yad Vashem Studies* 11 (1975): 49–65.

Marrus, Michael R. "The Holocaust at Nuremberg." *Yad Vashem Studies* 26 (1998): 5–41.

Mommsen, Hans. "Realization of the Unthinkable: 'Final Solution of the Jewish Question' in the Third Reich." *The Policies of Genocide: Jews and Soviet Prisoners of War in Nazi Germany*. Ed. Gerhard Hirschfeld. London: Allen & Unwin, 1986. 97–144.

New German Critique: Special Issue on the Historikerstreit 44 (Spring–Summer 1988).

Paucker, Arnold. "Resistance of German and Austrian Jews to the Nazi Regime, 1933–1945," *Leo Baeck Institute Year Book* 40 (1995): 3–20.

Stokes, L. D. "The German People and the Destruction of the European Jews." *Central European History* 6.2 (1973): 167–91.

Strauss, Herbert A. "Jewish Emigration from Germany: Nazi Policies and Jewish Responses." *Leo Baeck Institute Year Book*. Part I, 25 (1980): 313–61; Part II, 26 (1981): 343–409.

Tal, Uriel. "On the Study of the Holocaust and Genocide." *Yad Vashem Studies on the European Jewish Catastrophe and Resistance* 13 (1979): 7–52.

Wilhelm, Hans-Heinrich. "The Holocaust in National-Socialist Rhetoric and Writings—Some Evidence against the Thesis That before 1945 Nothing Was Known about the 'Final Solution.'" *Yad Vashem Studies* 16 (1984): 95–127.

LIST OF CONTRIBUTORS

Gisela Brude-Firnau, Professor of German, University of Waterloo, Waterloo, Ontario.

Steven R. Cerf, George Lincoln Skolfield, Jr., Professor of German, Bowdoin College, Brunswick, Maine.

Susan E. Cernyak-Spatz, Associate Professor Emerita of German, University of North Carolina at Charlotte, Charlotte, North Carolina.

Nancy M. Decker, Associate Professor of German, Rollins College, Winter Park, Florida.

Karin Doerr, Professor of German, Research Associate and member of the Editorial Board of the Montreal Institute for Genocide Studies, and Research Associate of the Simone de Beauvoir Institute, Concordia University, Montreal, Quebec.

William Collins Donahue, Assistant Professor of German and member of the Jewish Studies Faculty, Rutgers University, New Brunswick, New Jersey.

Linda Feldman, Associate Professor of German, University of Windsor, Windsor, Ontario; interviewer for the Visual History Foundation's Survivors of the Shoah Oral History Project (1995-98); and member of the city of Windsor's Yom Hashoah committee since 1996.

Thomas Freeman, Associate Professor of German, Beloit College, Beloit, Wisconsin.

Miriam Jokiniemi, Assistant Professor of German and Women's Studies; Fellow of the York University Centre for Jewish Studies, York University, Toronto, Ontario.

Nancy A. Lauckner, Associate Professor of German and member of the Judaic Studies Program, University of Tennessee, Knoxville, Tennessee.

Dagmar C. G. Lorenz, Professor of German, University of Illinois at Chicago, Chicago, Illinois; formerly Professor of German and member of the Executive Board of the Melton Center for Jewish Studies, Ohio State University, Columbus, Ohio.

Leslie Morris, Assistant Professor of German and member of the Advisory Board of the Center for Holocaust and Genocide Studies, University of Minnesota, Twin Cities, Minnesota; formerly Assistant Professor of German and Co-Director of Jewish Studies, Bard College, Annandale-on-Hudson, New York.

Laureen Nussbaum, Professor Emerita of German, Portland State University, Portland, Oregon; frequent faculty member of the Deutsche Sommerschule am Pazifik, Portland, Oregon.

Karen Remmler, Associate Professor of German Studies, Co-Director of the Weissman Leadership Center, and member of the Women's Studies, Critical Social Thought, and Jewish Studies Programs, Mount Holyoke College, South Hadley, Massachusetts; and course professor of German 43, Amherst College, Amherst, Massachusetts (spring 1996).

David Scrase, Professor of German and Director of the Center for Holocaust Studies, University of Vermont, Burlington, Vermont.

Florentine Strzelczyk, Assistant Professor of Germanic Studies, University of Calgary, Calgary, Alberta; formerly Assistant Professor of German, Queen's University, Kingston, Ontario.

Ronald Webster, Associate Professor of History and Discipline Coordinator, Atkinson College, York University, Toronto, Ontario.

INDEX

A

Ab heute heißt du Sara (Ludwig and Michel), 206
Die Abrechnung. Ein Neonazi steigt aus (Hasselbach and Bonengel), 148–49
accountability: legal, 49; scientific, 49
"Adopt-a-Course" financing strategy, 44, 45–46
Adorno, Theodor, 7, 33–34, 83, 94; -Celan exchange, 49
affective filter, in teaching the Holocaust, 211
Aichinger, Ilse, 64, 67
All Rivers Run to the Sea: Memoirs (Wiesel), 80
alterity and Otherness, in German Holocaust literature, xvi, 201–2, 205
Althans, Bela Ewald, 149
"Americanization of the Holocaust," 111, 216
Améry, Jean, 49–50, 167
Amichai, Yehuda, 230
Andorra (Frisch), 78, 80–81, 101, 178
Andreas-Friedrich, Ruth, 20
Anne Frank in Maine [film], 84
Anne Frank Remembered [film], 80, 83, 193
Ans Ende der Welt (Weil), 160–61
antifascism, postwar Germany, 141–42
anti-Jewish legislation, 204–5
anti-Judaism, 65, 69, 101
antisemitism, 69, 85, 93, 97, 147, 148–50, 196; in German literature, 61, 64; in Germany in 1930s, 202; as government policy, 205; history of, 6, 65, 194, 203–4; political, 125–26; racial, 19–20, 29, 65, 203; religious, 19–20, 29; theological roots of, 101
Anton the Dove Fancier (Gotfryd), 6–9
[The] Architecture of Doom [film]. See *[Die] Architektur des Untergangs*
[Die] Architektur des Untergangs ([The] Architecture of Doom) [film], 128
Arden Must Die (Fried), 66
Arendt, Hannah, 8, 33–34, 130
Are We All Nazis? (Askenasy), 21
art, Holocaust, 225–26
Aryanization, 7, 12
Ashkenazic Studies, 65, 70
Askenasy, Hans, 21
Auschwitz: Carmelite Convent at, 50; literature of, 8–10; number, 100; psychoanalytic reading of commandant's memoirs, 33; representation after, 225–26; standard works, 20–21; survivors, 62, 213–19; women's camp, 20–21
Auschwitz (Naumann), 98
"Auschwitz (Time Flies)" (in Spiegelman *Maus II*), 50
Auschwitz Trial (Frankfurt 1963–65), 19, 64, 97
Auschwitz: True Tales from a Grotesque Land (Nomberg-Przytyk), 8–9, 10, 227, 229
Die Ausgesperrten (Jelinek), 229. See also *Wonderful, Wonderful Times*
authenticity of voice, 229–30
autobiography, 212, 213–19

B

Bachmann, Ingeborg, 228, 231
Bammer, Angelika, 124
Bartov, Omer, 213
Baudrillard, Jean, 230
bearing witness, 158, 161
Becker, Jurek, 4, 63–64, 66, 84, 98–99, 128, 180, 181
Begley, Louis, 8–9, 10
Begov, Lucie, 213
Behrens, Katja, 147–48
belonging, 147
Benn, Gottfried, 33
Bentley, Eric, 95
Berenbaum, Michael, 110
Bergen-Belsen camp, 31, 49
Bergstein, Eve, 100
Berlin, 31–32
Berlin Underground 1938–1945 (Andreas-Friedrich), 20
Berlin Wall, 125, 142, 195, 201
Bernheim, Robert, 5
Beruf Neonazi (Profession Neo-Nazi) [film], 114, 149
Bettelheim, Bruno, 66–67, 84, 167
Biedermann und die Brandstifter (Frisch), 80–82
Billard um halb zehn (Böll), 178. See also *Billiards at Half-Past Nine*
Biller, Maxim, 50
Billiards at Half-Past Nine (Böll), 228. See also *Billard um halb zehn*
Birkenau camp, 100
Bitburg incident, 42, 50, 145–46, 213
Blair, Jon, 80
Blanchot, Maurice, 225–26, 231
"Blickwechsel" (Wolf), 85
B'nai B'rith, 9
The Boat Is Full [film]. See *Das Boot ist voll*
Bobrowski, Johannes, 178
Bogorad, Samuel, 3
Böll, Heinrich, 178, 228
Bonengel, Winfried, 148–49
Das Boot ist voll (The Boat Is Full) [film], 9, 81, 83, 84
Borneman, John, 128

Born Guilty (Sichrovsky), 144. See also *Schuldig geboren*
Borowski, Tadeusz, 20, 50
Der Boxer (Becker), 180
Der Brautpreis (Weil), 166, 168. See also *The Bride Price*
Brecht, Bertolt, 4–6, 7, 80–81, 178, 204
The Bride Price (Weil), 129. See also *Der Brautpreis*
Broch, Hermann, 94
Bronstein's Children (Becker), 64–65, 66. See also *Bronsteins Kinder*
Bronsteins Kinder (Becker), 128, 181. See also *Bronstein's Children*
Browning, Christopher R., xviii
"B sagen" (Weil), 163
Buchenwald camp, 200, 206–7
Bund deutscher Mädel, 113
Burgauer, Erica, 128

C

Calvino, Italo, 230
Canada: Berlin Embassy, 206; German Studies in, x; Human Rights Act, 149
Canadian Jewish News, 192
Carmelite Convent, Auschwitz, 50
Case Histories (Kluge), 228
"the Catastrophe," 231
Catholic Church. See Roman Catholic Church
Cat and Mouse (Grass), 4
Cayrol, Jean, 5
CBC Radio, Rosmus interview, 146
Celan, Paul, 8, 34, 63, 64, 67, 167, 230, 231–32; -Adorno exchange, 49; poetry of, 78, 82, 192, 200
Cesaire, Aimé, 230
Chelmno, 11
"Chicken Soup" (Gilman), 65
children: in Holocaust literature, 84–85, 98; of Nazi parents, 144–45; of survivors, 34, 45, 50, 77–78, 115–16, 147
"Chor der Geretteten" (Sachs), 82
Christian, passing as, 8, 10
Christian discourse, on the Jews, 65
Christian students, and forgiveness, 179

The Chronicle of the Łódź Ghetto, 1941–1944, 84, 99
cinema, as art form, 7
collaboration, 30
coming to terms with the past. *See* Vergangenheitsbewältigung
communication, and survivors, 67
communism, 9, 147
Communists, ix, 29–30
concentration camps, 30. *See also* names of specific camps
Confessing Church, 9
controversy: *The Deputy* (Hochhuth), 95; Goldhagen book, xviii; literary works, 92
core readings, 178–79, 180–81
"A Country, a Child, but Not the Country's Child" (Noll), 147
The Courage to Care [film], 9–10
The Courage to Remember (Simon Wiesenthal Center traveling exhibit), 180
course(s), xii, xx; assignments, 11–12, 22–23, 34, 52, 95–96, 115–16; case studies, 112; complaint about Holocaust content, 195–96; content, xiii–xvii, 93, 114–16, 125–27; evaluations, 35–36, 68–69, 78–79, 82, 100–101, 129, 132, 167–68, 180, 195, 218; goals, xiii, 4, 33–34, 108, 176; graduate seminars, 157, 175–76; guidelines, xix–xx; Holocaust-specific, 175; language of, 34–35, 59, 93, 109; materials, 143; modules, 48–51, 53; oral reports, 115–16, 177, 180; student-centered, 46–48; syllabi, xvii–xviii, 46; teaching units, xv–xvi, 60–62, 150; tests and examinations, 111, 130
crematoria poetry, 83
cultural studies: Holocaust, xv–xvi; postwar German, 140–50
culture: German, 124–25, 127, 140–50, 166; Jewish, 125–27, 146–47; Jewish American, 127
Czerniakow, Adam, 49

D

Dachau camp, 22–23, 31
Dafni, Reuven, 21
Dante's *Divina Commedia,* 98
Dante's *Inferno,* 10, 19
Darwish, Mahmoud, 230
David [film], 63
Dawidowicz, Lucy S., 80
Delbo, Charlotte, 36
Demant, Ebbo, 19
Demetz, Peter, 98
deniers, 19; Canadian, 100, 201; Holocaust, xi, 174–75, 181
deportation, 12, 30, 80, 164
The Deputy (Hochhuth), 4, 9, 101; controversy over, 95. *See also Der Stellvertreter*
Des Pres, Terrence, 84
The Destruction of the European Jews (Hilberg), 3, 110
Deutsch, Eva, 67, 180
Deutschkron, Inge, 20, 206
Deutschland: Zeitschrift für Politik, 192
dialogue, Jewish German, 129, 132
The Diary of Anne Frank (Frank), 66. *See also Das Tagebuch der Anne Frank*
"the Disaster," as term for Holocaust, 225
Dischereit, Esther, 128
Dispeker family, 159; wartime experience of, 159–60
Dispeker, Grete. *See* Weil, Grete
displacement, 230
diversity, as course theme, 201
documentation: system, xviii; versus literature, 10
Domin, Hilde, 63
"Don't touch me" (Weil), 167
The Double Crossing [film], 22
drama, genre of, 80–82, 95–98
Dry Tears (Tec), 8, 10, 21
Dürrenmatt, Friedrich, 178

E

Education of Fanny Lewald, 65
Eggebrecht, Axel, 19
Eichmann, Adolf, 33; banality of evil, 8
Eichner, Hans, 200

Eliach, Yaffa, 50, 80
emigration. See exile
emotions, of students, xix–xx, 33, 129–30, 132
Epstein, Eric, 17, 19
Epstein, Leslie, 84
Die Ermittlung (Weiss), 180. See also The Investigation
essay packages, xvii–xix
An Estate of Memory (Karmel), 21
The Eternal Jew [film], 114
ethnic cleansing, Bosnian, 21
Ettersberg, 200, 206
Europa Europa [film], 8, 10, 63, 113
euthanasia, ix, 7, 12
Evans, Gary, 194
evil, banality of, 8
"The Excursion of the Dead Girls" (Seghers), 64, 227
exile, xvi, 230; and emigration, 159; literature, 81 experience, 232; authenticity of, 229; and memory, 227
experiments: medical, 178; Nazi, 21, 33, 81
extermination, 12; camps, 115; machinery, 21

F

Facing Hate [Wiesel-Moyers interview], 80
False Front Ghetto and Transit Camp. See Theresienstadt
fascism, 35, 63–64, 145
Fassbinder, Rainer Maria, 50
Federal Republic of Germany. See Germany
Felstiner, John, 64, 82
Fest, Joachim, 110
filmmaking, Hollywood and European, 63
films: of the Holocaust, xiv, 3–4; use of, 21–22, 63, 100
Final Letters (Dafni), 21
"Final Solution," 8, 18–19, 31, 49
finance, "Adopt-a-Course" strategy, 44, 45–46
Finkielkraut, Alain, 226, 231
forced labor, 10
"foreignness," 228–29

forgiveness, and Christian students, 179
Fortunoff Archive (Yale University), 181
Frank, Anne, 49, 66, 79–80
Frankfurt Auschwitz Trial. See Auschwitz Trial (Frankfurt 1963–65)
Frankl, Victor E., 33
Freemasons, 30
Fried, Erich, 66
Friedländer, Saul, 50
Friedrich (Richter), 20
Frisch, Max, 80–82, 101, 178
"From the Cross to the Swastika" (Part I of The Longest Hatred [film]), 203–4
Fühmann, Franz, 85, 202
Fulbright Commission, 18, 116
Fulbright Landeskunde Seminar, 116
fund raising, potential donors, 44–45
Furcht und Elend des Dritten Reiches (Brecht), 4, 78, 80–81, 83, 178. See also The Private Life of the Master Race

G

Die Galizianerin (Schwaiger and Deutsch), 67, 180
"Garbage, the City and Death" (Fassbinder), 50
Generationen (Weil), 157, 162, 164, 168
genocide, ix, 29–30, 69, 81, 157, 161
Gentiles: cultural ties between German Jews and, 70; Holocaust significance to, 59; passing as, 8, 12
George, Manfred, 100
German Christians, 9
Germanists: as intended audience, xii, xviii; responsibilities of, 174–75
German-Jewish relations. See Jewish-German relations
Germans: eyewitnesses, 31; and Germanness, 216–17; in postwar Germany, 143; second generation, 214
German Studies, 124; definition, ix–xi; and Jewish Studies, 230; to "teach the Holocaust" in, 226
Germany: antifascism in GDR, 141–42, 149; contemporary, 193–94, 206; and Nazi past, 113, 148; norms in East and West, 148; "post-Holocaust," 213;

postwar history, 140–41; press restrictions on Nazi symbols, 194. *See also* postwar Germany
Der Gesang im Feuerofen (Zuckmayer), 180
Gesetz zum Schutze des deutschen Blutes und der deutschen Ehre (Law for the Protection of German Blood and Honor), 194
Gestapo, 31
Gestapo: Learning Experience about the Holocaust (Alternatives in Religious Education), 176, 181
Geyer, Michael, 150
Ghetto (Sobol), 30
ghettos, 30
Gies, Miep, 80
Gilman, Sander L., 65, 66, 128, 202
Giroux, Henry, 143
"Gloria Halleluja" (Weil), 162–63
Goebbels, Joseph, 5–6, 206
Goehr, Alexander, 66
Goldhagen, Daniel Jonah, xviii, 34, 50, 85, 116, 130; debate, xviii, 193
Gotfryd, Bernard, 6–7, 8–9
Grass, Günter, 4, 50
Great Depression, 203
Gross, Leonard, 20
grotesque, 178–79
"Guernica" (Weil), 166, 167
guilt: collective, 144–45; German, 34; and responsibility, 96, 144; survivor, 34
Gutmann, Al, 217
Gutmann, Ruth, 213–19

H

Habermas, Jürgen, 146
Hamburger, Michael, 64
Handke, Peter, 228
The Hangman [film], 22
Happy, sagte der Onkel (Weil), 162
Hart, Kitty, 66
Hasidic Tales of the Holocaust (Eliach), 80
Hasselbach, Ingo, 148–49
Haus der Geschichte der Bundesrepublik Deutschland, 213
Heimat [film], 145

Heine, Heinrich, 65, 67, 127, 130, 132, 192
Hellmund, Friedrich, 85
Hershman, Marcie, 7, 9
hiding, 10, 12; in Amsterdam, 162, 164, 166
Hilberg, Raul, 3–4, 12, 34, 110
Hilsenrath, Edgar, 67, 95, 101, 129, 180
Historikerstreit, 42, 145–46, 201, 227
history: of antisemitism, 6, 19, 65, 85, 194, 203–4; ethical issues, 176, 179; German Jewish, 65; of the Holocaust, xix–xx, 3, 17, 93, 110–11, 180; oral, 218; postwar German, 140–50; pre-Holocaust, 178; students' knowledge of, 43, 47, 176, 195; teaching strategies, 176–77
Hitler: as an orator, 95; rise to power, 29, 195
Hitler (Fest), 110
Hitler Jugend, 113
Hitler's Willing Executioners (Goldhagen), xviii, 50, 85, 116, 130
Hochhuth, Rolf, 4, 9, 10, 95–97, 178
Hoelzel, Alfred, 59
Holland, Agnieszka, 8, 10, 63
Holland (Netherlands), 213
Holocaust: Americanization of the, 111, 216; art, 225–26; centrality of in 20th century, 50–51; definition of term, ix, 50; historiography of, 97–98, 213; impact on politics, 49; individual's responses to, 49; issues, 108; living with the memory of, 165; relevance in contemporary Germany, 206; resistance to teaching, 50; significance for Germany, 117, 213; statistics, 112–13; unrepresentability of, xvi, 225. *See also* deniers; literature; teaching the Holocaust
The Holocaust and the Literary Imagination (Langer), 33
Holocaust Denial, 99–100
Holocaust discourse, xviii, 96; in Germany, 175
The Holocaust in History (Marrus), 96
The Holocaust: Introductory Essays (Scrase and Mieder), 5
Holocaust Memorial Resource and Education Center (Florida), 109, 116

Holocaust Studies, 4; ghettoization of, 212, 227. See also courses
Holocaust [TV series], 59, 96
homosexuals, ix, 30
Horak, Jan-Christopher, 100
Höss, Rudolf, 49
Hungary, deportation from, 80

I

Ich trug den gelben Stern (Deutschkron), 206. See also *Outcast*
identity: conflicts of, 147; diasporic, 230; Jewish, 147–48
Imhoof, Markus, 9
inability to mourn, 144–45
The Inability to Mourn (Mitscherlich and Mitscherlich), 144
Indelible Shadows (Insdorf), 83
The Informer (Brecht), 5
Insdorf, Annette, 83
In Search of Justice (Brecht), 5
Insiders and Outsiders: Jewish and Gentile Culture in Germany and Austria (Lorenz and Weinberger), 66
intellectualism, and survival, 50
interdisciplinarity, 124
Internet, 110, 181, 192–93
Intifadeh, 50
The Investigation (Weiss), 4, 10, 21, 33, 50, 64, 67, 97–98. See also *Die Ermittlung*
Invisible Cities (Calvino), 230
In zwei Sprachen leben, 201–2, 205

J

Jabes, Edmond, 230, 231
Jackson, Robert H., 85
Jacob the Liar (Becker), 4, 64, 98–99. See also *Jakob der Lügner* (Becker)
Jakob der Lügner (Becker), 84, 180. See also *Jacob the Liar* (Becker)
Jakob der Lügner (Jacob the Liar) [film], 83
Jakob Littners Aufzeichnungen aus einem Erdloch (Koeppen), 229–30
Jakobowsky und der Oberst (Werfel), 180
Jan Lobel from Warsaw (Rinser), 50

Jaspers, Karl, 95, 144
Jehovah's Witnesses, ix, 30
Jelinek, Elfriede, 228, 229
Jewish Council (Amsterdam), 160, 164
Jewish councils, 30
Jewish culture. See culture, Jewish
Jewish-German relations, 124–25, 128, 129–32, 165
Jewish Kapos, 30
Jewish life, before the Holocaust, 29
"Jewish Question," 49
Jewish Self-Hatred (Gilman), 65
Jewish Studies, 60, 62, 70, 93; and German Studies, 230
Jewish Theater (Amsterdam), 160, 163
The Jewish Wife and Other Short Plays (Brecht), 4–6
Jews: absence of, 226; Danish, 30; integration of into society, 159; life before the Holocaust, 29; as Other, 202–3, 205, 207; in postwar Germany, 117, 143, 165; as primary victims, ix, 85, 98; roundup of in Amsterdam, 161; secular, 127; in the U.S., 127
The Jews and Their Lies (Luther), 65
Jockisch, Walter, 162
Joëmis Tisch (Dischereit), 128
"Der Jude, ein Unglück für das Volk" (Brecht), 204
"Das Judenauto" (Fühmann), 85, 202–4
Jüdische Geschichte in Berlin (Rürup), 128
Jüdischer Verlag, 229
Jud Süß [film], 128
Jünger, Ernst, 33

K

Kadar, Jan, 7
Kafka, Franz, 132, 192
Karmel, Ilona, 21
Katz, Steven T., 202
Kay, Mania, 100
Kayser, Wolfgang, 64
Keneally, Thomas, 21, 85
Kiefer, Anselm, 82
Kieselsteine (Pebbles) [film], 66
King of the Jews (Epstein), 84

Kitsch, 96–97
Kitty: Return to Auschwitz [film], 66
Klemperer, Viktor, 78
Kluge, Alexander, 228
Klüger, Ruth, 62–63, 179
Kluger Verlag (Munich), 229
Koeppen, Wolfgang, 227–30
Kofman, Sarah, 225–26
Kogon, Eugen, 49
Kohl, Helmut, 42, 145–46
Kolmar, Gertrud, 192
"konzentrisches Schreiben," 147
Koonz, Claudia, 114
Korn, Benjamin, 148, 216
Kramer, Jane, 81
Kreisau Circle resistance group, 111.
  See also resistance, groups
Kristallnacht pogrom, 194–95, 213–14
Ku Klux Klan, 19
Kulturchronik (Inter Nationes), 192

L

Langer, Lawrence, 33, 98, 216
language: of courses, 34–35, 59, 93, 109, 126–29, 181, 193, 226–27; experience through, 225, 227; meaning of in context, 129; Nazi abuse of, 78
Lanzmann, Claude, 11
Lappin, Elena, 128
The Last Jews in Berlin (Gross), 20
The Last of the Just (Schwarz-Bart), 36
Law for the Protection of German Blood and Honor, 194
laws: anti-Jewish, 204–5; passed by Nazi Germany, 194
legal accountability, 49
legend, 50; in memoirs, 229, 230
Levins Mühle (Bobrowski), 178
Levi, Primo, 20, 49–50, 161, 167, 217, 227
Lewald, Fanny, 65
Lewenz, Lisa, 132
Lewis, Stephen, 205
Lieberman, Harold and Edith, 84
Lilienthal, Peter, 63
Lind, Jakov, 63, 67
literature, 17, 32–36, 61, 78; of the camps, 161; of children of survivors, 147; East German, 84; exile, 81; feminist perspective, 84–85; of the Holocaust, 3–4, 92, 175, 178–79, 229; and moral effect, 94; and New Criticism, 64; survivors' traumas, 162
Littner, Jakob, 229–30
Lixl-Purcell, Andreas, 218
Lodz Ghetto, 84
Lodz Ghetto: Inside a Community under Siege, 99
Loewy, Ernst, 162
The Longest Hatred: The History of Anti-Semitism [film], 5–6, 203
Lorenz, Dagmar C. G., 66
A Love in Germany [film], 10
LTI (Klemperer), 78
Lustig, Arnost, 20, 22
Luther, Martin, 65
Lyotard, Jean-François, 225–26

M

Madonna camp. *See* Majdanek camp
Maidanek camp. *See* Majdanek camp
Majdanek camp, 8, 42–43
Malina (Bachmann), 228
"Manna from Hell" (Kramer), 81
Mann, Thomas, 84
"Mario und der Zauberer" (Mann), 84
Marrus, Michael, 94, 96
Marxism, 63–64, 97
Maschmann, Melita, 49
Maus II (Spiegelman), 50
Mauthausen camp, 8, 160–61, 166
Mayer, Hans, 162
medical experiments, 178
"Meine Geigenstunden" (Wachenfeld), 202, 204–5
Meine Schwester Antigone (Weil), 84, 163–64, 166
Melton Center for Jewish Studies (OSU), 61
memoir, genre, 79–80
Memoiren eines Antisemiten (Rezzori), 84, 85
memory, 142, 225; and experience, 227; and history, 228, 231; living with,

165; and suppression of the Holocaust, 143
Milgram experiments, 21, 33
minorities, in Germany, 142
Mitscherlich, Alexander and Margarethe, 144–45
Moltke, Helmut von, 112
moral activism, and survivors, 9–10
moral effect, and literature, 94
morality: absence of, 8; disregard for, 19; and technology, 19
Mosse, George, 19–20, 128
Mothers in the Fatherland (Koonz), 114
motivation, student/teacher, 48
Moyers, Bill, 80
multiculturalism, 60, 201
Murdaugh, Elaine, 96
music, 82–83, 205
My Life as German and Jew (Wassermann), 65

N

"Die Nachmann-Juden" (Biller), 50
"Nacht und Nebel," 5
The Nasty Girl [film]. See *Das schreckliche Mädchen*
Nathorff, Hertha, 127, 128
National Socialism, 63–64, 65, 67, 69, 93, 193–94; reevaluation of teaching, 200–201
Naumann, Bernd, 98
The Nazi and the Barber (Hilsenrath), 95, 129. See also *Der Nazi und der Friseur*
Nazi Germany, laws passed, 194
Nazi literature, psychohistorical analysis, 33
Nazi Party, 111
Nazism, 146; abuse of language, 78; era of, 61–62; legacy of, 202; propaganda, 31, 194; symbols, 149
Der Nazi und der Friseur (Hilsenrath), 180. See also *The Nazi and the Barber*
neo-Nazism, 19, 21, 148–50, 202, 206; in Canada, 100, 149; East Germany, 149; revisionism of, 50
Netherlands, 80; as place of refuge, 159
Neuengamme camp, 31

Neue Sachlichkeit movement, 81
New Criticism, and Holocaust literature, 64
New Left, 63
New Right, 148–50; in the West, 149. See also right-wing extremism
New York Times, 192
New York Times Book Review, 192
Night (Wiesel), 8, 10, 20, 79, 80
Night and Fog [film]. See *Nuit et brouillard*
Night and Hope (Lustig), 20
Nolden, Thomas, 147
Noll, Chaim, 147
Nolte, Ernst, 146
Nomberg-Przytyk, Sara, 8–9, 10, 227, 229–30
North America: German government centers in, x; German Studies in, x; Holocaust teaching in, xi, 175
novel: and historical truth, 99; Holocaust through, 84–85, 92
NSDAP, rise of, 112
Nuit et brouillard (Night and Fog) [film], 5, 6, 22, 66, 67–68, 80
Nuremberg, 31, 79; Laws, 95; Trials, 85, 144

O

Oberski, Jona, 49
Olympia [film], 114
"The Ones Who in the Cold Sweat of Execution" (Broch), 94
Ophir, Adi, 98
Ordinary Men (Browning), xviii
Ormond, Henry, 19, 21–22
Osservatore Romano, 96
Other, Jews as, 202–5, 207
Otherness. See alterity and Otherness
Outcast (Deutschkron), 20. See also *Ich trug den gelben Stern*
Owings, Alison, 113
Ozick, Cynthia, 11, 227

P

paintings, 82–83
Patterns of Childhood (Wolf), 227, 228

Peck, Jeffrey, 128
pedagogy: interactive autobiography as, 211–19; objectives of German Studies programs, 191–92; teaching German culture, 142–43
"The People Who Walked On" (Borowski), 50
"Perfectly Normal" (Behrens), 147
perpetrators, x, 32–33, 36, 69, 92; trials of, 21, 97; and victims, 163, 165; in *The Wannsee Conference*, 8
persecution, 29–30, 163; of Jews as Other, 204–5. *See also* racism
Petrikau ghetto, 164
philosemitism, 146, 159
Pigeons on the Grass (Koeppen), 227, 228
Pius XII, 9, 95, 96
place, as theme, 230
The Plot to Kill Hitler [film], 112
Plötzensee Prison, 31
poetry, 7–8, 230; Adorno on, 7; crematoria, 83; genre, 82–84; German language, 8; SS, 31; translations of, 64
Poland, surviving in, 10
police, Jewish, 30
political antisemitism, 125–26
politics: impact of Holocaust on, 49; party platforms, 112
Polyglot, 192
post-Berlin Wall tremors, 125
postwar Germany: guilt, 142; *Historikerstreit*, 42, 145–46, 201, 227; history, 140–50; and Holocaust, 213; identity, 143; Jews in, 146–48; normalcy, 142, 146. *See also* Germany post-World War II, 78, 81, 85
prejudice, 178; and discrimination, 192
press, North American compared to German, 194
Pribic, Rado, 205
The Private Life of the Master Race (Brecht). *See also Furcht und Elend des Dritten Reiches*
Problemdichtung, 81
Profession Neo-Nazi [film]. *See Beruf Neonazi*

Q

The Question of German Guilt (Jaspers), 144

R

"The Rabbi of Bacharach" (Heine), 65, 67, 130, 132
racism, 163; after unification, 148; America compared to Nazi Germany, 218; ideological, 93; Nazi, 69, 81, 194
readings: core, 178–79, 180–81; historical, xix
Reagan, Ronald, 145–46
Reemerging Jewish Culture in Germany: Life and Literature since 1989 (Gilman and Remmler), 66, 128
refugees: autobiographies, 212; Jewish, 30
Reichskristallnacht. *See Kristallnacht*
Reitz, Edgar, 145
religion: and Holocaust, 49; teaching strategies, 176–77, 180
religious beliefs, Ruth Gutmann, 214, 218
Remembrance Day, 194
Remmler, Karen, 66, 128
"Report from Dachau" (Ryback), 85
representation, 126, 130, 132, 226, 230
rescuers, 9–10, 111; Polish, 21
resistance, 30, 83, 95; antifascist, 64; groups, 111, 164; risks of, 94; teaching strategies, 53; theme of, 9, 12, 92, 98–99, 111
Resnais, Alain, 5, 66, 67–68, 80
Resort 76 (Wincelberg), 84
responsibility: civil and moral, 96; and guilt, 96, 144
reunification, 140, 143
revenge, 178
revisionism, 19, 21, 62, 100; historical, 50; of neo-Nazi groups, 50; political, 50
Rezzori, Gregor von, 84–85
Richter, Hans Peter, 20, 205
Riefenstahl, Leni, 5–6, 66, 67, 113, 193
Right. *See* New Right
right-wing extremism, 116, 202, 206; students, 69–70. *See also* New Right

rigor, intellectual, 130, 131, 132
Rinser, Luise, 50
Roma, genocide against, ix, 30, 69
Roman Catholic Church, 9, 95–96, 101
Rosenfeld, Alvin, 216
Rosmus, Anna, 146
roundup of Jews, in Amsterdam, 161
Rürup, Reinhard, 128, 218–19
Ryback, Timothy W., 85

S

Sachsenhausen camp, 31
Sachs, Nelly, 8, 67, 78, 82
SS *St. Louis*, 22, 30
Salloch, Erika, 98
Salomon, Charlotte, 192
Santner, Eric, 213
Sartre, Jean Paul, 83
Schachnovelle (Zweig), 84
Schindler, Oskar, 21, 111–12
Schindler's List [film], 111, 116, 179, 193
Schindler's List (Keneally), 21, 85
Schirk, Heinz, 8
Scholl, Sophie, 112, 113, 164
"Das Schönste der Welt" (Weil), 167
Das schreckliche Mädchen (The Nasty Girl) [film], 113, 146, 193
Schuldig geboren. Kinder aus Nazifamilien (Sichrovsky), 113. See also *Born Guilty*
Schwaiger, Brigitte, 67, 180
Schwarz-Bart, André, 33, 36
scientific accountability, 49
Seelich, Nadja, 66
Seghers, Anna, 64, 94, 205, 227, 231
Senesh, Hannah, 49
The Seventh Cross [film], 100
The Seventh Cross (Seghers), 94–95
Seyhan, Azade, 143
Shandley, Robert R., xviii
The Shawl (Ozick), 11, 227
Shoah [film], 11, 83–84
Shoah. See Holocaust
The Shop on Main Street [film], 7
Sichrovsky, Peter, 113, 144, 147
Simon Wiesenthal Center, 99; traveling exhibit, 180

Sinti, genocide against, ix, 30, 69
slave workers, 10
Slavs, ix
Smith, Tom W., 211
Sobol, Joshua, 30
social responsibility, 92
Sojourners [film], 128
Die Sonnenblume (Wiesenthal), 179, 180
Sophie's Choice [film], 11
A Sorrow beyond Dreams (Handke), 228
Soul of Wood (Lind), 67
Spätfolgen (Weil), 166
Der Spiegel, 192
Spiegelman, Art, 50
Spielberg, Steven, 31, 116, 179
Srebnik, Simon, 11
SS, 31, 146
Staiger, Emil, 64
Stanford study, 33
statistics, Holocaust, 112–13
Stauffenberg, Claus von, 111–12; 20 July resistance group, 111. See also resistance, groups
Steiner, George, 83
Der Stellvertreter (Hochhuth), 178. See also *The Deputy*
Stephenson, Jill, 114
stereotypes: of Germans, 196; of Jews, 20, 48, 178, 203–4
Stern, Frank, 206
Stern, Susan, 128
stetl, Eastern European, 29
Stierle, Karlheinz, 97
"Storm over *The Deputy*" (Bentley), 95
Story of the Last Thought (Hilsenrath), 67
Strangers in Their Own Land (Sichrovsky), 147
Stroop, Jürgen, 33
students: attitudes of, 59–62; complaint about Holocaust content, 195–96; course centered on, 46–48, 51; emotions of, 33, 129–30, 132; German-American, 32; German-Canadian, 92, 200–201; knowledge of history, 43, 47, 176, 195; resistance to topics, 201; right-wing extremist, 69–70
Styron, William, 11
Suchomel, Franz, 11, 83

suffering, concept of, 216
survival: and intellectualism, 50; role of the lie in, 10; strategies, 163
Survival in Auschwitz (Levi), 20, 217, 227
survivors, 10, 66, 92, 99, 111, 164, 193; and autobiography, 212, 213–19; biographical material, 192; children of, 34, 45, 50, 77–78, 115–16, 147; and communication, 67; film about, 9–10; fund-raising strategies, 44–45; and Holocaust teaching, xi, xiv, 17–19, 31, 100, 181; moral obligation toward, 174–75; revenge of, 178; teachers, xiii–xiv, 17–18, 23; traumas, 162, 167; videotaped testimony, 31, 181, 218; writers, 80. *See also* rescuers
Survivors of the Shoah Visual History Foundation, 31, 45
Switzerland, in World War II, 81, 84
symbiosis: Jewish German, 125, 131, 132; negative, 147
synagogue, visit to, 177–78

T

Das Tagebuch der Anne Frank (Frank), 79–80. See also *The Diary of Anne Frank* (Frank)
Tales of the Master Race (Hershman), 7, 9
teaching the Holocaust, ix, xi, 30–31, 59, 61–62, 86, 101, 107; German government support for, x; meaning of, 225–26; pedagogy, ix, 142–43, 191–92; personal issues, 93; strategies, 53. *See also* Holocaust
technology: and morality, 19; and teaching, 180–81
Tec, Nechama, 8, 10, 21
Des Teufels General (Zuckmayer), 80–81
Theresienstadt camp, 19, 20, 22, 213
Theresienstadt: Hitler's Gift to the Jews (Troller), 20
Theweleit, Klaus, 33
Third Reich, 19, 31–32, 93, 192; Jews as Other in, 202–3; literary approach to, 178; women and, 113–14
This Way for the Gas, Ladies and Gentlemen (Borowski), 20

Throne of Straw (Lieberman), 84
The Tin Drum (Grass), 50
"Todesfuge" (Celan), 34, 64, 82, 200–201
Topographie des Terrors exhibition, 218–19
Toronto, Holocaust denial trial in, 201
totalitarianism, 81, 92
Toward the Final Solution (Mosse), 19–20
Tramhalte Beethovenstraat (Weil), 161
translations, 51, 63–64, 93; of poetry, 64; policy, xviii–xix; of texts, 227, 228–30
Transport from Paradise [film], 22
Traverso, Enzo, 128
Treaty of Versailles, 194
Treblinka camp, 11, 83
trial, Holocaust denial, 201
Trilogie (Delbo), 36
triumphalism, Nazi, 80, 84
Triumph des Willens (Triumph of the Will) [film], 5, 6, 7, 66, 67, 83
Triumph of the Will [film]. See *Triumph des Willens*
Troller, Norbert, 20
truth telling, 227, 229

U

unification, 125, 193, 195; xenophobia after, 148–50
United States: German Studies in, x; rejection of Jewish refugees, 30
United States Holocaust Memorial Museum (Washington, DC), 29–30, 79, 115; teaching guidelines, 108, 110, 117
universality, course theme, 201
university, as mall, 46
unrepresentability, of the Holocaust, xvi, 225
the unsayable, 225, 228, 231
the unspeakable, 225–26, 231
"unterwegs," 231–32
Unwilling Germans? The Goldhagen Debate (Shandley), xviii
"Un-Word" award of 1991, 205–6

V

Varnhagen, Rahel, 130
Vatican, during World War II, 95
"'Verbreitung falscher Nachrichten,'" 201
Der Verdacht (Dürrenmatt), 178, 181
Vergangenheitsbewältigung, 4, 34, 85, 125, 194, 214
Verhoeven, Michael, 9, 146
victimization, German-Canadian students' feelings of, 201
victims, 98; Jews as primary, ix, 85; moral obligation toward, 174; and perpetrators, 163, 165; survivor guilt, 34
videotapes, survivors' testimony, 31, 181, 218
violence, postunification Germany, 202
visits, synagogue, 177–78, 180
Visual History Foundation. *See* Survivors of the Shoah Visual History Foundation
voice, authorial, 229
voices, story of the Holocaust, 113

W

Wachenfeld, Sigrid, 202, 204
Wagner, Richard, 65
Wajda, Andrzej, 10
Wallenberg, Raoul, 30
Wandering Jew, 178
Wannsee Conference, 49, 160
The Wannsee Conference [TV docudrama]. *See Die Wannsee-Konferenz*
Die Wannsee-Konferenz (The Wannsee Conference) [TV docudrama], 8, 83, 179, 193, 194
Wannsee Villa, 31–32
The War Against the Jews: 1933–1945 (Dawidowicz), 80
Warsaw Ghetto, 30, 33
The Warsaw Ghetto [film], 22
Wartime Lies (Begley), 8, 10
war trials, 30. *See also* Auschwitz Trial; Nuremberg, Trials
Wassermann, Jakob, 65
The Wave [film], 21–22

Weil, Edgar, 159–60
Weil, Grete, 84, 129, 157–69
Weimar Republic, 20, 61
Weinberger, Gabriele, 66
Weinberg, Gerhard, 12
"Weiße Rose" resistance group, 164. *See also* resistance, groups
Die weiße Rose (The White Rose) [film], 9, 83, 112
Weiss, Peter, 4, 8, 10, 21, 33, 50, 64, 67, 97–98, 180
weiter leben (Klüger), 62–63, 179, 181
"Weizsäcker Rede," 85
Weizsäcker, Richard von, 201
Werfel, Franz, 180
werkimmanent school, 64
Wertheim department store, 206
When Memory Comes (Friedländer), 50
White Rose resistance group, 111. *See also* resistance, groups
The White Rose [film]. *See Die weiße Rose*
white supremacism, 69, 116
Wiesel, Elie, 8–9, 10, 20, 33, 49, 79–80, 161, 205
Wiesenthal, Simon, 179
Wincelberg, Shimon, 84
Wirtschaft und Wissenschaft, 192
"Witching Hour: Images of Germany—Sixty Years Later" (Korn), 148
Wolf, Christa, 85, 227, 228, 231
women: camp of, 8–9, 20–21; experience of the camps, 179; survivors, 192; and the Third Reich, 113–14
Women in Nazi Society (Stephenson), 114
The Wonderful, Horrible Life of Leni Riefenstahl [film], 114
Wonderful, Wonderful Times (Jelinek), 228–29. *See also Die Ausgesperrten*
The World Must Know (Berenbaum), 110
World War I, 20
World War II, 17, 64; German soldier in, 85; Vatican during, 95
World Wide Web resources, xiv, 108, 110, 181

X

xenophobia: after unification, 148–49; of Luther, 65

Y

Yale University, Fortunoff Archive, 181
Yiddish culture, 29
Yiddish Studies, 60, 70–71
Yiddish words, 129
Yom Hashoah, 17–18; committee, 45

Z

Zeilen, Joachim, psychoanalytic reading of Auschwitz commandant's memoirs, 33
Die Zeit, 192
Zerbrochene Geschichte (Blasius and Diner), 128
Zinnemann, Fred, 100
Zuckmayer, Carl, 80–81, 180
Zündel, Ernst, 149
Zweig, Stefan, 84
Zwillinger, Frank, 63